MW01032100

1967

1967

The Year of Fire and Ice

VICTOR BROOKS

Skyhorse Publishing

Skyhorse Publishing books may be purchased in bulk at special discounts for sales promotion, corporate gifts, fund-raising, or educational purposes. Special editions can also be created to specifications. For details, contact the Special Sales Department, Skyhorse Publishing, 307 West 36th Street, 11th Floor, New York, NY 10018 or info@skyhorsepublishing.com.

Skyhorse® and Skyhorse Publishing® are registered trademarks of Skyhorse Publishing, Inc.®, a Delaware corporation.

Visit our website at www.skyhorsepublishing.com.

10 9 8 7 6 5 4 3 2 1

Library of Congress Cataloging-in-Publication Data is available on file.

Cover design by Rain Saukas

Print ISBN: 978-1-5107-1676-6
Ebook ISBN: 978-1-5107-1678-0

Printed in the United States of America.

CONTENTS

Preface

During the summer of 1973, as the Watergate scandal emerged as headline news and Arabic leaders were preparing a surprise attack on Israel that would ignite the oil crisis that would nearly paralyze American transportation by autumn, one of the most popular musical performing groups of the 1970s released a new album and a new single. The album was titled *Now & Then* and was produced by Richard Carpenter who, along with his sister Karen, fronted a group of that family name. The Carpenters were cashbox gold in the early to mid-seventies and had already tapped into the burgeoning young adult market with their anthem for young newlyweds, "We've Only Just Begun." Now the Carpenters invited their huge core audience to buy an unusual album that featured contemporary hits of the early seventies, such as "Sing" and "Heather," on one side, and predominately sixties "oldies" such as "Johnny Angel," "One Fine Day," and "Dead Man's Curve" on the other. That side also included a single 1970s hit, the Carpenters' number 2 *Billboard* charted "Yesterday Once More," which was blocked from the top spot by Jim Croce's iconic "Bad, Bad Leroy Brown."

Karen Carpenter struck a major chord in the psyches of young people who had grown up in the 1960s when she sang that "when I was young I'd listen to the radio, waiting for my favorite song; when they played it

I'd sing along; those were such happy times and not so long ago." Now she reveled in the fact that her favorite music was "back again like a long-lost friend" with the emergence of "oldies" stations in the seventies.

At about the same time that "Yesterday Once More" was peaking on the music charts, twenty-nine-year-old producer George Lucas was releasing a visual trip back to the sixties with *American Graffiti*. The film centered around a single night in the lives of a small group of teenagers in a small California city where major adolescent decisions—such as relationship building and choosing whether to go away to college or remain in the hometown community—are made and unmade, all to the tune of a driving musical score that backs the dialogue from beginning to end. Posters at movie theaters invited the audience to include themselves in the action with the slogan "Where Were You in '62?"

Several decades after "Yesterday Once More" and *American Graffiti*, television producer/writer Matthew Weiner introduced a twenty-first-century audience to the lure of America in the sixties with his multiple Emmy-winning series *Mad Men*, which followed advertising executive Donald Draper through that decade in what emerged as a ratings bonanza for the AMC network.

Even after five decades, the simple term "the sixties" seems to evoke emotional responses in those Americans who lived through the era. It also sparks genuine interest in those people who are too young to remember the decade. However, while there is no shortage of books about that decade, at present only four years—1964, 1965, 1968, and 1969—have received full treatment as broad-based narratives of American life. This book, *1967: The Year of Fire and Ice*, is an attempt to give the year 1967 its rightful place as an extremely significant time in the sixties, one that produced more than an average portion of positive and negative events.

I have written two books dealing with young people in the 1960s: *Boomers: The Cold-War Generation Grows Up*, and *Last Season of Innocence: The Teen Experience in the 1960s*, while my most recent book, *The Longest Year*, focuses on America in 1944. Thus *1967: The Year of Fire and Ice* draws from elements of those projects. The decision to write a book that focused on 1967 emerged while teaching my popular course on the sixties at Villanova University. It always amazed my students that this single year produced the first Super Bowl, one of the most exciting baseball seasons in history, the emergence of full television broadcasting in color, one of the most iconic record albums (*Sgt. Pepper*), the Summer of Love, the Six-Day War, and the first serious step toward détente between the Soviet Union and the United States.

I have attempted to write *1967: The Year of Fire and Ice* from the perspective of a society that at that point still had no idea that Lyndon Johnson would withdraw from the presidential race the following spring; that the "light at the end of the tunnel" in Vietnam would be extinguished by the Tet Offensive in January of 1968, or that the thousand-to-one-shot Boston Red Sox will edge out seemingly far more talented teams to take on the St. Louis Cardinals in a spectacular World Series.

As for my own background for viewing 1967, I began the year as a teenager commuting to LaSalle University from a Philadelphia suburb as a dual major in history and teacher education. My father was a college professor who had served as a major in the Army Air Forces in World War II and was the only survivor of an air crash, requiring twice-weekly treatments at a veterans hospital until his death in 1998. My mother met my father when she worked in the hospital where my father was sent to recuperate from his injuries; she grew up in the city of Utica in upstate New York, where the hospital and air base were located. My family also included a younger brother, who was in high school, and twin sisters, who were in elementary school. Like many American families, our first color television set arrived only days before the onset of 1967. All six family members, augmented by friends who still had black-and-white TV sets, sat in awe as we realized that the Xs and Os on *Hollywood Squares* were actually yellow and that Mr. Spock and Dr. McCoy on *Star Trek* actually wore blue tunics.

While spending much of 1967 in school could be a bit of an insular experience, this was reduced by several factors in my life. During the fall I spent every weekday until 3:00 p.m. as a student teacher at Wagner Junior High School in North Philadelphia. I taught Eastern Hemisphere Geography to hugely overcrowded classes of seventh graders in a school forced to employ split shifts because of a lack of classrooms. This enjoyable, rewarding, and exhausting experience of dealing with group of forty or more adolescents hopefully broadened their minds. It certainly did mine.

Another form of expanded experience was our family's frequent summerlong trips to Europe. At a time of far less transatlantic travel than is currently the case, I was able to meet both adults and young people everywhere from shops in the Carnaby Street of "swinging London" to the edge of the Iron Curtain in a divided Germany. My father's legitimate fear of flying opened another experience, as leisurely voyages to and from Europe on such passenger ships as the *Leonardo da Vinci* or *Michelangelo* offered ten- to fourteen-day opportunities for me to interact with young people from diplomat families representing the Soviet Union and other East European societies. Some of these conversations produced genuine affinity, such as my discovery that a Russian student had been undergoing a Soviet version of "duck and cover" exercises against possible American attack on the same day of the week that my class was conducting the same drills against *their* aircraft.

While I have accessed a large number of books that include some narrative of the 1967 experience, my main research goal in this project was to view the events of that year from the perspective of the people who lived through it. A substantial element of my research was devoted to understanding 1967 from the journals and magazines that Americans read at that time. This included serious newsweekly magazines such as *Time, Newsweek,* and *U.S. News and World Report,* and heavily illustrated sources such as *Life* and *Look,* all of which were major news sources in typical American households. I perused original issues of more specialized journals such as *Ladies Home Journal, Saturday Evening Post, Fortune, Sports Illustrated,* and *TV Guide.* I also focused on literature geared to young people, including *Mad Magazine,* which provided surprisingly relevant satire on American lifestyles; *Seventeen,* which focused on issues other than dating and fashion; and *Glamour,* which attracted a college student/young career audience. A broadened view of popular culture was enhanced through a variety of journals such as *Teen, Teen Screen, Teen*

Age, and *American Girl,* while *Ebony* magazine reflected the concerns of an African American community experiencing the still mixed blessings of recent civil rights legislation.

Much of what you will read in this book has been enormously enhanced by my graduate assistant Alexa Piccoli, who, though preparing to embark on a career in counseling, has proved an invaluable historian in preparing the draft of this work. Alexa has demonstrated her almost certain success as a counselor by her cheerful engagement in a project well outside her own studies, while at the same time providing advice from a different perceptive than my own.

I have also been blessed by the fact that my three children—Matthew, Gregory, and Stephen—have all been interested in at least some aspects of the past, be it music, sports, films, or politics. The youngest member of my family, fourth-grader Liam, just came aboard when he asked me to explain the meanings in Don McLean's "American Pie," so he can pass the information on to his fellow nine-year-olds.

On a professional level, I would like to express my gratitude for institutional support at Villanova University from my department chair, Dr. Edward Garcia Fierros, and the Dean of Arts and Sciences, Dr. Adele Lindenmeyr. I also would like to express my sincere gratitude to my editor at Skyhorse Publishing, Niels Aaboe, who was wonderfully supportive and understanding about the sometimes stressful world of publishing.

Prologue
Autumn 1966

The great nocturnal invasion of American homes began at dusk on a Monday evening in October 1966 along the East Coast and spread inexorably westward during the next three hours. For the 187 million Americans living in the United States, the invasion centered around strange creatures almost universally smaller than an average adult human being. These miniature creatures dressed in bizarre clothing depicting other times, other places, even other dimensions. Miniature females sought entry into homes dressed as pint-sized versions of America's favorite women with supernatural powers—Samantha Stevens of *Bewitched*, or, as the companion/servant/nightmare of an American astronaut, a being from a bottle known as "Jeannie," played by Barbara Eden. Diminutive male invaders often wore the green face of bumbling giant Herman Munster or the pointed ears of the science officer of the USS *Enterprise*, Mr. Spock. These miniature invaders were sometimes accompanied by still youthful but taller adolescents who may or may not have worn costumes as they chaperoned their younger siblings but invariably seemed to be holding a small box equipped with earplugs that allowed these teens to remain connected to the soundtrack of their lives, the "Boss Jocks" or "Hot 100" or "Music Explosion" radio programs.

These teenagers were different forms of invaders in the adult world of late 1966, as they seemed semipermanently attached to their transistor radios, spending four, six, or even eight hours a day listening to rapid-fire disc jockeys who introduced, commented upon, and played current hits such as "Last Train to Clarksville" by the Monkees, "96 Tears" by ? and the Mysterians, "Have You Seen Your Mother, Baby, Standing in the Shadow?" by the Rolling Stones, and "Reach Out I'll Be There" by the Four Tops.

As the miniature "home invaders" were often invited by their "victims" into their living rooms to receive their candy "payoffs," they encountered adults watching *The Lucy Show, Gilligan's Island, The Monkees,* and *I Dream of Jeannie*. The fact that nearly half of Americans in 1966 were either children or teenagers made it extremely likely that at least one or possibly even two of the programs airing on the three major networks would feature plotlines attractive to youthful viewers.

The most famous home that received the costumed "invaders" was 1600 Pennsylvania Avenue. Three years earlier that address had featured two young children as its residents, but the current residents were now looking forward to becoming first-time grandparents after the recent wedding of their daughter. While Lady Bird Johnson welcomed the diminutive visitors who passed through far more security than average homes, President Lyndon Baines Johnson was recovering from the massive jet lag and exhaustion incurred during a recent 10,000-mile odyssey across the Pacific Ocean.

A few days before Halloween, Lyndon Johnson had become the first president since Franklin Roosevelt to visit an active battle zone by traveling to a war-torn South Vietnam. While a quarter century earlier Roosevelt had been ensconced in the intrigue-laden but relatively secure conference venue of Casablanca, Johnson's Air Force One had engaged in a rapid descent toward Cam Ranh Bay in order to minimize the time the president could be exposed to possible Viet Cong ground fire.

Johnson, dressed in his action-oriented "ranch/country" attire of tan slacks and a matching field jacket embossed with the gold seal of the American presidency, emerged from the plane with the demeanor of a man seeking to test his mettle in a saloon gunfight. Standing in the rear of an open Jeep, the president clutched a handrail and received the cheers of seven thousand servicemen and the rattle of musketry down a line of a nine-hundred-man honor guard. Meanwhile, a military band played "The Yellow Rose of Texas." Johnson's speech—considered by many observers to have been his best effort in three years in office—compared the sweating suntanned men in olive drab fatigues to their predecessors at Valley Forge, Gettysburg, Iwo Jima, and Pusan. He insisted that they would be remembered long after by "a grateful public of a grateful nation."

Now, at Halloween, Johnson had returned to the White House, more determined than ever to (in his sometimes outlandish "frontier speak" vocabulary) "nail the coonskin to the wall" in concert with a relatively small but enthusiastic circle of allies, including Australia, South Korea, the Philippines, and Thailand. All were dedicated to thwarting a Communist takeover of South Vietnam and possibly much of Southeast Asia. While European allies had decided to sit out this conflict, Johnson had been able to forge an alliance in which young men from Melbourne, Seoul, and Manila were joining American youths from Philadelphia to San Diego in a bid to prevent North Vietnam and its Viet Cong allies from forcibly annexing a legitimate but often badly flawed South Vietnamese entity.

Unlike Halloween of 1942, when even the youngest trick-or-treaters had some semblance of knowledge that their nation was involved in a massive conflict that even affected which toys they could buy, what was for dinner, or whether they would have the gasoline to visit their grandparents, the United States in October 1966 displayed little evidence that a war was on. Neighborhood windows did not display blue or gold stars signifying war service. Dairy Queen stands did not run out of ice cream due to a sugar shortage, McDonald's restaurants were in the process of offering even larger hamburgers than their initial 15-cent versions, and there were no contemporary cartoon equivalents of the Nazi-Japanese stereotypes in the old Popeye and Disney cartoons. In October of 1966, "The War" still primarily referenced the global conflict of a generation earlier. Names such as Tet, Hue, My Lai, and Khe San were still obscure words referenced only as geographical or cultural terms by a minority of young soldiers "in the country" in South Vietnam.

Halloween 1966 was in many respects a symbolic initiation of the long 1967 that this book will chronicle. Post–World War II American culture had gradually chipped away the edges of the traditional January 1 to December 31 annual calendar. Nearly sixty million American students and several million teachers had begun the 1967 school year in September as they returned to classes in a new grade. The burgeoning television industry had essentially adopted the same calendar, as summer reruns ended soon after children returned to school, so that the 1967 viewing season began several months before New Year's Day. Car manufacturers began discounting their 1966 models in the autumn as new 1967 autos reached the showroom far ahead of calendar changes. While the college basketball season did not begin until December, about three weeks later than its twenty-first-century counterpart, the campaigns for the National Hockey League 1967 Stanley Cup and the corresponding National Basketball Association Championship title began far closer to Halloween than New Year's Day. This reasonable parameter for a chronicle of 1967 would seem to extend roughly from late October of 1966 to the beginning of the iconic Tet Offensive in Vietnam during the last hours of January 1968.

While the undeclared conflict in Vietnam had not yet replaced World War II as *the* war in many Americans' conscious thought, no sooner had the president returned from Southeast Asia than a new threat to Johnson's presidency emerged. Since his emergence as chief executive in the wake of the Kennedy assassination three years earlier, Johnson had driven a balky but Democratic-dominant Congress to one of the most significant periods of legislation activity in the nation's history. Bills enacting civil rights legislation, aid to schools, public housing subsidies, highway construction, space exploration, and numerous other projects wended their way through Congress, often in the wake of the president's controversial treatment of uncommitted lawmakers through a combination of promises and goadings. By the autumn of 1966, supporters and opponents of the Johnson's Great Society began to believe that, for better or worse, the president was beginning to envision a semipermanent social and political revolution in which current laws would be substantially enhanced while new reforms were proposed and enacted. However, a week after Halloween, this prospect collided with a newly emerging political reality.

The Goldwater-Johnson presidential contest two years earlier had not only resulted in the trouncing of the Arizona senator, but essentially provided the Democrats with a two to one majority in both houses of Congress. While some northern Republican lawmakers were more politically and socially liberal than a number of Southern Democrats, party discipline still obligated these southern politicians to support their leader. At least in some cases, the Great Society legislation kept churning out of the Congress, notably with the startling 100 to 0 Senate vote for the 1965 Higher Education Act. Now, as Americans voted in the 1966 elections, the seemingly semi-moribund GOP came back dramatically from its near-death experience.

When the final votes were tallied, the Republicans had gained eleven governorships that added to the fifteen they already held, which now meant that the majority of states were led by a GOP chief executive. The relatively modest party gain of three Senate seats was overshadowed by a spectacular increase of forty-seven seats in the House of Representatives, which more than repaired the damage of the 1964 fiasco. Newspapers and news magazines featured stories purporting that "the GOP wears a bright new look." Politics in '66 sparkled the political horizon with fresh-minted faces, and the 1966 election has made the GOP presidential nomination a prize suddenly worth seeking. The cover of *Newsweek* displayed "The New Galaxy of the GOP" as "stars" that "might indeed beat LBJ in 1968."

This cover story featured George Romney, "the earnest moderate from Michigan"; Ronald Reagan, "the cinegenic conservative from California"; and other rising stars of the party. Edward Brooke, the first African American US senator since Reconstruction, "Hollywood handsome" Charles Percy from Illinois, Mark Hatfield of Oregon, and even the newly energized governor of New York, Nelson Rockefeller, were all mentioned. Notably absent from this cover story "galaxy" was the man who easily could have been in the White House in autumn 1966, Richard M. Nixon. According to the news media, the former vice president's star seemed to be shooting in multiple directions. One article dismissed him as "a "consummate" old pro "who didn't win anything last week and hasn't won on his own since 1950," while another opinion held that the Californian had emerged as "the party's chief national strategist" as he urged the formula of running against LBJ and in turn most accurately predicted the results.

All around the nation, analysis of the 1966 election supplied evidence that the Democratic landslide of two years earlier was now becoming a distant memory. Only three Republican national incumbents running for reelection lost their races across the entire nation. Republicans now held the governorships of five of the seven most populated states. Romney and Rockefeller had secured 34 percent of the African American vote in their contests, and Brooke garnered 86 percent of the minority vote in his race.

While the GOP had lost 529 state legislature seats in the legislative fiasco of 1964, they had now gained 700 seats, and a Washington society matron described the class of new Republican legislators as "all so pretty" due to their chiseled good looks and sartorial neatness—"there is not a rumpled one in the bunch." Good health, good looks, and apparent vigor seemed to radiate from the emerging leaders of the class of 1966.

George Romney, newly elected governor of Michigan, combined his Mormon aversion to tobacco and spirits with a brisk walk before breakfast to produce governmental criticism of the Vietnam War that caught national attention. His Illinois colleague, Senator Charles Percy, was described as a "Horatio Alger" individual, a self-made millionaire with the "moral fibers of a storybook character." The equally photogenic Ronald Reagan looked a good decade younger than his birth certificate attested, and alternated stints in his government office with horseback riding and marathon wood-chopping sessions. All of these men were beginning to view 1967 as the springboard for a possible run at the White House, especially as the current resident of that dwelling seemed to be veering between a brittle optimism and a deep-seated fear that the war in Southeast Asia was about to unravel the accomplishments of his Great Society.

While the new galaxy of emerging Republican stars was reaping widespread public attention after the election of 1966, two men who had come closer to actually touching the stars were gaining their own share of magazine covers and media attention.

James Lovell and Buzz Aldrin spent part of late 1966 putting exclamation points on Project Gemini, the last phase of the National Aeronautics and Space Administration's plan to fulfill John F. Kennedy's challenge to land Americans on the moon before the 1960s ended. One of the iconic photos of late 1966 occurred when Lovell snapped a photo of Aldrin standing in the open doorway of their Gemini spacecraft, with the Earth looming in the background. James Lovell Jr. and Edwin "Buzz" Aldrin were marking the end of the run-up to the moon that had been marked by the Mercury and Gemini projects and which were now giving way to the Apollo series, which would eventually see men setting foot on the moon.

Journalists in late 1966 chronicled the sixteen astronauts who traveled eighteen million miles in Earth orbits as participants of "Project Ho-Hum," or engaged in"clocking millions of miles with nothing more serious than a bruised elbow."

Life columnist Loudon Wainwright compared the almost businesslike attitude of both the astronauts and the American public in 1966 to six years earlier, when citizens waited anxiously for news of a chimpanzee who had been fired 414 miles out into the Atlantic. They admired its spunk on such a dangerous trip, then prayed for Mercury astronauts who endured the life-and-death drama of fuel running low, hatches not opening properly, and flaming reentries that seemed only inches from disaster. Now, in 1966, James Lovell, who had experienced eighty-five times more hours in space than John Glenn a half decade earlier, could walk down the street virtually unnoticed. By late 1966, American astronauts seemed to be experiencing what one magazine insisted was "the safest form of travel," but only days into the new year of 1967 the relative immunity of American astronauts would end in flames and controversy in the shocking inauguration of Project Apollo.

Late 1966 America, to which Lyndon Johnson returned from Vietnam and James Lovell and Buzz Aldrin returned from space, was a society essentially transitioning from the mid-1960s to the late 1960s in a decade that divides, more neatly than most, into three relatively distinct thirds. The first third of this tumultuous decade extended roughly from the introduction of the 1960 car models and the television season in September of

1959 and ended, essentially, over the November weekend in 1963 when John F. Kennedy was assassinated and buried.

This period was in many respects a transition from the most iconic elements of fifties culture to a very different sixties society that did not fully emerge until 1964. For example, the new 1960 model automobiles were notable by their absence of the huge tail fins of the late 1950s, but were still generally large, powerful vehicles advertised for engine size rather than fuel economy. Teen fashion in the early sixties morphed quickly from the black leather jacket/poodle skirts of *Grease* fame to crew cuts, bouffant hairdos, penny loafers, and madras skirts and dresses. Yet the film *Bye Bye Birdie*, a huge hit in the summer of 1963, combined a very early sixties fashion style for the teens of Sweet Apple, Ohio, with a very fifties leather jacketed and pompadoured Conrad Birdie in their midst.

Only months after *Bye Bye Birdie* entered film archives, the mid-sixties arrived when the Beatles first set foot in the newly named John F. Kennedy airport in New York, only a few weeks after the tragedy in Dallas. As the Beatles rehearsed for the first of three Sunday night appearances on *The Ed Sullivan Show*, boys consciously traded crew cuts for mop-head styles and teen girls avidly copied the styles of London's Carnaby Street fashion centers. By summer of 1964, *A Hard Day's Night* had eclipsed *Birdie* in ticket sales and media attention.

While the early sixties were dominated by the splendor and grandeur of the Kennedy White House, the wit and humor of the president, the effortless style of Jacqueline Kennedy, and the vigor of a White House of small children, touch football, and long hikes, the mid-sixties political scene produced far less glamour in the nation's capital. Ironically, Lyndon Johnson was far more successful in moving iconic legislation through a formerly balky Congress, yet the Great Society was more realistic but less glamorous than the earlier New Frontier. While the elegantly dressed Jack and stunningly attired Jackie floated through a sea of admiring luminaries at White House receptions, Johnson lifted his shirt to display recent surgery scars and accosted guests to glean legislative votes while the first lady did her best to pretend that her husband's antics had not really happened.

Much of what made mid-sixties society and culture fascinating and important happened well outside the confines of the national capital. Brave citizens of diverse cultures and races braved fire hoses and attack dogs in Selma, Alabama, to test the reach of the Great Society's emphasis on legal equality, while television networks edged toward integrating prime-time entertainment. Those same networks refought World War II with *Combat, The Gallant Man, McHale's Navy,* and *Broadside.* James Bond exploded onto the big screen with *From Russia With Love, Goldfinger,* and *Thunderball,* and the spy genre arrived on network television with *The Man from U.N.C.L.E., Get Smart,* and even *Wild, Wild West.*

The mid-sixties soundtrack rocked with the sounds of Liverpool and London as the Beatles were reinforced by the Rolling Stones, the Zombies, the Kinks, the Troggs, and the Dave Clark Five. American pop music responded with Bob Dylan going electric with "Like a Rolling Stone" and the Beach Boys' dreamy *Pet Sounds.* Barry McGuire rasped out the end of civilization in "Eve of Destruction," while the Lovin' Spoonful posed a more amenable parallel universe with "Do You Believe in Magic?"

The American sports universe of the mid-1960s produced a number of surprising outcomes that would significantly influence competitions in 1967 and beyond. For example, the 1964 Major League Baseball season featured a National League race dominated for all but the final week by one of its historically most inept teams. After the 1950 Philadelphia Phillies "Whiz Kids" soared to a league title, and a four-game sweep loss to the New York Yankees, the franchise spent most of the next decade mired in the National League cellar. Then a good but not exceptional team roared out to a spectacular start and, by mid-September, was printing World Series tickets with a seven-game lead with twelve games remaining. Then the Phillies hit a ten-game losing streak that included two losses when an opposing player stole home in the last inning. Meanwhile, the St. Louis Cardinals, who played badly enough to convince their owner to threaten to fire their manager at the end of the season, went on a winning streak, overtook the Phillies to win the pennant, then beat the New York Yankees of Mickey Mantle, Roger Maris, and Yogi Berra in a dramatic seven-game set.

Meanwhile, on the West Coast, a relatively stern-looking coach old enough to be the grandfather of his players was assembling a team that would carry UCLA to NCAA basketball championships in 1964 and 1965, virtually never losing a game in the process. Then, in the spring of 1965, coach John Wooden received news that the most highly sought-after high school player in the country, Lew Alcindor of Power Memorial High School in New York City, was leaving the East Coast to join the UCLA Bruins as a member of the freshman team. That team ended up winning the 1967 NCAA championship and became the final piece in one of the greatest collegiate basketball teams in history.

Finally, during this middle sixties period, Joe Namath a brash, unpolished quarterback from Beaver Falls, Pennsylvania, turned his back on northeastern colleges and enrolled at the University of Alabama. His subsequent sensational but controversial college career with the Crimson Tide would lead to victories in premier bowl games and his status as the most prized draft pick for the rival National and American football leagues. His acceptance of one of the largest signing bonuses in history—to join the New York Jets of the upstart AFL—would set in motion a series of negotiations that would shock the football world. In the summer of 1966, the rival leagues announced a merger that would culminate with an AFL–NFL championship game, quickly designated as the "Super Bowl." The first such game would be played January 1967.

While all this was going on, a very real war was raging in Southeast Asia. The fifteen thousand largely advisory American troops in place in South Vietnam in 1963 had, by late 1966, risen toward the half-million mark. Death totals were rising regularly at the time of Lyndon Johnson's dramatic appearance at Cam Ranh Bay.

By Halloween of 1966, American forces had been engaged in extensive combat in Vietnam for almost a year. Twelve months earlier, a massive Communist offensive intended to slice South Vietnam in two was initially thwarted by elements of the American Air Cavalry at the bloody battle of Ia Drang Valley. Though the enemy drive was blunted, the American death toll leaped from dozens to hundreds within a few days. Interest in the war from both supporters and opponents began rising rapidly, as television networks committed more time and resources to coverage of the conflict as well as pro-war and anti-war demonstrations that were taking place across the nation. By the end of 1966, the Vietnam War was the major American foreign policy issue, and it would grow even larger during the next twelve months. The question that still remained in late 1966 was how the conflict in Southeast Asia would affect an economic expansion that had created increasing prosperity through the entire decade of the 1960s.

As Americans prepared to celebrate the beginning of what promised to be an eventful new year, the news media was filled with summaries of society in 1966 and predictions for the future. The closing weeks of the year had produced a continuing economic surge that had pushed the Dow Jones Industrial Average past the 800 mark. Unemployment was hovering in a generally acceptable 3.5 percent range, with a feeling that there were more jobs than applicants for most positions requiring a high school diploma or above. The $550 billion Gross National Product of 1960 had climbed to $770 billion. *Fortune* magazine noted that "the great industrial boom of the last six years has lifted factory output by 50 percent and total output by 33 percent."

A frequent topic for journalists in late 1966 was the impact of an extended period of prosperity on the family and social life of an America now more than two decades removed from the challenges of war and depression. For example, twenty-five years after Pearl Harbor, the often uncomfortable reality of shared housing among extended family or even strangers—imposed by the Great Depression and then World War II— was almost totally absent in modern America. In fact, almost 98 percent of married couples now lived in their own household. The low marriage rate of the 1930s had rebounded to a 90 percent marriage rate among modern Americans. There was a nearly 70 percent remarriage rate among divorced citizens. Among the 25 percent of married Americans who had gotten divorced, about 90 percent now reported marital success the second time around.

The overwhelming tendency among young Americans to get married had been a key element in the iconic "baby boom" that had been a central element of family life for twenty years. Although the birth rate was just beginning to slip, the four-child household was basically the norm in contemporary society. Yet in this generally prosperous family environment, sociologists reported two problem areas: many children did not seem to have a concept of "what daddy did" in an increasingly office-oriented workforce, and in turn were less than enthused when "mommy sometimes worked too." This was a situation quite different from the overwhelming "reality" on television comedies based on "typical" families.

All in all, 1967 already was beginning to look like a roller-coaster ride for more than a few Americans.

CHAPTER I

Now in Living Color—Television in 1967

Several weeks before the official start of the 1966–1967 television season, network executives made two announcements that would significantly affect television viewing for the next half century. In the wake of the startling news that the two rival professional football leagues were about to merge, the public was informed that the first AFL–NFL championship game in January 1967 would be broadcast by two rival networks. A huge competition between NBC and CBS was ignited as viewers were enticed to watch one network or the other. The game was already becoming designated as the "Super Bowl," the first step in creating professional football as the most lucrative entertainment event available for network telecast, with the day of the game an unofficial American national holiday.

The second announcement, with even more massive economic and entertainment impact, was that ABC, NBC, and CBS were about to change their primarily monochrome telecasts into what NBC officials branded as "living color." In effect, the majority of home television sets were obsolete, as they would permit only a ghostly monochromatic image of programs that would now be available in the stunningly bright colors of the new broadcasting capabilities. Families that did not purchase the roughly $400 and up color sets were essentially reduced to watching Dorothy Gale's adventures only in Kansas, with the far more spectacular action in Oz only a shadow experience. Part of the "fire and ice" divide in the America of 1967 would be in living rooms and family rooms, between those individuals now able to access a rainbow on their television sets and those who still had to make do with multiple shades of gray.

The onset of virtually universal color broadcasting was the third wave in the relationship between television and American society since the end of World War II, and would be the major technological breakthrough until the emergence of VCRs in the 1980s. After several years of experimental television broadcasting in a limited number of cities, a recognizable three-network broadcasting industry began to emerge, with ABC, NBC, and CBS offering some predictable format of television services in the fall of 1948. Almost all television was done live, with very little of the programming scripted. Popular shows included audition-oriented talent programming such as *Arthur Godfrey's Talent Scouts* and *Stop Me If You've Heard This One*; prime-time cooking and fashion shows such as *The Dione Lucas Cooking Show* and *Paris Cavalcade of Fashions*; and limited sports shows, such as *Monday Night Boxing* and *Gillette Cavalcade of Sports* on Fridays. There were huge portions of the day when the only programming was the local station's signal pattern, and only sporadic programming after 9:00 p.m. on most nights.

By roughly 1954, recognizable, often iconic scripted series were beginning to dominate viewing, which in turn encouraged families without television sets to buy the relatively expensive appliance. Many 1960s critics viewed the early to middle 1950s as the "Golden Age" of television in what seemed a cornucopia of entertainment, from *I Love Lucy* to *Dragnet* to Milton Berle to Jackie Gleason. Early prime time included such educationally valuable shows as *Mr. Wizard* and *Kukla, Fran and Ollie*, followed by the mixed child/adult audience for *The Lone Ranger*, *The Gene Autry Show*, and *The Adventures of Rin Tin Tin*.

No one was exactly sure when the Golden Age of television reached its peak, but by the mid-1960s much of this era seemed long over. Meanwhile, the main advances in television seemed to be that the screens had jumped from mostly twelve-inch sets to twenty-one inches. Portable televisions had also become available, allowing viewing in virtually any part of the house. Few households that watched television did not have access to one or more of the sets.

During the run-up to the great switch over to color in the 1966–1967 season, the relatively few families that were willing to spend the triple or quadruple price to attain a color set were treated to a handful of programs and events that seemed to most families to be a poor return on the investment. The National Broadcasting Cooperation, which featured the most colorcasting and its soon-to-be iconic multihued peacock, enticed viewers with the Tournament of Roses Parade, the Rose Bowl, the World Series, and its most popular long-term program, *Bonanza*, in color. A product of the day's technology, the colorcasts seemed to offer too many green faces and orange hairdos, with primitive color adjustment buttons. Too many programs were still in black and white and not really enticing on a mass scale. This standoff was complicated by the fact that two of the three major networks were engaged in a feud over exactly how to make the switch from monochromes to color telecasting. The NBC network favored "compatible" broadcasting, in which one television set could show both color and black-and-white programs until monochrome sets were phased out by attrition. Their CBS competitor was more inclined toward sets developed exclusively for color transmission in a very rapid turnover, in which black-and-white televisions might become obsolescent when the big switch occurred. In reality, the two competitors each received a partial victory. These two networks, joined by the still slightly junior American Broadcasting Company, agreed to a total conversion to colorcasting for the 1966–1967 season, while the NBC-favored "compatible" sets would become the exclusive outlet for the new color broadcasting. This would allow viewers still comfortable with monochrome service to continue to use their current television sets.

The first major event of something dated "1967" occurred over a roughly two-week period in the autumn of 1966 when, as per telecasting policy, the 1967 television season premiered nationwide. While there were still many more monochrome sets in use than new color models, a combination of a substantial upward curve of color sales and the willingness of color set owners to frequently invite friends, relatives, and neighbors into their living rooms to partake in the still-novel viewing experience ensured that by the end of the 1967 TV season, a large percentage of Americans had watched their first color broadcasts.

Despite the ability to perceive suit or dress color and the added hues of indoor or outdoor soundstages, much of the viewing audience was still enthralled by variety and situation comedy programs centered around celebrities from earlier in the decade or even back into the 1950s. The 1967 television season still featured long-term standbys such as Jackie Gleason, Ed Sullivan, Garry Moore, Lucille Ball, Red Skelton, Bob Hope, Danny Kaye, and even "Mr. Television" himself, Milton Berle. These celebrities had been the bedrock of television broadcasting for much of the previous two decades and were among the most recognizable names in American culture. These were the programs traditionally viewed in living rooms with entire families watching. These family variety shows were supplemented by the two quiz shows that had survived the virtual annihilation of that genre in the late 1950s, when scandals torpedoed *Twenty-One, The $64,000 Question, Tic-Tac-Dough*, and other "big payoff" programs, all of which had been discovered to be rigged. Because *What's My Line* and *I've Got a Secret* had much smaller payoffs yet maintained large audiences, this duo formed the core of surviving family viewer quiz programs. They were supplemented by the snoop fest of early reality programming, the hugely popular *Candid Camera*, in which sheer embarrassment seemed to guarantee high ratings.

While most of this core of family prime-time programming was essentially based on a stage and often live broadcasts, the more heavily scripted, film-based situation comedies had undergone an enormous transition by 1967. During the late 1950s, a group of family-oriented situation comedies became almost synonymous with the whole concept of family life in the Eisenhower era. *Make Room for Daddy, The Donna Reed Show, Leave It to Beaver, Father Knows Best, The Adventures of Ozzie and Harriet,* and *My Three Sons* were all family-based riffs on lighthearted adventures that in many cases could have been based on different streets of the same community. These programs represented the explosion of suburbia during the postwar years. Other than having smaller numbers of children than their real-life counterparts and the plotline that Fred MacMurray was a single parent on *My Three Sons*, these shows seemed to mirror much of white middle-class family lifestyles of the period.

As the late sixties beckoned, only *My Three Sons* was still on the air, and situation comedy seemed to be exploding everywhere other than traditional suburban family adventures. It is difficult to ascertain whether suburban families grew tired of seeing themselves on television or viewers from other places, races, or ages wanted to be counted as well, but the situation comedies on TV in 1967 would have been almost unrecognizable in living rooms a decade earlier.

The two most popular comedies developed against a traditional suburban backdrop featured, as their lead female stars, a witch and a genie. Samantha Stevens at least had a surface "normal life" with a daughter, an advertising executive husband, and meddling parents, but a mere wiggle of her cute nose radically altered the traditional plotline and left reality in the rearview mirror. However, while Elizabeth Montgomery's *Bewitched* character at least spent most nights in a bedroom with two incarnations of husband Darren (Dick York and Dick Sargent), Barbara Eden's Jeannie in *I Dream of Jeannie* spent most of her time in a magic bottle, on call from Larry Hagman's Tony, who was more interested in his astronaut activities and only developed romantic feelings for her in later seasons.

Interestingly, most of the remaining situation comedies steered very far from split-level homes and lawn mowers. Some aspect of rural or small-town lifestyles permeated most of the hit comedies of the season. The two longest-running hit situation comedies were *The Andy Griffith Show*, featuring the title character as a sheriff in a small North Carolina town, and *The Beverly Hillbillies*, which transplanted down-on-his-luck hick Buddy Ebsen to Southern California when he discovered oil on his otherwise worthless land. These early 1960s shows were still popular enough in 1967 to produce equally successful spin-offs, including an urban middle-aged couple purchasing a farm in *Green Acres*, three young ladies and their mother coping with rural romance in *Petticoat Junction*, and a rural marine recruit coping with military life in *Gomer Pyle*. All five of these situation comedies had huge audiences in 1967, and the more they were panned by largely urban television critics, the more convinced their audiences were of a cultural divide in American culture.

While rural/small-town situation comedy was still thriving in 1967, the iconic portrayal of many of the values from the 1950s and early 1960s had diminished significantly. At the turn of the decade, the 1959–1960 television season, the three networks produced a record thirty-seven prime-time programs that depicted some elements of the Old West. From well-dressed, hard-hitting sheriff Bat Masterson, to the Yukon goldfields of *The Alaskans*, to the single-parent homestead on *The Rifleman*, cowboys had been king at the end of the 1950s. Now, in 1967, just as colorcasting could far better transmit the majesty of the West, the genre's representation had shrunk significantly.

A few survivors of the golden era of TV westerns still flourished with hard-core but aging audiences. Marshal Matt Dillon still possessed his quick draw on *Gunsmoke* and Ben Cartwright and his sons still ranched the Ponderosa in *Bonanza*, but most of the remaining westerns sought success by distancing themselves from the plotlines and characters of the past. The producers of *Daniel Boone* exchanged cowboy hats for coonskin caps and moved the action back a full century, when the West began in Pittsburgh. Fess Parker essentially pulled his iconic 1950s Walt Disney Davy Crockett coonskin cap and long rifle and created a successful niche in frontier life. While *Daniel Boone* went back to the eighteenth century, the producers of the hugely popular *The Wild Wild West* essentially melded the 1960s James Bond craze with a version of nineteenth-century high-tech, in which Robert Conrad battled retro versions of Goldfinger or Dr. No with a western backdrop. *F Troop* turned the classic John Ford *Fort Apache* and *She Wore a Yellow Ribbon* cavalry-fort epics into comedy, with Ken Berry as the well-meaning but clueless commanding officer of an isolated fort. There, both the garrison and the native residents are running a giant con, with staged fake battles and a joint lust for loot. Another recent entry into the shrinking western genre was the largely successful *Big Valley*, which shamelessly exchanged Lorne Greene's single-father role into Barbara Stanwyck's single-mother matriarch of a spread seemingly larger than the Ponderosa. This ABC mirror image of NBC's *Bonanza* provided a profitable proving ground for young talents Lee Majors and Linda Evans, portraying step-siblings in the edgy world of frontier cattle raising combined with a complex family structure.

By 1967, much of the action lost by the shrinking of those thirty-nine western programs at the beginning of the decade had been channeled into the duo of spies and space.

The world of espionage and spies was an important component of the Cold War between the United States and its largely Western European allies and an eastern bloc dominated by the Soviet Union and the People's Republic of China. While the onset of nuclear weapons had made a nuclear exchange between America and Russia a lose-lose situation, each side was engaged in a global chess match to gain any advantage possible in this twilight confrontation. Ironically, much of the impetus for the spy image of the mid- to late 1960s had been initiated by a physically unimpressive, chain-smoking, British man about town who had used family connections to spend World War II as an intelligence officer in the Royal Navy. During the 1950s, Ian Fleming created a far more handsome version of himself in a hugely successful series of novels centered around James Bond, Agent 007. By the 1960s, Bond fans included John F. Kennedy, and the books were adapted to motion pictures, beginning with *Dr. No* in 1962.

The James Bond film series featured a predictable but hugely popular format in which Sean Connery as Agent 007 would confront an archvillain, usually from a shadowy organization known as SPECTRE. The consequences of Bond's failure would be a spectacular enemy attack, usually on some iconic American target. The third installment in the series, *Goldfinger*, released in 1964, pushed the franchise from success to near-cult status as archvillains Auric Goldfinger and Pussy Galore conspired to set off a nuclear device in the gold depository at Fort Knox, only to be foiled by Bond at the last second. *Goldfinger* spawned toys, games, fashions, and a major interest among the networks in shifting much of their action series stable from the Wild West to the contemporary Cold War. The follow-up success of *Thunderball* in 1965, and the upcoming release of *You Only Live Twice* in

1967, meant that by the 1966–1967 television season, spies, intrigue, and Cold War confrontation were pushing shoot-outs in Tombstone or Dodge City to the margins. The characters in these spy series exemplified much of the "fire and ice" that was a signature of the era.

By 1967, the two most successful television adaptations of the Bond films were both on NBC, *The Man from U.N.C.L.E.* and *I Spy*. Each of these series took the "hot" and "cool" sides of James Bond and apportioned them between two equal but different characters. Despite the singular term in the title, this series quickly developed as essentially "the men from U.N.C.L.E." and focused on an American with a playboy persona, Napoleon Solo, and the more scholarly, detached Soviet/Ukranian representative Illya Kuryakin. Surprisingly for the Cold War era, the United Network Command for Law Enforcement was a truly international organization and featured agents from virtually every continent. The major threats in the series were not Soviet spies, but a seemingly unending supply of megalomaniacs, each with eccentricities and each determined to rule the world. Their umbrella organization was THRUSH, which featured both agents and uniformed soldiers who always seemed to outgun the U.N.C.L.E. forces until the final scene.

While the earlier episodes centered around Robert Vaughn's Napoleon Solo character, with David McCallum's Illya as a secondary personage, McCallum's cool accent and moppish Beatles' haircut attracted legions of younger fans. In the "hot" versus "cool" duality of the era, Napoleon, though cool under pressure, often took risks to develop relationships with women who invariably either unknowingly led him into a trap or were enemy agents themselves. On the other hand, Illya virtually never fell into this pitfall and maintained a polite but cool demeanor with females. One episode even included his real-life wife, Jill Ireland.

By early 1967, *The Man from U.N.C.L.E* was the seventh most popular network program and had achieved enough success to produce a spin-off, *The Girl from U.N.C.L.E.* This series starred Stephanie Powers as April Dancer, the first full-fledged female U.N.C.L.E. agent, and British actor Noel Harrison played her alternatively bemused and exasperated partner, Mark Slate.

April Dancer became virtually the prime model for 1960s mod fashions, with multiple changes each episode of boots, miniskirts, and quirky hats. She almost never fired a weapon, instead using an awesome display of martial arts combined with gas-dispensing compacts and lipstick tubes to defeat classic THRUSH megalomaniacs. April Dancer's character was so popular with young female viewers that *U.N.C.L.E.* was asked to do a photo shoot for *Seventeen* magazine, in which she cavorted through a mock episode (always called an "Affair" in both *U.N.C.L.E.* series) that featured a different "groovy" outfit on each page.

Both *U.N.C.L.E.* series were hugely popular with young audiences and presented a virtual global travelogue as each segment opened with a caption of "Somewhere in . . ." The locales ranged from exotic to mundane, from Paris in one episode to an Iowa cornfield in another. By 1967, the two *U.N.C.L.E.* programs were must-see viewing for a huge segment of the young American population. All of the lead characters were prominently featured in youth-oriented magazines. However, the NBC studios had another solid spy hit in their stables that at times evoked far more controversy and realism than Napoleon, Illya, or April could.

The enormous success of *Goldfinger* in theaters and subsequent popularity of *U.N.C.L.E.* in its first season encouraged NBC executives to take a risk in launching a rather different spy show in late 1965. The program, cryptically titled *I Spy*, would not be centered on a fictional global network but around two members of the CIA who would be confronting much more realistic threats to American security. The two agents were Kelly Robinson, a relatively successful tennis pro, and his personal trainer Scott Alexander, who would actually be a multilingual Ivy League–educated agent. The series featured the same close, trusting relationship as between Napoleon and Illya, but added substantial new dimensions to the spy genre. First, unlike *U.N.C.L.E.*, which was shot on a Hollywood lot and relied on stock footage for its glamorous episode sites, *I Spy* would be shot on location in foreign locales, in the tradition of the James Bond films. This was a major deviation from most network programming, but initially paled from the other innovation: Kelly would be portrayed by veteran actor Robert Culp, while Scott would be played by the emerging African American comedian, Bill Cosby.

As soon as the show went on the air, *I Spy* generated kudos from critics for its realism, plotlines, and exotic backdrop. The show also elicited howls of protest from some southern station owners, who substituted cartoons in that time slot rather than subject their audiences to such a level of racial equality. During the series, Kelly and Scott formed an even deeper relationship than Napoleon and Illya, as *U.N.C.L.E.* director Mr. Waverly usually sent significant reinforcements if the odds became too steep. The *I Spy* duo worked largely without this form of safety net.

The NBC network's trio of spy dramas was given added spice by one of its most popular comedies, a spoof of the espionage game titled *Get Smart*. Comedian Don Adams played Maxwell Smart, a bumbling version of Napoleon Solo or James Bond who was the chief field agent for a mysterious organization called CONTROL. His support network seemed to be largely limited to the head of the agency (Ed Platt), who was simply called "Chief," and sultry real-life model Barbara Feldon, who was known as "99." Much of the comic plotline centered around conflicts with an enemy organization, KAOS, which was even more bumbling than CONTROL, and the romantic interest of Feldon for the not particularly handsome Smart, who seemed oblivious to her attention. The often over-the-top use of two- or three-word sentences and incomprehensible "techno" speech became a major American social phenomenon, as people satirized the dialogue in everyday conversations.

While NBC enjoyed four solid ratings winners in its quartet of spy programs, their two major rivals countered in 1967 with soon-to-be iconic thrillers of their own. CBS had already incorporated spy elements into its hit western *Wild Wild West*, and ABC's series *Voyage to the Bottom of the Sea* merged science fiction and espionage, but it was not until the 1967 season that those networks had full-fledged spy competitors to NBC's stable of hit shows.

The American Broadcasting Company discovered its most iconic spy drama through the back door of summer replacement programming. In an attempt to entice summer viewers away from the rival networks' reruns in late spring of 1966, the network replaced the canceled series *The Long Hot Summer* with Britain's ITV network hit, *The Avengers*. In an ironic series of twists, *The Avengers* had been Britain's single commercial network response to the Bond craze on that side of the Atlantic when they paired off Patrick Macnee as a dapper but deadly secret agent with Honor Blackman as a tough-minded female counterpart. The adventures of John Steed and Cathy Gale proved to be a smash hit in Britain as it progressed in a relatively no-nonsense action-oriented format. The popular pairing ended when Blackman left the show to play the lead female role of Pussy Galore in the James Bond hit *Goldfinger*.

In the wake of Blackman's defection, series producers and writers decided to replace her with tall, willowy theater star Diana Rigg, who played the wealthy socialite widow of a famous explorer and man about London. The new billing was framed as John Steed, a "top professional" agent of an unnamed ministry spy agency, and Emma Peel as a "talented amateur" who seemed to have social access to everyone in British high society. The reconfigured series exchanged hard-bitten criminals for eccentric and wealthy millionaires and added an undercurrent of humor as Steed and Peel stepped over a steady stream of bodies.

The Avengers was designed only for a British audience, but when ABC aired the program as a summer replacement, critics and audiences raved about the plotlines and the "Britishness" of the show. Since Britain was still years away from telecasting in color, when ABC announced it wanted to pencil the program into its January 1967 replacement lineup, the show had to be shot in "colour," and the writers added an even broader dimension of British manners and eccentricities into the new episodes. By using Carnaby Street mod fashions like Emma Peel's iconic single-piece jumpsuits and boots, *The Avengers* became a window on Britain for huge numbers of American viewers. As Steed and Peel waded through some of the most bizarre villains in television history, dispatched mainly by Steed's reinforced steel bowler hat and umbrella and Peel's martial arts prowess, *The Avengers* became the first British-produced full-length program to became a notable prime-time hit in America. The couple would become an iconic part of 1967 popular culture.

While ABC went overseas to respond to their rival network's success in the spy game, CBS executives remained closer to home and approved producer Bruce Geller's proposal for an action/adventure/espionage drama that would become an iconic franchise into the twenty-first century. Geller planned his new series, *Mission Impossible*, as a chess match between an entire team of "cool" American agents pitted against an often hot-blooded mixture of Communist dictators, Third World caudillos, and psychotic American gangsters.

In the initial 1966–1967 season, the "Impossible Mission Force" was commanded by actor Steven Hill as "Mr. Briggs" (he would eventually be replaced by Peter Graves), who began each episode visiting locations ranging from a record store to a hotel front desk. There, he would receive a record or tape in which the never-seen head of IMF would present the latest crisis, suggest the tasks ahead, and remind Briggs that the tape would self-destruct ten seconds after the message was completed. The next scene would feature Briggs in the den of his gorgeous apartment, sorting through photo dossiers of potential selections of the team, which was usually composed around femme fatale Cinnamon (Barbara Bain), master of disguise Rollin (Martin Landau), strongman Willy (Peter Lupus), and tech wizard Barney (Greg Morris). Other members would be added to the team, depending on the mission. The script writers probably had a field day assigning appropriate place names to fictional nations that were either behind the Iron Curtain or somewhere in Latin America.

Mission Impossible was extremely fast paced and exciting compared to many 1960s television series, and relied heavily on the "ice in their veins" cool heroes who were often only centimeters or nanoseconds away from exposure or death but still maintained their composure. A unique sidebar to the plotline was the insistence that either the team or the individual members always be informed that they could choose to turn down any mission at any time, while also being informed that if they were caught, the Secretary (of an unnamed organization) would deny that the team ever existed. Fifty years later, the *Mission Impossible* brand was still quite viable in the Tom Cruise film series.

The spy orientation of action programs that essentially filled the void left by the demise of early sixties westerns was complemented by the emergence of a solid core of network science fiction offerings that in many respects became as iconic as the espionage genre. Perhaps the most iconic moment in television science fiction up to that moment occurred when an "away team" beamed down to an utterly desolate planet and became the victims of a creature that could create an image of the *Enterprise*'s chief medical officer's former flame.

"The Man Trap" was not the first episode of *Star Trek* in order of filming, but it gave viewers a hint of the size of the USS *Enterprise* and its crew when several personnel were killed by the first commercial break. Since NBC initially seemed to be blasé about presenting episodes in the order in which they were filmed, the home audience was kept on the edge of their seats attempting to create some coherence from a series that incorporated three different pilot episodes in a very nonlinear march to the stars. Dr. Leonard McCoy, the object of an alien shape-shifting salt-craving creature disguised as his former girlfriend, turned out to be the third chief medical officer in one of the three "first episodes" sprinkled throughout the first season.

Yet once a growing legion of fans began to connect the dots on what producer Gene Roddenberry termed "Wagon Train to the stars"—where phasers replaced six-shooters and warp drive replaced stagecoaches—a healthy segment of the younger population settled in to "go where no man has gone before." Through the clever use of "star dates" in Captain James Kirk's verbal, ongoing log entries, viewers were only informed that they were witnessing adventures somewhere between two and three centuries beyond the 1960s, yet were still brought back to comfortable ground as the frequent time-travel experiments seemed to send the USS *Enterprise* back to the twentieth century more than any other era.

Star Trek never came close to rivaling the network ratings of *Gunsmoke* and *I Love Lucy*, but it was the first science fiction program that created a franchise of multiple follow-up television series and theatrical films that in many ways transformed the relationship between television and the silver screen.

The 1967 television season saw the origin of "Trekkies" and included an above-average supply of the iconic episodes in all of the franchise's incarnations. In many respects, this program embodied the emerging reality of a generation gap, as legions of older viewers simply could not comprehend the plots or the gadgets, while younger members of the same family reveled in transporters, phasers, warp drives, and Vulcan science officers.

In a Cold War that brought the possibility that there would be no old age for younger members of society, Gene Roddenberry's view of the future was an essentially optimistic one, even if Klingons and Romulans hovered around the edges of civilization.

Star Trek was one of the major programs of 1967 that played above its weight category. It had enormous difficulty attracting viewers over forty, yet enticed much of the population below that age. It also enhanced the impact of several other science fiction–oriented programs on NBC's rival networks and, at least for 1967, created a substantial subgenre in network programming.

Although *Star Trek* was the first truly iconic science fiction program of the mid- to late 1960s and helped fill the gap created by the demise of *Twilight Zone* and *The Outer Limits*, a few years earlier a producer named Irwin Allen had already provided a science fiction alternative to the shrinking world of TV westerns.

Allen jumped into the post-Sputnik space race in 1961 by coming out with a modestly budgeted, hugely publicized film titled *Voyage to the Bottom of the Sea*. Allen combined ecological disaster, Cold War tension, and technical wizardry in a film that featured aging film stars Walter Pidgeon, Joan Fontaine, and Peter Lorre with younger television stars Barbara Eden, Michael Ansara, and Robert Sterling. He spiced the mix with early rock-and-roll star Frankie Avalon and placed the group abroad a futuristic submarine named the *Seaview*.

The plot centered around Pidgeon as brilliant scientist Harrison Nelson, who uses his newly created brainchild submarine to attempt to fire missiles to extinguish a fire wrapping the world around the Van Allen radiation belt. As every navy in the world attempts to stop him and internal enemies attempt to sabotage the mission, Nelson saves the world—all in spectacular Technicolor and Cinemascope.

This hybrid of James Bond and science fiction proved popular enough that ABC signed Allen to create a television series based on the film. However, while *Voyage to the Bottom of the Sea* achieved modest success on ABC, competing CBS approached the producer to create a space version of Swiss Family Robinson for its prime-time schedule.

Lost in Space was set near the end of the twentieth century, at a time when overpopulation on Earth had encouraged governments to sponsor a program to send world-renowned astrophysicist Dr. John Robinson to Alpha Centauri. There, he would establish an Earth colony that was to attract huge numbers of settlers. By its 1967 second season, the program, newly telecast in color, was a serious rival to *Star Trek* in attracting young audiences. The parents in the Robinson expedition were well-known to viewers. June Lockhart, who played Timmy's mother in the hit series *Lassie*, was the mother, while John Robinson was played by Guy Williams, the star of *Zorro* only a few years earlier.

While Williams and Lockhart shared top billing, by the second season in 1966–1967 most of the plotlines were dominated by a budding romance between eldest daughter Judy (Marta Kristen) and command pilot Don (Mark Goddard). Another major plotline featured younger daughter Penny (Angela Cortwright) and young son Will (Billy Mumy), who quickly emerged as the two most popular characters on the program.

By 1967, the two most influential adults on *Lost in Space* were a strange duo of Dr. Smith—a bumbling foreign agent who had sneaked aboard the *Jupiter V* to destroy the ship on takeoff, and then found himself trapped aboard—and a highly intelligent robot who never received a name but became the family protector. *Lost in Space* was popular even though the plots were quite predictable, as some form of alien creature would either attack or kidnap Will and Penny, "robot" would rescue them, and unwilling Dr. Smith (Jonathan Harris) would run away or attempt to make a deal with the villains. Throughout 1967, many school playgrounds and corridors resonated with the robot's stern warning to Billy Mumy,

"Danger, danger, Will Robinson!" that always preceded the emergence of the alien villain of the week.

While *Star Trek* and *Lost in Space* took science fiction in new directions on prime-time television, the writers and producers of an emerging daytime drama turned the world of soap operas in an entirely new direction in 1967. A few months into 1966, producer/writer Don Curtis convinced ABC to attempt to bolster its relatively lackluster stable of soap operas with a daytime daily series that avoided "normal" middle-class issues and skirted more toward gothic plotlines. The new series was titled *Dark Shadows* and set in Collinsport, Maine, primarily in the mansion of reclusive, wealthy members of the Collins family. The initial catalyst for plotlines was an orphaned young lady by the name of Victoria Winters, who secures her first job as a nanny for the Collinses' youngest son.

While *Dark Shadows* achieved some audience attention due to its non-traditional location and hints of darker things to come, the series exploded into national recognition when Curtis broke completely with soap opera plotlines and introduced a resident vampire into the family, two-hundred-year-old Barnabas Collins. After Barnabas is mistakenly brought back to life, he veers between romantic affection for Victoria (Alexandra Moltke) and Victoria's waitress friend Maggie Evans (Kathryn Leigh Scott). As the body count among town residents and the Collins family shoots up, audience share climbed and national news outlets picked up on the excitement. Younger viewers, bored by the infidelities and petty arguments of most characters in daytime dramas, raced home from school to watch hero/villain Barnabas (Jonathan Frid) pick off his own Collins descendants. In late summer and early fall, *Dark Shadows* gained even more popularity when it shifted to color and ventured into a new plotline in which Victoria participates in a séance that throws her back in time to 1795. There, she witnesses the events that turned Barnabas into a creature of the night. The colorcasts added hugely to the sumptuous period costumes and sets and created fascinating new roles for the actors as they all assumed the identities of the 1795 plotline.

From Barnabas Collins to Captain James T. Kirk to John Steed and Mrs. Peel to the men from U.N.C.L.E., the 1967 television season was producing genres that would eventually be recreated in film versions a half century later. The television images of the year of fire and ice that witnessed the transformation of television from monochrome to stunning color would undergo a further reincarnation on the silver screen of a new century.

CHAPTER II

Vietnam:
The Stride of a Giant

On January 1, 1967, just as dawn was warning of another torrid day in the deep-green tableau that was the Republic of South Vietnam, a trim, athletic, middle-aged American solider clambered out of his bed in the villa of a French wine merchant, engaged in a rapid-fire set of sit-ups and push-ups and, clad in a bathrobe, ambled over to his in-house communications center to survey the latest combat information from all corners of his command. After a breakfast of one egg, two pieces of toast, and a cup of black coffee, General William Westmoreland donned a starched and pressed version of standard combat fatigues and ducked into the back seat of a black air-conditioned staff car that began maneuvering through the overcrowded environs of Saigon City. He was on the way to Tan Son Nhut airport, the nerve center of the American expeditionary force in the embattled entity called South Vietnam.

General Westmoreland was blessed with a combination of good looks, presence, and military bearing that at first glance might remind someone of George McClellan, Robert E. Lee, or Douglas MacArthur. He seemed destined to be a notable battlefield commander. At that moment, Westmoreland commanded a force of 400,000 American servicemen, a contingent that would rise by another 100,000 before the year ended. That number far exceeded the forces under McClellan or Lee and was comparable to MacArthur's frontline ground force two decades earlier.

It was roughly fourteen months after the first significant American engagement at Ia Drang in November of 1965, relatively the same point in the Vietnam conflict as the Battle of Antietam in the Civil War and the battles of Kasserine Pass and Guadalcanal in World War II. Ironically, Westmoreland's first major step to his present command had occurred at Kasserine Pass when, as a young artillery battalion commander, he had blunted German Field Marshal Erwin Rommel's gambit to break through a final American defense line at Thala.

Westmoreland had risen from battalion command to four-star general, but commanded an army engaged in operations that were far different than those that engaged Germany's legendary "Desert Fox." The topography and environment of Vietnam was far closer to Guadalcanal than Antietam or Kasserine Pass, but while Guadalcanal was a relatively compact island on which the American Navy gradually controlled most ingress and egress, South Vietnam was approximately the size of Florida, and was merely the lower half of a quite large peninsula extending downward from the heart of the Asian continent. The United States was only a little more than a decade removed from a somewhat similar conflict in Korea. That war had been fought in far more open terrain than Vietnam and along a more clearly defined battle line, in which the majority of the South Korean population supported their government against the fanatic northerners of Kim Il-sung.

While the Korean War had begun with a Pearl Harbor–like Sunday morning surprise attack across the north/south border and brought American combat forces almost immediately into the fray, there simply was no Lexington and Concord, Fort Sumter, or Pearl Harbor in this new Southeast Asia conflict. Almost from the moment in 1954 when the Geneva accords turned Vietnam from a French colony into a Communist-dominated North and a non-Communist South, Ho Chi Minh began formulating plans for forceable reunification if the recalcitrant southerners did not succumb to the inevitablity of unification. By the early 1960s, vast numbers of pro-Communist southerners, commonly described as the Viet Cong, were gradually escalating operations against a series of southern governments averse to falling under "Uncle Ho's" mantle. Soon after John Kennedy's assassination in 1963, new president Lyndon Johnson began countering each Viet Cong escalation with another contingent of American forces, culminating with the dispatch of major American combat units in 1965. Starting with the bloody battle of the Ia Drang Valley, which pitted the American Air Cavalry against the enemy in the autumn of 1965, US forces were able to prevent the enemy from slicing South Vietnam in two but could never coax the Communists into a set-piece battle large enough to permanently cripple Ho's intentions.

The twelve months preceding January 1967 had been a period of massive buildup for American forces, with Westmoreland's command soaring from 155,000 to more than 400,000, a commitment that was straining the army and the Marine Corps to their limits. Johnson, meanwhile, was being pushed ever closer to the politically unpopular expedient of mobilizing the National Guard and reserves, a move guaranteed to turn an already marginally unpopular conflict into a potentially election-changing massive unrest and protest. By early 1967, Johnson's political future and Westmoreland's military career were increasingly dependent on the general's battle plan, called "search and destroy," which was centered around constant assaults on enemy base camps, supply depots, communication centers, and command structures. American air and ground forces were mobilized to strike any place, any time. In 1967, the president would provide his battlefield commander with about 8,000 reinforcements a month to gradually expand operations, but Westmoreland's task was complicated by two aspects of the war that hugely influenced operations.

First, Johnson and Westmoreland were essentially fighting a war in a nation that was in most respects technically at peace. Even though a majority of Americans would at least tacitly support the conflict until late summer, there was also a general consensus, tacitly accepted by the military, that individual armed forces personnel could not be expected to serve in Vietnam for the duration of a conflict that seemed to have no end in sight. Therefore, soldiers posted to Vietnam would experience a tour of duty of only a single year (thirteen months for marines). The day that year was completed, soldiers would be whisked back home on jet passenger liners complete with stewardesses and beverages. Thus, for most of the war, there would be few World War II or Korean War grizzled veterans, but rather a constantly changing cast of late-teen and early-twenties Americans who were passing through Vietnam between school experiences, jobs, and relationships. They were soon replaced by a less experienced version of themselves.

Second, in an attempt to maintain some sense of morale in a war with few road signs to total victory, these young people "in country" would, whenever possible, be provided with an environment that was at least some imitation of life at home. This concession would require a huge amount of support personnel to maintain some provision of decent food, housing, and recreation for the troops. Thus, Westmoreland's combat strength of true frontline soldiers and marines would be proportionately smaller than in previous American conflicts, and his "frontline rifle men" would be somewhat smaller than his World War II–era counterparts.

The Vietnam campaign of 1967 would be conducted by an American contingent of 400,000 soldiers, sailors, airmen, and marines, which would be augmented by approximately 8,000 personnel a month over and above replacements for Americans who had been killed, wounded, or had finished their tour of duty. Westmoreland also technically commanded an Allied force centered around a South Korean division; an Australian battalion; and contingents from Thailand, New Zealand, and a few other allies supported by elite South Vietnamese marine, air force, and other special forces. In all, his reliable combat forces totaled half a million men at the beginning of the year. However, the Military Assistance Command Vietnam (MACV) commander enjoyed a numerical superiority far below the (traditional) ratio of a ten to one superiority when taking the offensive in a guerrilla or insurgency conflict. Despite heavy casualties in 1966, the North Vietnamese were infiltrating about 8,400 regulars a month, while the Viet Cong were recruiting about 3,500 southerners a month. This pushed the Communist army to just over 300,000 men, or a 5:3 ratio, far below textbook guerrilla war doctrines.

While the search-and-destroy concept was most widely publicized in print and on television reports, strategy also included aspects of the supposedly rival "ink blot" concept of "clear and hold," in which ever-widening zones of South Vietnam would be pacified, secured, and expanded in an ever-spreading ink blot on a map. American forces in 1967 would be conducting operations that had a certain precedence in a nearly successful British strategy in the later stages of the American War of Independence. In the wake of the disastrous defeat and surrender at the Battle of Saratoga in 1777, the British head of military and foreign affairs, Lord George Germain, approved a plan in which His Majesty's forces would abandon the rebel capital in Philadelphia, maintain a large garrison in the major port of New York, and send much of the field army south to Georgia to begin recapturing the colonies. The plan was to move northward province by province, with the ultimate objective to gradually recover all of the colonies below New England, offer extremely generous peace terms to the rebels, and leave a rump rebel nation trapped between British Canada and the newly welcomed back rebel colonies from New York southward. Only the French fleet at Yorktown, Virginia, ended the British march northward, but the plan inflicted some of the worst American defeats of the year at Savannah, Charleston, Camden, and numerous smaller engagements.

Westmoreland's search-and-destroy operations would have enough success during 1967 to convince the North Vietnamese politicians to authorize the risky and ultimately bloody Tet Offensive early the next year, which for a time turned the conflict from an insurgency into a conventional confrontation in which the Americans won the military battle and the Communists won the public relations aftermath.

When Colonel Harold Moore's 1st Battalion, 7th Cavalry landed by helicopter in Landing Zone X-Ray in the Ia Drang Valley on November 14, 1965, the Communist insurgency had gained control of about 40 percent of South Vietnam's territory and roughly half of the population. Secretary of Defense Robert McNamara privately considered the Vietnamese operation to be a "bottomless pit," while Lyndon Johnson was just beginning to see the conflict as a major threat to his cherished Great Society domestic reforms. If Johnson had not authorized massive land, sea, and air reinforcements, it is a strong possibility that New Year's Day 1967 would have witnessed a united Communist "people's republic" of Vietnam. The nation would have morphed from a corrupt, chaotic but at least somewhat open nation into an Orwellian nightmare of thought police, "reeducation" camps, frequent executions, and a cult of personality in leadership.

The enormous American troop buildup during 1967 would ultimately contribute to the failure of a president to be reelected, raise the prospects for a Republican in the White House in the next election, and stay the hand of the introduction of the Indochina "killing fields" until the following decade. Yet for that year, before the Tet Offensive and Walter Cronkite intoning that the war was unwinnable, there was still a sense that a massive intrusion of American men, material, money, and ingenuity could produce a tolerable outcome, possibly better than the barely tolerable draw that was the Korean conflict. In 1967, American soldiers were not fighting while their diplomats wrangled; there were no Pork Chop Hill bloodbaths where Americans died trying to tidy up truce lines for a war about to end. Theoretically, the Americans could technically lose the war, but so far the GIs and marines seemed to either win the battles or win by default when the enemy simply disappeared.

Contrary to the ensuing films, novels, and analyses, one thing the Vietnam War was not was a replay of Korea. A year after massive commitment of American forces to that peninsula, the war had degenerated into a World War I–era trench stalemate, with 1916 terms such as "no-man's land" and "over the top." The second full year of massive American operations in Vietnam was always centered around movement, whether in squad-size patrols or in massive air landings. In Korea, the helicopter carried wounded men to MASH units; while the service continued in Vietnam, for the most part helicopters were attack instruments on the prowl for the enemy and game changers in tight spots on the battlefield. To the incredibly young (average age nineteen) Americans in Vietnam, Korea was their older brother or youngish uncle's war. Their 1967 world was dreams of Corvette Sting Rays, color TV, Motown, and the Rolling Stones. They carried their own soundtrack into combat on their transistor radios, put peace symbols on their helmets, and called their young platoon leaders "L-TEE." They expected to win the war, quite possibly during their own tour of duty, and it was up to leaders from William Westmoreland down to junior officers to cash in on their bravery-tinged innocence. Like a baseball or football season, or a stint wearing braces, or a single year in high school, this war was, if nothing else, not personally interminable. Unlike their fathers, who dreamed of "End the War in '44" or "Home Alive in '45" or even "The Golden Gate in '48," these men and women had their own personal "game ender," their own "Date of Expected Return from Overseas" (DERO), and in 1967 there was still some belief that DERO would be superseded by date of victory.

At the time, General Westmoreland believed that he had enough American and Allied forces in country to allow the South Vietnamese army (ARVN) to focus on the pacification of the countryside while American search-and-destroy missions would keep the North Vietnamese and Viet Cong forces constantly off balance. Particular attention would be given to assaulting base areas and destroying the supply dumps, training facilities, communications centers, and weapons caches without which the insurgency might begin to implode. In effect, the American commander was making a trade-off by remaining on the defensive along the borderlands of the demilitarized zone between North and South Vietnam and the supply conduits across the borders of Cambodia and Laos, while at the same time imposing maximum pressure on enemy bases within South Vietnam. The expectation was that if and when the Communist forces chose to engage the Americans in a frontal battle in order to protect their bases, superior firepower and mobility would inflict enormous casualties and produce a crossover point at which the enemy was losing more men than could be infiltrated from North Vietnam. The two major questions were whether the Communists would actually stand and fight to protect difficult to replace equipment and facilities, and whether the American and Allied forces stationed along the entry points from Cambodia, Laos, and North Vietnam could hold their adversaries at bay.

One week after New Year's Day 1967, Westmoreland's battle plan went into operation as "Operation Cedar Falls" lunged into action. The first major target for the offensive was the town of Ben Suc, a community on the Saigon River only twenty miles upstream from the capital city. Just over two years earlier, as South Vietnam seemed to be in its death throes before the massive infusion of American forces, a major Viet Cong force had defeated a South Vietnamese battalion, marched into town, executed anyone holding antisocialist leanings, and begun drafting local residents into the Communist army. Soon Communist forces spread outward to dominate an area of about 120 square miles centered around the town, the Thanh Dien forest preserve and the Thi Tinh and Saigon rivers. Two weeks before Christmas 1966, a Viet Cong force attempted to blow up the Binh Loi bridge over the Saigon River to cut off the capital from the north and west, while another strike force attacked the massive military airport, Tan Son Nhut, destroying almost a dozen combat planes.

On the hot, muggy morning of January 8, 1967, Operation Cedar Falls responded to the growing Communist threat to Saigon as elements of the 1st Infantry Division (the Big Red One). The 25th Infantry Division (Tropic Lightning) and the 196th Light Infantry Brigade burst into the Iron Triangle actively looking for a fight. The initial attack force was a battalion of the 1st Infantry Division, the "Blue Spaders," commanded by Lieutenant Colonel Alexander Haig, who would emerge a little over a decade later as one of the key members of the Reagan Administration. He commanded an assault force of 500 men transported by sixty Huey helicopters and supported by ten gunships that descended on Ben Suc in two huge V formations. A helicopter assault had become the 1960s version of a huge cavalry charge, and if surprise was achieved, as it was this day, it would be difficult for the enemy to hold their ground.

Rocket-firing helicopters peppered the nearby woods while other ships dropped leaflets informing townspeople that defectors from the enemy regime would be more than welcome. Meanwhile, elements of the Tropic Lightning division occupied a nearby rubber plantation as Viet Cong forces retreated through the woodlands. Lines of prisoners were herded back to the helicopter pads, awaiting a fate that could range from full amnesty to execution, depending on their captors' mood back in Saigon.

Once Ben Suc had been evacuated, the full offensive power of Cedar Falls began to emerge in what news personnel insisted was "the largest operation of the war." A massive force of 30,000 American and South Vietnamese troops began poking, digging, and even crawling through sixty square miles of prime Viet Cong real estate, much of it underground and cleverly concealed. One reporter noted "the most remarkable tunnel system; innocent looking from the air but in reality an underground village immune to artillery and air bombardment, a warren of manholes connect each room with the underground complex and its food stores, kitchens, and sleeping quarters." Another underground complex "contains galleries that zigzag so it is impossible to fire a shot at a target more than a few feet away; every few hundred yards a concealed trap leads to a second or even third level of galleries, lit by portable electric generators smuggled in from Saigon." One correspondent quoted an American soldier as admitting that in this almost Alice in Wonderland environment, "occupation on the ground means nothing" as above-ground soldiers admired American "tunnel rats" who actually went below to seek out the enemy.

These often diminutive volunteers "for one of the most dangerous fighting services a man can perform" crawled through tunnels wearing visored caps with an attached lamp and microphone. At the very least they were confronted by poisonous scorpions and bats, at worst by a Viet Cong ambush. As they inched forward, they planted explosive charges and crawled back to the surface until the next American advance uncovered another tunnel system. One team of "rats" from the 196th Infantry Division discovered a bonanza in one extensive tunnel sixteen feet below the woods. Viet Cong forces there had abandoned a small hospital, medical supplies, maps, diagrams of American barracks and headquarters in Saigon, and plans for raids at the Tan Son Nhut air base. Vietnam reporters and military leaders compared these systems to the tunnel network constructed by the Japanese for their final defense of Iwo Jima twenty years earlier. Yet unlike Iwo Jima—where over 20,000 Imperial soldiers died while killing more than 7,000 American marines for a fairly small rock in the Pacific—Operation Cedar Falls, extending over a vastly larger battleground, resulted in the deaths of a relatively modest 700 enemy soldiers and seventy-two Americans. There were no last-ditch stands by the Communists, who were willing to abandon huge supply dumps in the expectation that everything could be replaced by resupply from Hanoi, theft from the South Vietnamese, or simply bribes to the right officials.

On the positive side of the ledger, American forces had checkmated a potential enemy threat almost within sight of the outer suburbs of Saigon, even at the cost of forced evacuations of peasants that tended to enhance enemy recruiting drives among the rural population. One threat to the capital city had been at least temporarily checked, but to the northeast of Saigon, Communist reinforcements coming over the border from Cambodia were creating another crisis for the South Vietnamese government.

William Westmoreland had strong roots in World War II operations and these roots emerged anew in plans for Operation Junction City. The general was constantly searching for ways to utilize superior American firepower to checkmate enemy threats. In February 1967, he decided to play one of his trump cards. Communist forces pouring across the border from Cambodia, to the northeast of Saigon, had established a horseshoe salient (a battlefield feature that juts into enemy territory) aimed at Saigon, and the American commander intended to nullify that threat by launching the most massive American airborne operation since World War II.

If Junction City unfolded as Westmoreland hoped, a huge segment of South Vietnam designated as War Zone C would be returned to government control while, as a bonus, there was some intelligence reporting that identified that region as the headquarters of Senior General Nguyen Chi Thanh, the senior officer of COSVN, the Communist headquarters for South Vietnam.

Operation Junction City would be the largest major action of the war to this point and would rival significant airborne operations of World War II, as a multidivisional force of 30,000 men would attempt to throw a horseshoe-shaped net around a thousand-square-mile Vietcong stronghold. At the least, it was expected to disrupt any enemy plans to invade Saigon before that city's garrison was fully prepared to engage them.

One of the highlights of Junction City was the decision to use a significant paratroop contingent to make the first combat jump since the Korean War, while in turn initiating the largest helicopter concentration in history to add a different airborne dimension to the attack. The American news media leaped at the idea of covering a massive World War II–like offense as a break from the small-scale ambush activities that seemed to blend one into another. Newsmen accompanying the paratroopers of the 173rd Airborne Brigade noted the tie-ins to the operations against the Germans and Japanese two decades earlier. The eight hundred paratroopers in the first wave belonged to a unit that had jumped onto the island of Corregidor in the battle to recapture the site of the last stand of the doomed American garrison in the Philippines in the disastrous weeks after Pearl Harbor. Scenes of World War II drama seemed to be brought back to life as one correspondent noted of the paratroopers, "loaded, the men were so encumbered they moved in slow motion. When they lay on the ground to smoke, they were as helpless as beached whales and had to be helped back to their feet. They talked a little and joked some, but after they jammed themselves into the bellies of the C-130s they didn't talk anymore. The huge planes shuddered and throbbed and leaped off into the morning."

The men carried on these lumbering planes represented a wider age range than the young foot soldiers who plied the rice paddies in infantry patrols. Sergeant Leon Hostak had jumped into a Korean apple orchard sixteen years earlier and was met by massive enemy sniper fire. Now, mammoth B-52s were pummeling the target zone to discourage a repeat of that earlier scenario. The commander of the assault force, Lt. Colonel Robert Sigholtz, had joined the paratroopers right after Pearl Harbor and was now entering his third war. Chief Warrant Officer Howard Melvin, meanwhile, was one of the few men left in the entire army who was embarking on his fifth combat jump. Melvin would be in charge of the heavy drop portion of the operation, the 200 tons of supplies that would accompany the assault forces ranging from 105 MM howitzers to 10,000-pound trucks that required three hundred-foot parachutes to keep them from sinking into the ground. This was the first time the army had ever dropped truly heavy trucks and guns, and more than a few people were anxious to see how this risky maneuver played out. While the men were fully involved with the World War II heritage of their military craft, they were clearly products of the 1960s television generation, as from Colonel Sigholtz on down they wore red and white circular disks proclaiming "we try harder," a wink to the television advertising campaign of the Avis rental car company celebrating its energy in competing with the larger Hertz competition.

Unlike the jumps on Sainte-Mère-Église, France, and Nijmegen, Holland, in 1944, where significant units dropped onto a fully alerted enemy ground unit, the "Avis" men were able to beat back a screen of enemy snipers and establish a solid flank protection for an operation that had no real antecedent in the war against the Axis powers. The skies over the vast green meadows outside the town of Katum were suddenly darkened by a massive aerial flotilla of 250 helicopters. As the choppers circled the fields only a mile from the Cambodian border, attack helicopters skittered just above the grass as eight battalions of combat troops hopped off and sprang into action. The Americans overran base camps that featured showers, offices, and even machines that turned worn-out truck tires into the sandals that were standard footwear for thousands of Communist soldiers.

In a purely tactical sense, Junction City was a clear-cut victory, as the eighty-two-day operation produced an official tally of just over 2,700 Viet Cong killed in action, compared to 282 fatalities for the attackers, many of whom were South Vietnamese soldiers. One of the most spectacular engagements in this lengthy American sweep of the Cambodian/Vietnamese borderlands occurred when a heavily manned firebase was constructed by American army engineers at Prek Klok, near a camouflaged Viet Cong headquarters. Alert American officers then formed a large barrier of armored personnel carriers, set in a circle march like a nineteenth-century wagon train encamped in hostile frontier territory.

On the night of March 10, 1967, one of the more spectacular battles of Junction City erupted as the Viet Cong 272nd Regiment slammed into the encampment after a massive mortar barrage. The Communists, usually known by the stealth of their movements, regressed to a World War II–like human wave assault worthy of battles on Guadalcanal in 1942. On the other side, the American defenders were supported by massive artillery from nearby firebases. Attack aircraft were soon swarming overhead in a flare-studded aerial assault. At a cost of three dead American defenders, Prek Klok was held as more than two hundred attackers' bodies sprawled over the battlefield.

Operation Junction City was a modestly successful and sometimes visually spectacular campaign, but this offensive would prove to be a microcosm for the American experience in Vietnam in 1967. During the twelve-week operation, the American offensive permanently removed perhaps 3,000 to 4,000 enemy troops from the chessboard of the war, but in the same time span about 31,000 fresh Communist troops had entered the fray. In that same season, the numbers of Americans opposing the war had inched up another point or two in national polls, as they feared the conflict had devolved into an unwinnable stalemate. It was gradually becoming apparent that there was not a limitless number of Junction City–equivalent operations in an American military involvement that would be put to a national plebiscite in November of the next year.

A generation earlier, in the far more all-encompassing Second World War, the seemingly impossible task of pushing the Japanese menace all the way back from the fringes of Hawaii to Tokyo was difficult in the face of the ultimately self-defeating Nipponese strategy of suicidal attacks. The reality began to emerge in August of 1942 when Imperial banzai attacks on American marines barely holding a small airstrip on the island of Guadalcanal routinely resulted in twenty or thirty enemy fatalities for every dead leatherneck. In subsequent campaigns, every time the Japanese seemed to hold a nearly impregnable defensive position, they would lose patience and disintegrate in a wall of American firepower.

The watchword of Japanese strategy in the Pacific War was the banzai attack, when Imperial forces that often occupied almost impregnable defensive positions poured out of their hideouts and charged into Americans supported by tanks, machines guns, and air support. The most spectacular of these events occurred in July 1944 on Saipan, when the

Japanese commanders, after slowing the American advance to a crawl, lost patience and decreed a "gyokusai," which was in essence a banzai charge on steroids. Over 4,000 troops left excellent defensive positions and, often armed with only swords or baseball bats, charged at American soldiers and marines in an action that several defenders likened to a cattle stampede in a western movie.

The members of the gyokusai operation were able to kill 401 Americans, including one regimental commander, but the next morning the defenders tallied 4,311 Nipponese corpses in an action that delayed American victory by perhaps one day.

Even in the more recent Korean conflict, North Korean and Chinese soldiers, while not actually engaged in suicide attacks, still launched human wave assaults against the Americans that caused them untold numbers of casualties.

Most of the senior officers in Vietnam had served in one or both of these conflicts, and they were hoping that their numerous operations could set up large-scale versions of the Prek Klok encounter. Yet although the Americans won most of their encounters with the enemy in early 1967, with large swaths of territory taken, the enemy was not deterred and did not even consider negotiating a compromise. Meanwhile, popular support for the war was slowly eroding.

CHAPTER III

Super Bowl to Hoops Mania

On New Year's Day 1967, much of the population of the United States huddled in front of television sets, many of them new color models received as holiday presents, and watched what was in effect a four-team tournament to determine eligibility for what would soon emerge as the premier sporting event in the nation. Six months earlier, the leaders of two bitterly feuding professional football leagues called a halt to the pigskin war and announced that the rival American Football League and National Football League would shortly merge into a single entity, with the inaugural event of that merger being a championship game that league officials started describing as a "super" bowl game.

Compared to Major League Baseball, which could trace its roots back nearly a century with the formation of the Cincinnati Red Stockings (originally Redlegs) Baseball Club, true professional football did not emerge until the 1930s, and had begun to attract crowds approximating those of college football powerhouses only during the past decade. The National Football League's emerging guardian angel was a television industry that had gaping holes in weekend daytime schedules and discovered that the hard-hitting action of football was a great autumn and early-winter complement to the spring and summer drama of baseball. By the late 1950s, autumnal weekends were split between college football on Saturdays and professional football on Sundays. The combination of live gate receipts and ever-larger paying crowds encouraged both investors and cities that desired "major" status to line up to somehow break into the tight circle of a dozen NFL franchises.

The NFL owners grudgingly conceded the creation of expansion franchises in Dallas and Minneapolis, but this still left a substantial circle of investors who wanted to know why their city was not included in this minimal expansion. The most vocal member of this excluded circle was oil baron H. Lamar Hunt, who gathered a group of like-minded gentlemen who decided that if the NFL would not provide them entry, they would use their wealth to create a rival American Football League in the tradition of the creation of the American League in baseball six decades earlier.

The AFL hit the ground running in 1960 as the "cool" alternative to the "stodgy" existing league, and featured snazzy uniforms and a two-point conversion option after a touchdown. The AFL initially competed directly with the senior league in only three cities, which was quickly scaled to two when Hunt left Dallas after only one season for a new home (Kansas City) and a new name (Chiefs). Meanwhile, the Raiders were kept safely across the bay in Oakland, California, and the New York Titans (Jets) set up shop near the growing suburbs of Long Island. The AFL quickly acquired a network affiliation when NBC, drooling at the profits of CBS with its NFL and ABC with its NCAA affiliation, came up with a novel weekly doubleheader program as eastern teams kicked off at 1:00 p.m. and western teams delayed until 4:00 p.m. Eastern time.

This television schedule proved to be a brilliant strategy, especially since the NFL had a rigid blackout rule in which fans in league cities were limited to viewing only their team's seven away games, with no televised game at all, even from other cities, when their team played at home. Thus, until the launch of the AFL, a football fan in Philadelphia, for example, only had access to seven professional football games per season. That all changed in 1960, when the AFL provided the local NBC outlet twenty-eight of the upstart league's contests which, if not as emotionally captivating as the boys in green and white, still provided a great window into the stars and action of such distant teams as the Denver Broncos and Oakland Raiders. In turn, the NFL blackout rules were so rigid that even when the Eagles played the emerging powerhouse Green Bay Packers for the NFL championship in December 1960, the game was blacked out within a fifty-mile radius of Franklin Field. The only concession was an 11:30 p.m. tape delay, by which time everyone already knew the outcome of the game.

While the two leagues engaged in simmering warfare for six years, it soon became clear to most NFL owners that the upstarts were not going away anytime soon. By summer of 1966, rationalization of profits clearly dictated some sort of merger advantages to both leagues. The senior league gained generous entrance fees from the AFL owners in return for full recognition. Part of the agreement stipulated that three established NFL teams be transferred to the upstart entity, with the trio of owners being generously rewarded for their concession. Eventually, the Baltimore Colts, Cleveland Browns, and Pittsburgh Steelers would shift to the junior circuit of a slightly modified entity called the American Football Conference, which would now engage in regular contests with the National Football Conference of a totally merged league.

While many aspects of the merger would move at a relatively leisurely pace, the most surprising aspect of the 1966 merger announcement was that after the two former rivals played their respective championship games in December, they would then meet in the Los Angeles Coliseum for a professional championship game that quickly attained the label of "Super Bowl." One interesting sidelight of this new championship contest was that since CBS and NBC each owned rights to one of the former rival entities, both networks would carry the initial game before a rotation system was put in place a year later.

A new era in American sports history would begin in early 1967, but the first order of business was that the two league championship games would now determine who would play in this novel contest. Early on New Year's afternoon the eastern and western conference champions of the AFL trotted out onto a Buffalo, New York, field, which was surrounded by piles of snow but provided relatively tolerable playing conditions. Young Bills coach Joe Collier had assembled a formidable squad for the 1966 season, centered around future United States congressman Jack Kemp. The team had a balanced attack, with running back Bobby Burnett (who had won the Rookie of the Year award), rookie split end Bobby Crockett, and receiver Elbert Dubenion, who caught fifty-two passes during the season. The opportunistic team had scored nine touchdowns on interceptions, punts kickoff returns, blocked punts, and recovered fumbles.

In contrast to the Bills, Kansas City Chiefs coach Hank Stram had gotten his team to the championship game by avoiding stupid mistakes. Stram's team was loaded on offense and defense, starting with quarterback Len Dawson, easily considered the premier field general in the AFL. He had an enviable choice of passing to sure-handed receiving star Otis Taylor or handing off to speedy running back Mike Garrett. Fullback Curtis McClinton, meanwhile, could both catch and run. The defense was anchored by most likely the best lineman of the season in either league, Buck Buchanan, who was one of the most intimidating players in professional football.

The Bills were able to hold their own for a quarter as each team scored a touchdown on a pass reception, with Dubenion's 69-yard scamper outdoing the Chiefs Fred Arbanis' 29-yard catch. Starting in the second quarter, however, the Chiefs unleashed a 24–0 offensive blitz while Buck Buchanan seemed to be permanently attached to Kemp as he tried to find a receiver. Soon the fairly modest crowd of 42,000 fans began thinking of warm living rooms instead of cold benches and Buffalo's dreams of playing in the first Super Bowl diminished as rapidly as the crowd.

Buffalo fans who left earlier may have arrived home in time to watch nearly twice as many fans pack the Cotton Bowl in the second half of the Super Bowl qualifying tournament. Over 75,000 screaming Cowboys fans were desperate to see their newcomer franchise maul the Green Bay Packers, one of the original teams in the NFL. They never got to see a mauling, but they did get to watch a game that would be far more exciting than the Super Bowl. "Dandy" Don Meredith, the jocular quarterback with a country twang, began his duel with no-nonsense Packer field general Bart

Starr as emerging legendary coaches Tom Landry and Vince Lombardi paced the field like rival generals in a battle. The Cowboys could run, pass, block, and tackle, but they suffered from lapses on kickoff and punt return coverage, and Landry's coaching style hinted at a small element of complacency that the martinet Lombardi would never have tolerated.

After Packer halfback Elijah Pitts scored on a short pass from Starr, Cowboy kickoff returner Mel Renfro promptly fumbled the catch and suddenly Dallas was down by fourteen points. The Cowboys quickly struck back with a short goal line plunge by running back Dan Reevers and a following score by fellow backfield mainstay Don Perkins, and the two teams settled down to a duel that would last all afternoon. The Packers hung on desperately in the second half as their 21–17 lead at intermission seemed impossible to extend in any significant way. Each team engineered two scoring drives in the second half, but the Cowboys could only match the Packers' two touchdowns (with a missed extra point) with a touchdown and a field goal, and their ability to nearly double the Packer rushing yardage was negated by Starr's nineteen for twenty-eight completion rate, compared to Meredith's mediocre fifteen for thirty-one. The duel on this relatively mild first day of 1967 in Dallas would be replayed on the last day of the year in a Green Bay, one that provided one of the coldest days in the history of organized sports, but for now the Packers were on their way to Pasadena and Super Bowl I.

Seldom has a single sporting event received the hype that accompanied the premier contest between the AFL and NFL champions. First, the league decided to postpone the planned alternate-year television network coverage of the game until 1968 so that the inaugural contest would be broadcast by both NBC and CBS. For weeks before January 15, stars of major television series would voice-over the closing credits of their shows with appeals to watch the best coverage of the game on their parent network. Members of millions of households planned gatherings in front of their new Philco, GE, or RCA color television sets, never realizing that the practice would eventually turn Super Bowl Sunday into one of the few days that almost all American restaurants closed rather than compete with home Super Bowl parties.

On January 15, in generally mild, sunny but slightly smoggy weather, 63,000 fans entered a crowded but far from sold out 90,000-seat Los Angeles Coliseum and swapped opinions on whether the brash new AFL representative could possibly hold its own against one of the iconic franchises of the NFL.

Fred "The Hammer" Williamson, a future successful film star, raised Chiefs' fans spirits when insisting that although he respected the Packers, "The Green Bay receivers don't rate with the top receivers in our league and Bart Starr, who is he anyway?" On the other hand, Lombardi and most of his team were confident that as long as they took the Chiefs seriously, they could beat them. The coach did take the precaution of reminding his players that their efforts would reflect on the whole NFL portion of the merged league.

Although the Chiefs sacked Starr twice in the first Packer drive, the Green Bay field general atoned on the second possession with a six-play 80-yard drive climaxed by a 37-yard touchdown pass to wide receiver Max McGee, who outraced Williamson to the goal line after making a sensational one-handed grab. During the second quarter, Len Dawson engineered his own long 66-yard drive that ended when fullback Curtis McClinton scampered fourteen yards into the end zone. Another drive by Dawson gave the Chiefs a successful chance at a field goal less than a minute before the first extravaganza-laden Super Bowl halftime "event."

After Lombardi received the shocking halftime statistics that the Chiefs had actually outgained his team 181 yards to 164 and led in first downs 11 to 9, the super-intense veteran of the famed Fordham University "Blocks of Granite" confronted his team, player by player, and questioned whether the real World Champion Green Bay Packers had actually shown up on this January afternoon.

For a few minutes Len Dawson seemed on his way to shocking the football world when he led the Chiefs into Packer territory at the beginning of the second half, but then free safety Willie Wood stepped neatly in front of Dawson's next pass and raced down to the Chiefs' 5-yard line. A touchdown by Elijah Pitts came on the very next play. Bart Starr now had a 21–10 lead and a corps of skilled pass receivers at his disposal, and while the Packers were scoring two more touchdowns, the Chiefs only made it back into Packer territory one more time for one final play. In turn, "Hammer" Williamson never really received a chance to find out why his prediction turned out so badly, as he spent much of the game injured and on the bench, only able to glare at the Packers' "second-rate" receivers.

On this warm California afternoon, Vince Lombardi, Bart Starr, and the Green Bay Packers had solidified their claim to be the premier professional football team of the 1960s. Yet only a few miles away, in the Westwood neighborhood of Los Angeles, a late-middle-aged man equally as intense as the Packers' coach was becoming known as the "Wizard of Westwood" for his ability to dominate the rapidly growing world of college basketball. If Lombardi had his Bart Starr to lead his team, John Wooden was now sitting on his UCLA Bruins team bench with an ever-present folded-up game program in his hand and directing the choreography led by a basketball prodigy named Lewis Alcindor.

John Wooden was an active member of the Presbyterian church whose Calvinist sense of purpose was softened by an occasional small smile, something he was certainty entitled to after he began to achieve basketball "wizard" status three years earlier, when his Bruins team led by Gail Goodrich and Walt Hazzard beat a powerful Duke squad in the NCAA tournament championship. Now, after the blip of a good but not sensational 18–8 in 1965–66, Wooden was about to unleash a group of sophomores who, due to the archaic freshman eligibility rules still in force, had been ineligible to add enough firepower to most likely beat Texas Western the previous April.

At the time, basketball magazines were writing gushing preseason accounts such as "First Look at the New UCLA Dynasty," in which the core of a very good 1965–66 squad, Mike Lynn, Edgar Lacy, and Mike Warren, would be melded with one of the last great freshman basketball teams in history, centered around Lew Alcindor and another phenomenon recruited almost as passionately, Lucius Allen. As one preview magazine noted, "everyone has been blasting bugle calls on this team ever since the ghost of Horace Greeley spoke to Lew and told him that east is east but west is best." As UCLA fans tried to remain calm while outsiders insisted that the newcomer from New York was the next Wilt Chamberlain or Oscar Robertson, rival coaches began preparing their fans for almost sure losses, hinting that "we should be thankful we weren't humiliated 139–54."

Rival newsmagazines began carrying articles and pictorial essays showing Alcindor playing musical instruments, lounging on campus with his girlfriend, and dominating Wooden's highly structured practices. Readers were reminded that the new varsity player carried Power Memorial High School to three straight New York City championships and a winning streak of seventy-one games as he left eighth grade as a 6-foot-8 phenomenon and simply kept growing and maturing.

Alcindor was invariably described as either "lonely" or "a loner," a nineteen-year-old student who wore size 51 pants ("the only pants larger are for a redwood tree") and had been so overprotected by high school teachers and coaches that he had left school with few friends and a reputation for being detached and aloof. Yet now, well into his second year of college, the emerging superstar was far more candid, complaining that "the world isn't made for anyone over six-foot-two," and shifted his commentary from sports to personal heroes such as Marcus Garvey, Malcolm X, John Coltrane, and Miles Davis. As articles titled "Big Lew Confronts His Lonely World" or "Lew Alcindor: Alone In A Crowd" appeared, he abandoned dorm hijinks for an off-campus apartment, music practice, and a relationship with a girlfriend who admitted, "I usually had my way with boys but not with Lew."

Wooden, Alcindor, and the hugely talented UCLA squad were powerful, but would be challenged on the way to the championship by a number of other basketball powers that, at least on paper, conceded nothing to the Bruins. Looming large in the rearview mirror was the "Baron" Adolph Rupp's powerful Kentucky team that had not met the speed of champion Texas Western in the Southeastern Conference league schedule, but returned All-Americans Pat Riley and Louis Dampier from a 27–2 NCAA finalist. A bit farther east on Tobacco Road, Vic Bubas's 24–6 Duke squad, fronted by Bob Verga, and Larry Brown's North Carolina Tar Heels, blessed with a double All-American presence of guard Bob Lewis and forward Larry Miller, still stood in the Bruins' way.

While Kentucky, Duke, and North Carolina were all rated as potential final four teams, three other southern teams were emerging to challenge the traditional SEC–ACC dominance of the region. One was reigning champion Texas Western, where thirty-five-year-old coach Don Haskins had pulled off one of the most startling championships in hoops history and was still generally conceded to be a final four prospect, led by the warp-speed passing of Bobby Joe Hill. The second of this trio was the University of Louisville, which was dismissed by Kentucky students and alumni as a glorified community college, but coach Peck Hickman still had probably the best player in the Commonwealth in burly 6-foot-8 Wes Unseld, who had little choice if he wanted to play big-time basketball in the state, as "Baron" Rupp had not quite gotten around to recruiting nonwhite players. The third southern powerhouse that had talent but played just outside the lines of the elite conferences was the University of Houston Cougars, who suffered from that same "independent" status as the reigning national champions. Unlike the Don Haskins Miners playing in relatively overbooked El Paso, the Cougars held court in an increasingly glitzy Houston, home of oil barons, the new Astrodome (the "eighth wonder of the world"), and coach Guy Lewis's prize star, Elvin "Big E" Hayes. Lewis had coached the Cougars to the finals of the Far West Regional in 1966 and was already dickering with UCLA for a mega-hyped game between Alcindor and Hayes in the Astrodome for 1968.

One element that the inner circle of collegiate powerhouses lacked in 1967 was an expected contender from the Northeast and Midwest, which still boasted a giant share of both schools and home television sets.

Most preseason basketball preview magazines picked the Midwest as the weakest region in college basketball in 1967, as one publication warned of a "Big Ten year that seems less than vintage" and picked only Northwestern to finish in the top twenty-five from that league. Another journal insisted that Michigan State was the only school that had any possibility of crashing the upper tier of college hoops that year. The main hope for midwestern college basketball fans hoping to see a team from their region gain national attention was a look to the near past, when in 1963 the nation watched an all-Midwest national championship game between two non-Big Ten teams, the Cincinnati Bearcats and the champion Loyola Ramblers. The Ramblers largely initiated a half-century phenomenon in NCAA basketball, in which a relatively small Catholic school that either did not field a football team or played the sport at a relatively lower level than college hoops somehow stunned the nation by winning the crown. This process has been carried to the present: Villanova University stunned the North Carolina Tar Heels in 2016 with a last-second basket. In 1967, the small college team believed to have the greatest chance at a major tournament run was the University of Dayton Flyers, generally picked between fifth and seventh in preseason polls.

The East had the same dilemma as the Midwest, as no team from that region seemed a likely bet to reach the final four in March. The Providence Friars were generally conceded to be the best in the East, as they boasted a consensus first- or second-team All-American in smooth Jimmy Walker, who was likened to prolific NBA star Oscar Robertson, while Boston College, coached by NBA legend Bob Cousy, and St. John's, with All-American Lloyd (Sonny) Dove, also looked like teams capable of mid-level runs in the tournament.

Largely because of a lack of nationally televised games, the 1967 college basketball season excitement was largely generated by local attention interspersed with occasional weekend afternoon television of rare intersectional contests. The UCLA Bruins seemed to be the stars of these occasional national games, as Wooden's squad spiced up their league schedule with home games against Duke and Notre Dame and road trips to Illinois and Loyola, all naturals for wider telecast audiences. Still, until the eagerly waited seedings for the NCAA tournament, most of the excitement lay within regions or even single cities. For example, Philadelphia had five major college basketball teams with La Salle, St. Josephs, and Temple in an otherwise low-profile Middle Atlantic Conference, University of Pennsylvania in the Ivy League, and Villanova, like many other Eastern Catholic schools, an independent. However, the magic of the regular season occurred as all of these schools also formed an informal Big Five mini league in which each team agreed to play a minimum of ten games in the Penn Palestra, which featured three weekly doubleheaders and an internal round robin that produced standing room only in a smoke-filled, hot, 9,000-seat arena. Such doubleheaders might see La Salle play powerhouse Syracuse at 7:00 p.m., followed by a 9:00 p.m. "holy war" between Villanova and St. Joseph. Since Philadelphia was blessed with three independent television channels desperate for programming, area fans were treated to nearly fifty Palestra games plus two or three dozen of the schools' road contests. While this was a semi-unique situation carried out to lesser levels in other multi-school urban areas, college basketball in 1967 was far more provincial than five decades later. American college hoops fans saw far more of their local teams than powerhouse schools outside the area, and thus one of the most tantalizing aspects of a still comparatively compact NCAA tournament was the chance to see national stars that had only occasionally been glimpsed on TV during the regular season.

The 1966–67 basketball season—not unlike the 1961 baseball season when Roger Maris, Mickey Mantle, Yogi Berra, and Whitey Ford carried the Yankees to such an explosive season that a powerful, over-100-game-winning Detroit Tigers finished in a relatively distant second place—was basically about who would get to play UCLA for the championship. All season long the Bruins streak kept extending and Lew Alcindor was proving to be very much as advertised. Sports magazines began calling Alcindor "the most heralded college player of his day" while admitting that the enigmatic superstar "will face many problems on and off of the court." John Wooden gave his star a successful mixture of fatherly advice and room to become himself. Wilt Chamberlain lauded Alcindor's choice of UCLA and shared advice on being a seven-foot basketball star in a world of less-talented mortals as his own team was tearing apart the NBA. While the rest of the PAC-8 vied for the runner-up position in a league they could not win, coaches across the rest of the nation hoped to at least get a crack at the Bruins in the national title game.

Yet as the climax of the college basketball season approached, the tense atmosphere pervading the transition from the regular season to the NCAA tournament was just a bit more subdued than its half-century-later counterpart. The absence of a shot clock and three-point option allowed superior teams suffering through an inferior performance to simply stall and hang onto their lead as the underdog rolled up fouls grasping for the ball. The lack of a three-point option to pare any substantial lead also didn't help. Lew Alcindor had turned into a hoops Zeus with a supporting cast that could beat almost any team in the nation even without him.

The semifinals of the final four created a stir as the next four preseason rankers after UCLA, Duke, Kentucky, Texas Western, and Louisville had all lost before the final weekend of play. The next highest ranking team, the Dayton Flyers, led by emerging superstar Don May, were able to get by twelfth-ranked North Carolina to score their spot in the Easter Saturday night championship game. Yet most of the news media was promoting the other semifinal game between the Lew Alcindor–led Bruins and 6-foot-9, 250-pound Elvin (Big E) Hayes and his powerful Houston Cougars.

For one of the few times that season, a player opposite Alcindor scored both more points and more rebounds, but the trio of Lynn Shackelford, Lucius Allen, and Mike Warren far outplayed their Houston counterparts and the Bruins coasted to a relatively easy 73–58 victory. On the eve of Easter, as many families decorated eggs for holiday baskets, the Flyers entered the championship game as significant underdogs in a game that was less hyped than the regular season Alcindor–Hayes rematch in the Houston Astrodome nine months later. The Bruins had a deeper bench and numerous secondary targets beyond Alcindor, so that while the Flyer defense was modestly successful in holding the UCLA center to twenty points, there always seemed to be a Bruin under the basket as coach Don Donohoe used a pressure defense to keep his team in the game. Wooden kept shifting his own attack plans as a modest lead gradually crept into double figures and, ultimately, a 79–64 victory. After a year's absence from the championship trophy, Wooden's team ignited a streak that would continue far into the 1970s, as this fabulously talented quintet would simply keep regenerating itself with new faces and the same intense-looking coach wielding his folded program like a magic wand.

Three thousand miles from UCLA's sparkling new basketball temple, an equally tall young man who could dominate a game at least as much as Lew Alcindor was routinely stuffing balls down into the nets of a poorly lit, Depression-era arena where hoops shared pride of place with flower, car, and boat shows. Wilton Chamberlain, who had advised Lew Alcindor to attend UCLA, and hinted at what it might be like to become the super-star of his sport, was now back in his hometown of Philadelphia, eager to exact revenge on a Warriors organization that had summarily dismissed his favorite coach and then traded their 7-foot-1, 230-pound titan of roundball.

Five years earlier, Chamberlain had averaged a league record fifty points a game for the Philadelphia Warriors, and near the end of the season in tiny Hershey Farm Show Arena amassed a spectacular 100 points against the New York Knicks in front of a cozy crowd that barely reached 3,000 fans. The Warriors' ownership promptly decamped for San Francisco, where Chamberlain endured a fan base that—while not with-out admirers—included spectators who called him an oversized goon who could dunk but had little interest in feeding off to his teammates with pithy comments such as "I can't love a seven-foot loser." Now, by the opening of the 1966–67 season, fired coach Alex Hannum was reunited with his star player in a franchise that played in a second-class arena, had until recently been called the Syracuse Nationals, and were now tearing apart the rest of the compact ten-team National Basketball Association as the Philadelphia 76ers.

Unlike a half century later in a league with triple the number of teams, the NBA of 1967 was a limited admission club of 120 talented players who were modestly compensated by twenty-first-century professional sports standards and occasionally even coached by a playing member of their team, such as Bill Russell of the Boston Celtics. Players were more likely to earn modest extra money for simply endorsing a particular prod-uct. They rarely appeared on national television commercials and often lived in middle-class neighborhoods shared by some of their fans.

Whatever the name of the Philadelphia basketball franchise, they could never seem to get beyond the Boston Celtics in the playoffs, but this par-ticular year the team coasted to a 68–13 record with Wilt Chamberlain easily winning the Most Valuable Player award, even though his scoring average was only half the level of five years earlier. Wilt was now truly a team player, and when it came time to confront the Celtics in the league semifinals, the team swept the first three games, endured a heartbreaking four-point loss in Boston Garden, and won the Eastern Conference with a 24-point blowout in the smoky environs of Convention Hall.

Three thousand miles away, Philadelphia's previous franchise actually had a slightly tougher time against a usually tough Bob Pettit–led St Louis Hawks. Yet in an oddity that would mark this professional basketball season, the Hawks had slid into the postseason with a 39–42 record as simply the best of the also-rans in a league dominated by the 76ers, Celtics, and Warriors.

The Hawks players may have had trouble getting the ball into the net, but when the Warriors came to Kiel Auditorium, the fans developed the shooting accuracy of foreign object marksmen. While Boston fans hurled eggs and tomatoes at 76ers players and Philadelphia fans countered with eggs, potatoes, and coins against the Celtics, Warriors players dodged a fan barrage of candy bars, cigarette lighters, and finally rocks, which eventually forced team owner Franklin Mieuli to hire uniformed guards to stand behind his team's bench and at least distract the St. Louis marksmen. The Hawks were duly eliminated in six games, as team ownership began making plans to move the team to Atlanta, and the league finals were left to a unique final series in which two versions of Philadelphia professional basketball teams would play one another for the championship of a still cozy ten-team NBA.

The visiting Warriors arrived in their former hometown in all the sartorial splendor for which the sixties would be famous. The team owner wore a sky-blue blazer over a smart turtleneck while his players wore black coats with Warriors Golden Gate emblems and their names and team numbers on their breasts. The Western champions were an eclectic team that included five players actively engaged in church or youth work, a starting guard who had a barber's license, and a star forward who wrote poetry. They also arrived hampered by two starters with broken hands and a third with a serious ankle injury. The home team 76ers were not as well dressed nor as physically banged up, but Wilt Chamberlin's sheer size and 6-foot-9, 240-pound Luke Jackson's girth and gleaming shaved head could each attract their own kind of attention in a crowd.

Alex Hannum and his Warrior counterpart Bill Sharman eliminated midsized players from much of the action as the 76ers often coupled the two huge men with a diminutive trio of guards, including All-Star Hal Greer, Wally "Wonder" Jones, and Matt Guokas against a San Francisco Bay team backcourt of Jim King, Jeff Mullins, Paul Neumann, and Al Attles while Nate Thurmond took on all comers under the net.

These unusual divergences from the common quintets on the floor seemed to immediately favor Philadelphia as the 76ers emerged the victors in a no-defense 141–135 shoot-out and then crushed their opponents 126–95 before the teams headed for the Bay Area.

The two teams managed to split their series near the Golden Gate and then the Warriors showed some possibilities in beating the 76ers in Convention Hall in game five. However, while the loss forced Philadelphia to skip the champagne and fly back cross country, Hannum's team ultimately were able to uncork the bottles after a hard-fought 125–122 contest that brought the usually rabid Philadelphia sports fans one of only two professional sports championships during the entire decade of the sixties.

One impediment to hometown fans raising championship banners in their home towns was that only four American cities had all four major league sports as 1967 began. The most notable offender was professional ice hockey, as the NHL had only six franchises, two of which were in Canada. The tiny band of New York, Boston, Chicago, and Detroit hemmed the sport into a relatively small geographic empire, and the publishers of *Sports Illustrated* admitted that issues of their magazine with hockey-themed covers were usually the lowest sellers on newsstands. A significant portion of this dilemma would be addressed after the 1966–67 Stanley Cup was decided, but during the early spring of that season, American NHL fans would be put to the ultimate test in the emerging playoff picture.

The lords of hockey simply could not bring themselves to admit all six teams to playoff contention, so the Boston Bruins and Detroit Red Wings were left to ponder their summer as two international pairings provided a New York Rangers–Montreal Canadiens, Chicago Blackhawks–Toronto Maple Leafs final four that could theoretically produce a North American sports championship series with no team from the states or, conversely, no team from Canada.

The New York Rangers were still inhaling the heady air of moving up from the previous season's last-place disaster to a playoff spot. Local scribes gushed over the excitement of Gotham's skaters as they eyed the "generous" $5,250 per player share held out for the Stanley Cup winners. Montreal team captain Jean Beliveau, on the other hand, dismissed the lure of crass financial gain as he insisted "we represent all of French Canada and we know that a lot of people count on us." Even English-speaking players who found a roster spot on the Habs (the Montreal Canadiens) admitted that they were quickly caught up in a tradition that was passed down to every young player, a tradition that only two things in hockey are worthwhile: playing for Les Canadiens and winning the Stanley Cup.

The Rangers' quick rise from the ashes of the previous season provided mixed emotions of hopes for a miracle and the reality that it was exciting to simply be back in the playoffs. Both emotions swirled around the team and the city when, in the opening game in Montreal, the Canadiens scored five goals in nine minutes and parried desperate Rangers counterattacks for an eventual 6–4 triumph. The Canadiens hoped for a sweep, the Rangers hoped for competitive games, and each got their wish as the Habs scored consecutive 3–1, 3–2, and 2–1 hard-fought victories that seemed likely to ensconce the Stanley Cup in Quebec. Meanwhile, Rangers fans could console themselves with a possibly bright future.

The Toronto Maple Leafs seemed set to suffer the same fate as the Rangers, as the Leafs had finished nineteen points behind a Chicago team that featured legendary Bobby Hull, All-Star Doug Mohns, and an expectation that they alone could take on Montreal successfully for the Cup. Yet the Maple Leafs shocked the hockey world by turning the regular season on its head as the Blackhawks folded against a Toronto team that had three equally talented lines, superb checking, and the luck of facing the two Blackhawks superstars playing with worsening injuries. When members of the two teams engaged in the ceremonial handshaking line at the end of the series, the Blackhawks were leaving to pack their bags for home while the Maple Leafs were about to give Canada an all-dominion final.

This pairing of two Canadian teams battling for the Stanley Cup while US teams and fans watched at a respectful distance proved to be the Maple Leafs' greatest triumph for the next half century. An easy four-goal Canadiens victory 6–2 in the Forum convinced many hockey fans that 1967 was definitely not going to be the year of the Maple Leaf. Then Toronto simply exploded and won four of the next five games, highlighted by a 3–2 overtime victory.

While Toronto fans celebrated their brief moment of glory, the NHL owners had decided to change the face of hockey by initiating the most ambitious expansion program in the history of North American sports. Like a giant icy amoeba, a sport lodged almost exclusively in Canada and the northern reaches of the United States welcomed six investors with deep pockets to join this exclusive fraternity and moved the sport itself into seemingly alien territory, where the only ice and snow residents encountered were in their beverages. This expansion binge included only one city that experienced below-freezing temperatures all winter, and the Minnesota North Stars location became part of their name. This would eventually become an issue decades later when the franchise was moved to Dallas, morphing initially into the South Stars and eventually the carefully neutral Stars. The Philadelphia Flyers, Pittsburgh Penguins, and St. Louis Blues were located in cities that experienced a climate roughly like that in New York and thus had some modest infrastructure of winter sports and a smattering of youth hockey leagues. The boldest move was to award franchises to the Bay Area, with the origin of the California Golden Seals, and the even balmier Los Angeles region, which received the Kings franchise.

Professional hockey now had more teams than the NBA, but while basketball was a huge sport across the nation, neophyte hockey fans had to be introduced to the game step-by-step. A copy of the *National Hockey League Official Magazine and Program* for the Philadelphia Flyers in autumn 1967 included the obligatory game program numbers and names of players, pictures of team members and club officials, and several ads for color television sets. However, the fifty-cent publication featured a multiple-page *Know Your Hockey—The Worlds Fastest Sport*, which illus-trates offside and icing calls, admits that "as nearly as possible" a rink should be 200 feet long and 85 feet wide, even if some arenas do not feature that configuration, and still lists helmets as optional (and still unusual). The program also featured an extensive article on the history of the Lester Patrick trophy, which would now take on added significance as it was awarded for "outstanding service to hockey in the United States of America," and was closed to Canadians, who still dominated the game. However, as professional hockey ended its season and prepared for the brave new world of successive expansions that placed a thirty-first franchise in decidedly unfrozen Las Vegas in 2017, the Boys of Summer were heading north from spring training. One of the most exciting baseball seasons in history was about to commence.

—

CHAPTER IV

The Party Game

On Wednesday morning, November 4, 1964, Lyndon Baines Johnson awoke from a series of catnaps to prepare to accept the official congratulations of Senator Barry Goldwater after the Arizonan's concession speech. Johnson had spent most of the night chain-smoking, he was never far from a generous supply of coffee and liquor, and his haggard appearance made him look far older than his fifty-six years. Yet lack of sleep could not dampen his euphoric mood as near complete vote tallies confirmed that he had won one of the most one-sided elections in American presidential history. Barry Goldwater had managed to win his home state of Arizona and five states of the deep South, but Johnson had carried the other forty-four states, a phenomenal improvement over John F. Kennedy's razor-thin margin of victory four years earlier. A media barrage that hammered Goldwater as a warmonger, culminating with the iconic "flower petal" television commercial that depicted a little girl picking petals from a flower with a nuclear countdown in the background of a projected Goldwater presidency, established the Texan as the ultimate man of peace to lead America in a nuclear-armed world. Goldwater's theme of being "a choice, not an echo" by presenting a true alternative to the policies of the Democrats was now essentially dead on arrival. Lyndon Johnson was now poised to govern in perhaps the golden age of the American experiment.

Lyndon Johnson's landslide win in November 1964 was in most respects a national plebiscite on the Texan's highly publicized "Great Society" program that he began to implement once he took over the presidency. While Johnson's address to Congress after the assassination of President Kennedy in Dallas included an obligatory disclaimer that he would have given "everything" he had if Kennedy had only lived, the speech also included a hint that the new president could use his vast legislative experience to cajole Congress into moving forward with his predecessor's largely stalled domestic reform program. In essence, the "New Frontier" was now expected to make way for the "Great Society."

Once President Johnson was guaranteed an additional 1461 days in office, the already frantic pace of the first year of his presidency seemed to enter warp drive as bills ranging from civil rights expansion to educational reform to beautifying American highways made their way from the White House to the Capitol and then back to the Oval Office for a final signature in relatively intact condition. While John Kennedy (and his family) added a glamour and excitement seldom seen in the White House before or since, the former Massachusetts senator was more of a negotiator than a bully, and took the long view that he could get most of his New Frontier programs passed during the eight years he expected to be president. Now his vice president, a man Kennedy could barely tolerate beyond his ability to help him win the White House, was back in the catbird seat he had enjoyed as Senate majority leader. If all went well, he would have over nine years to make a permanent mark on every aspect of American life.

The president, who expected to be chief executive for the rest of the sixties and the early seventies, was embarking on a social, political, and cultural crusade from a background much closer to most Americans' experiences than his fallen predecessor. While John Kennedy was attending private boarding schools and rapaciously exploring the lives of important individuals (often from a sickbed), Johnson was alternating between school classes he hated and backbreaking farm work he hated even more. While Kennedy traveled between Harvard Yard and the Court of St. James of his ambassador father, Johnson sweated through a barely recognized college with marginal accreditation, all the while also dealing with children even less affluent than he was. Then, when Johnson hoped and expected to be his party's nominee for the 1960 presidential post, he was virtually forced to give up his powerful Senate position to become one of the most ignored, shunned vice presidents in modern history. The anonymity of being John Kennedy's second-in-command is depicted with startling clarity in the film *Thirteen Days,* which centers on the Cuban Missile Crisis of 1962. During the film, which features constant meetings and discussions in the White House, Johnson's character is almost always in a nonspeaking background role. He was essentially watching history being made with no one bothering to ask him what he thought, knew, or cared about.

Then, after Dallas, the tall Texan finally gained center stage and, to some public surprise, his vision of sixties America expanded even further than that of his predecessor. When Johnson experienced his first official inauguration as elected president in 1965, he fully expected that his power to influence American politics and policies would be more likely enhanced than diminished two years later in 1967. The primary foundation for this optimism was that at the time of his inauguration, Johnson was in effect the leader of a party that had totally dominated American politics for more than three decades.

Since the election of 1932, when Herbert Hoover was decisively beaten by Franklin Delano Roosevelt in the wake of the Great Depression, the White House had been a Democratic residence, the single exception being the eight years served by war hero Dwight D. Eisenhower who, in 1952, could have secured the nomination of either party. Professional Republican politicians Alf Landon, Wendell Willkie, Thomas Dewey, and Richard Nixon had all attempted to secure the White House before Barry Goldwater's latest attempt. Nixon, in fact, had come very close in 1960. Yet for a generation, from the early 1930s to the mid-1960s, the Democratic Party largely called the tune of national policy while the Republicans either fought often futile delaying battles or engaged in compromises that went more than halfway to meet Democratic objectives.

The closest thing to a Republican Renaissance during this period was the two election victories of Dwight Eisenhower, which at least provided the Republicans with hope for the future, but Ike was obliged to deal with a Congress that usually had large Democratic majorities. The nation never really came close to a one-party state during these decades, but more than a few scholars and politicians wondered if the Republicans, who had dominated national policy from 1865 to 1929, were slowly being consigned to semipermanent minority status.

The 1964 election seemed to be the culminating event in the broad domination of the Democrats over the American political and social agenda, and Johnson used his soaring popularity to push forward a monumental expansion in the role of the government in daily affairs. Using the soon-to-be iconic "Johnson treatment," the burly chief executive would verbally and physically "surround" politicians who held a needed vote and flatter, cajole, threaten, and virtually bribe an individual to come around to his point of view. As the "treatment" expanded outward, the federal cornucopia overflowed beyond any level that could be believed a few years earlier. A civil rights initiative that was dead in the water on the eve of Kennedy's trip to Texas was split into two parts and enacted as the Civil Rights Act of 1964 and the Voting Rights Act of 1965. These eliminated a long list of outrages, from refusal to serve a customer in a restaurant to an assault on the notorious literacy tests that could turn a list of 1,000 potential African American voters to a "passing" handful of six or seven.

The nation's education system was so overwhelmed by the postwar baby boom that local school districts and colleges were overcrowded, underfunded, and barely meeting the day-to-day crises that expanded enrollments presented. Thus, a major aspect of the Great Society was educational funding and expansion, both driven by a president who had taught in elementary and high school environments. The Education and Secondary Act of 1965 sailed through both houses of Congress; the subsequent Higher Education Act secured an astounding 100–0 vote in the Senate.

As Johnson gained confidence as an elected and not accidental president after November 1964, the Great Society became an ever-expanding cornucopia of federal largesse, from highway beautification to school lunches to medical care for needy and elderly Americans. In turn, the enormous prosperity of the mid-1960s allowed these programs to be instituted relatively painlessly for the nation's pocketbook. The Republican minority in Congress was caught in an inevitable position of appearing to be scolds when their members opposed bills that the majority of Americans supported and liked. Yet if the Johnson administration was capable of proposing and passing a domestic welfare agenda that was gradually edging toward the generous social safety net in Scandinavia, American foreign affairs were a different matter. Ten thousand miles away, the Communist insurgency in South Vietnam, which Johnson called "that bitch of a war," had escalated from an American advisory role to outright combat.

Soon, an almost Alice in Wonderland reality started to emerge in Congress, as one of Johnson's allies on the war, Senator Richard Russell, adamantly opposed the civil rights bills, while another of his Senate confidants, William Fulbright, was one of the most determined foes of the conflict in Southeast Asia. As the president kept preaching the ability of the nation to have "guns and butter"—that is, fight the war while expanding domestic services—the Democratic Party began losing its consensus.

One of the ironies of the mid-1960s was that as the Vietnam War widened, President Johnson started receiving more support for his foreign policies from Republican members of Congress than from his own party. While the party game of 1967 had few hard or fast rules, the Republicans, with some notable exceptions, were aligning with the president and the southern members of his party in support of his "domino" theory, which held that failure to confront Communist aggression in Vietnam would eventually force a Western pullback out of Southeast Asia, all the way to Australia or even Hawaii. The fear was that these "wars of liberation" would turn Asia into a huge Marxist empire. At the same time, however, Republican leaders began to sense that Johnson was losing much of the voter support he had garnered in the 1964 election. They sensed that 1968 would provide a real opportunity to regain the White House.

In January 1967, the 90th Congress convened amid a mood of growing resentment and uncertainty. Even after the strong showing of the GOP in the fall 1966 elections, the Democrats still held a sixty-four to thirty-six majority in the Senate and a shrinking but still formidable 246 to 187 majority in the House of Representatives. While Congress would present a far less diverse composition than its 2017 equivalent, it was clearly more inclusive than five decades earlier. The members' religious background was still predominately Protestant, with 399 members of that faith, but there were now 108 Catholics, eighteen Jews, two Greek Orthodox, and two simply listed as "no affiliation." World War II and the Korean conflict still loomed large in military background, as 385 members had served in the armed forces, a common experience that softened some of the party differences among them. African Americans now held five seats in the House of Representatives, while Edward Brooke of Massachusetts had just been elected as the first black senator since Reconstruction. In a nation where middle-class salaries usually ranged from $5,000 to $10,000 a year, thirty-two members of Congress were listed as millionaires, and the lawmakers' salary of $30,000 a year was an enviable income for most Americans. While the majority of House and Senate members came from either a law or business background, there was still some degree of occupational diversity in the group that included seventy-one teachers, fifty-seven farmers, five physicians, and one clergyman. This prevented the legislature from becoming an exclusive bankers' and lawyers' club.

Since the Republicans had placed only one member of their party in the White House in nearly half a century and the 1964 contest had been one of the most disastrous in party history, there was considerable debate in 1967 about who had the best chance to defeat Lyndon Johnson in 1968. One certainty was that even though Barry Goldwater remained popular among rank-and-file Republicans, there was no chance that he would gain a second opportunity to head the election ticket. Goldwater had carried only six states in 1964, and even if the Republicans did not capture the White House in 1968, they at least had to make a more respectable showing. The Goldwater disaster in 1964 created a bonanza for political pundits and the news media to begin assembling lists of potential challengers in 1968, with articles such as "Top Republicans Talk About Their Choice in 1968" and "Race for the Republican Nomination: How It Looks Now" initiating handicapping of a field largely centered around the emerging stars of the 1966 election. *U.S. News and World Report* insisted that "hope of victory is high among Republicans. They believe that with the right candidate they can elect a president in 1968." Another article quoted a party leader as admitting "the scent of victory keeps us eager. We are willing to listen to anyone. We want to win. We can already smell the bacon frying."

Many party leaders frowned on forming regional blocs in 1968. They wanted to avoid the bitter factional divisions that made the 1964 election a Republican disaster. One midwestern party official insisted, "we sense that we have a chance and we don't want to lose it." Ironically, while Republicans celebrated their gains in Congress after the 1966 election, only one member of that body was emerging as a serious candidate for the presidential nomination. That was Senator Charles Percy of Illinois, a photogenic poster person for the new breed of Republican lawmakers. Ironically, while Percy's name was on almost all the short lists for the 1968 presidential nomination, in 1967 he was forced to share the limelight with his possibly even more photogenic twenty-one-year-old daughter.

Just after Percy was elected to the Senate in fall 1966, his daughter, Sharon, rocked the partisan world of politics by announcing her engagement to John D. Rockefeller IV, a tall, lanky, twenty-nine-year-old Democrat who had recently been elected to the West Virginia House of Delegates. The nephew of Republican governors in New York and Arkansas, Rockefeller and Sharon Percy were now becoming the magazine cover stars of 1967 while at the same time enhancing Charles Percy's status as a person to watch in the next election campaign. As one correspondent insisted, "if the convention goes into a real snarl, Mr. Percy's name could emerge as a compromise candidate."

While Charles Percy was emerging as the leading congressional-based candidate for the 1968 convention, the twenty-six sitting Republican governors in 1967 offered a wide choice of possible opponents to thwart Johnson's reelection. Among this group was a trio of state executives who were drawing particular attention: Nelson Rockefeller of New York, George Romney of Washington, and Ronald Reagan of California. Each of these governors had been confronted with state-level issues that promised to become national ones: civil rights, urban violence, rising tax burdens, and a rapid rise in the cost of government.

In a purely political sense, Nelson Rockefeller was, in 1967, the most famous of these three figures. At age fifty-nine he was dean of all American state governors in terms of service in office. He was first elected in 1958, reelected in 1962, and then reelected again in 1966, although by a smaller majority each time. Rockefeller had reason to think in large terms: His family had created charitable foundations, donated the site of the United Nations building, and built the iconic Rockefeller Center in New York City. During his nine-year career he had massively improved the purity of the Hudson River, which during the 1950s had become an open sewer. Rockefeller also guided a billion-dollar antipollution bond issue through the state legislature. A $2.5 billion bond was helping to finance the expansion of highways, bus systems, railroads, and the New York City subway system. He was also influential in promoting a statewide higher education system that was beginning to rival California as the iconic college system in the United Sates. Between 1957 and 1967, the State University of New York (SUNY) had grown from twenty-seven primarily teacher training schools, enrolling 38,000 students, to fifty-seven college and university centers with an enrollment of 140,000. It would reach 185,000 by 1970. The system's modest $400-a-year tuition matched the tuition in California. SUNY would become a *Time* magazine cover story early in 1968. The governor's strong support for minority rights and fluent command of Spanish were additional assets in the Republican hope to entice African American and Latino votes away from Johnson.

A thousand miles west of Albany, George Romney was finishing his fifth year as governor of Michigan and, like Rockefeller, solidifying his potential base as a liberal Republican posed to take the GOP back to the White House. In what seemed almost a polar opposite universe compared to fifty years later, Romney was governor of a state in which Detroit and smaller cities were coping with the immigration of huge numbers of southerners eager to work in the booming automobile industry. Romney had the great good luck of being responsible for allocating priorities in a state budget that was currently running a $137 million surplus—a situation that, like

Rockefeller, allowed Romney to avoid identification as a flinty, Scrooge-like Republican miser, especially as he distributed over a billion dollars in school and child aid to comprise nearly half the Michigan state budget.

George Romney was rugged, active, photogenic, and happily married, and the news media vied to chronicle life in a governor's mansion filled with warm, attractive people. On the other hand, Romney carried two impediments toward the upcoming election season. First, the governor was a high-profile Mormon in a nation where any denomination outside of mainstream Protestantism was at best a bit suspect. In a 1967 political system that still featured backroom deals made over ample adult beverages and clouds of smoke, Romney seemed just a bit of an outsider. Equally detrimental to his presidential candidacy was a major political gaffe that he committed after an extensive tour of the Vietnam war front. The governor returned from Southeast Asia relatively optimistic, but as the tide against the war began to rise, he insisted that he was "brainwashed" by military handlers and largely revoked his support for the war. This about-face was a lose-lose situation, as Romney enraged war supporters by revoking his support while at the same time encouraging anti-war voters to believe that he was an opportunist who would say anything to get elected. If he was so eager to change his mind on one important issue, there would be a question about his reliability on other important decisions.

In many respects, the most intriguing newcomer to politics in 1967 was Ronald Wilson Reagan, the newly inaugurated governor of California. In an era when most political leaders gradually ascended a career ladder from relatively minor offices to more national recognition, Reagan jumped directly from the entertainment industry to politics in a single dramatic leap. In a sense, *Back to the Future*'s Dr. Emmett Brown's hilarious double take in 1955 when time traveler Marty McFly informs him that Reagan is president of the United States was already creating massive media attention in 1967. Reagan had begun to emerge as a serious political operative when his impassioned television plea for Barry Goldwater on election eve in 1964 was one of the few bright spots of the candidate's campaign. Now, just over two years later, the former actor was chief executive in a state where Democrats controlled both houses of the legislature and had called for shrinking government size in a California that largely existed in larger-than-life activities. He soon gained mixed attention when he began cutting the number of state employees, raised taxes on income, and proposed college fees (the same $400 fee as SUNY) in what had always been a free system.

Reagan quickly incurred the wrath of labor leaders, college administrators and faculty members, and a large segment of the minority population. Despite this, his genial demeanor, excellent speaking voice, and seeming lack of a mean-spirited nature energized Republicans on both state and national levels. Reagan sat at the governor's desk in what was now perhaps the most high-profile state in the nation, and his rise was one of the major political stories of 1967.

Three thousand miles to the east, a rather bland-looking lawyer was beginning to set his sights on far more than his latest brief. While the news media of 1967 trolled Congress and governors' mansions for clues to who would face Lyndon Johnson in 1968, a slightly graying middle-aged man in a nondescript business suit walked through the man-made canyons of New York City and entered a building at 20 Broad Street, where he took the elevator to his office on the twenty-fourth floor. He was a partner in a six-person law firm but his name stood out compared to Mudge, Rose, Guthrie, Alexander, and Mitchell on the office suite entrance. Unlike his partners, he had spent most of the 1950s in the White House as vice president to Dwight David Eisenhower. Now, bored to tears with the tedium of corporate law, Richard Milhous Nixon sat in a relatively small office, facing an influx of mergers, petitions, and corporate business issues, and plotted his return to the center of the American political game.

Only five years earlier, after losing a tight race to Edmund Brown for the governorship of California, Nixon had snapped at reporters, exclaiming that they wouldn't have Nixon to push around anymore. Now Nixon's lucrative law practice was a barely tolerable annoyance that distracted him from a chance to redeem the achingly close defeat in the iconic 1960 election. The former vice president may have been a full partner in a law firm, but in the past year he had found the time to visit thirty-five states and campaign for eighty-six Republican candidates running for an assortment of offices.

Richard Nixon was back in the political game and was less than coy about his determination to win the presidency. Yet this new Nixon was less gruff and argumentative and insisted, "if I am to be the nominee, I must earn the nomination, I don't want to have it handed to me as a reward for service rendered to the party." He insisted that "we want the best man as a nominee. We want to win the election."

Yet Hugh Sidey, a correspondent for *Life* magazine who interviewed Nixon in 1967, felt that the former vice president wanted more than just a Republican in the White House after the upcoming election. "It has been seven years since Nixon saw the sights and felt the pulse of official Washington. He savors those memories as he stares down the shadowed financial canyon. His voice is a little wistful. It is plain to see the great ache within him has grown over the past years, not diminished." The question still to be answered was whether this man who had come so close to the presidency in 1960 and now held no political office at all could emerge from a large pool dominated by men either in Congress or the governors' mansions.

If the historically one-sided presidential election of 1964 had virtually guaranteed that Barry Goldwater would permanently remove himself from any future presidential candidacy, it seemed for most of 1967 that the man sitting in the White House simply had to formally announce his candidacy for reelection to gain the Democratic Party bid for the nomination. Yet between New Year's Day and New Year's Eve of that year, Johnson's presidency gradually found itself in competition not so much with the Republican adversaries as with the ghosts of the New Frontier and anyone who in any way attached themselves to the spirit of Camelot.

In the immediate aftermath of John Kennedy's assassination, President Johnson exerted enormous energy in persuading Robert Kennedy to remain as attorney general and share in the task of embracing JFK's near Lincolnesque hagiography. Yet Robert Kennedy's quiet, almost scholarly personality meshed poorly with the burly, bullying, often profane new president, and Bobby gradually became isolated, as much of his brother's "court" left the administration to focus on enhancing John Kennedy's legacy. White House Counsel Theodore Sorensen, presidential aide and historian Arthur Schlesinger Jr., and other more junior officials began attaching themselves to Robert Kennedy in the hope that the new senior Kennedy would somehow emerge to restore Camelot in the not too distant future.

The first step in the campaign to replace the Great Society era with a restored New Frontier began when Robert Kennedy successfully campaigned for a Senate seat in New York, then used that seat as an emerging government in exile. On March 7, 1967, William J. vanden Heuvel, an aide to the new junior senator from New York, told an audience at Syracuse University that widespread dissatisfaction existed in the Democratic Party over the Johnson administration's foreign policy, especially the Vietnam issues. The next day Sorensen told a Princeton University audience that Lyndon Johnson would be following a "historic pattern" if he did not choose to run in 1968, as "of all the vice presidents who originally succeeded to the White House, as Lyndon Johnson did, by their predecessor's death, not a single one had ever sought to be reelected for a second full term," citing Theodore Roosevelt, Calvin Coolidge, and Harry Truman as examples. The day after that interesting piece of presidential lore was passed to an audience, Kennedy historian Arthur Schlesinger informed members of the Americans for Democratic Action that "the Johnson administration does not wish to negotiate now to settle the war in Vietnam."

As these loyalists were sowing doubt about a Johnson candidacy for 1968, at least nine new books about Robert Kennedy were in some level of preparation, while a "national citizens" organization emerged, promoting Kennedy for presidential considerations. Anti-war senator William Fulbright was "nominated" as his potential running mate. Meanwhile, the subject of this public relations offensive hedged his bets on a future candidacy by informing a gathering of state Democratic leaders that he would work for a "Johnson-Humphrey" ticket in 1968, while adding a slightly less enthusiastic codicil that "it is important to continue a Democratic administration for the next four years."

All summer and autumn of that year, as riots erupted in American cities, draft calls expanded, draft deferments for graduate students were ended, and Great Society programs languished in congressional committees, Lyndon Johnson was gradually being squeezed between a Republican party that sensed the Goldwater fiasco could be avenged in 1968 and Robert Kennedy's insistence that he would not oppose the president for the nomination. This seemed to contrast sharply with the rise of a virtual Kennedy government in exile, from New York to Washington to California. Charles Percy, George Romney, Ronald Reagan, Nelson Rockefeller, and Richard Nixon were all emerging as candidates that might put the ghosts of the 1964 disaster at rest, and while none of these men expressed any great desire to force a unilateral exit from Vietnam, they were not saddled with the role of commander in chief, as Lyndon Johnson was as the 1968 election cycle loomed. It seemed that guns and butter were not compatible forever and America might well lose an economic boom or a war or both. The five Republican candidates for the White House could function as a team of rivals committed to putting the Grand Old Party back in the White House with no need to fully draw their swords on one another.

On the other hand, the Democrats might have lost the majority of governors' mansions, but they still held the House, the Senate, and the presidency, even if their 1964 magical consensus was beginning to unravel. Johnson still fully expected to run for, and win, the presidency in 1968, yet he kept his sights focused on Robert Kennedy and the men of Camelot. The gods who orchestrated the party game of 1967 were fickle, however, and soon after the fourth anniversary of the end of Camelot, a silver-haired Minnesota senator who auditioned for careers from priesthood to ice hockey player would decide to enter the presidential lists. Eugene McCarthy would turn the party game in a new direction.

CHAPTER V

Soundtrack 1967

In December of 1959, as America prepared to welcome in the new decade of the 1960s, more than a few adults were delighted to note that one of the most disruptive influences of the 1950s appeared to be on social life support. Ever since Bill Haley, Elvis Presley, Little Richard, and other young performers had challenged the bland fifties "pop" music with their jarring sound of rock and roll, many adults figuratively covered their ears and hoped that the fad would go the way of 1920s raccoon coats or 1940s zoot suits.

During the previous four or five years, teenagers had made the Big Beat the anthem of their frantic lifestyles, threatening the primacy of real singers such as Rosemary Clooney, Perry Como, and Nat King Cole, as electric guitars joined black leather jackets and ducktail haircuts as signs of adolescent rebellion. Now, as the fifties were about to end, even though Danny and the Juniors only a year earlier had produced a huge hit song insisting "Rock and Roll Will Never Die," the genre now actually did seem to be dying.

As America prepared to enter the sixties, rock and roll was devastated by the deaths of Buddy Holly and Ritchie Valens, the marriage of twice-divorced Jerry Lee Lewis to a girl who had just entered adolescence, and the transition of Elvis Presley from superstar to army private. On New

Year's Day 1960, the top 40 charts were dominated by film themes such as *Exodus*; former rockers Connie Francis and Bobby Darin, who had shifted over to more adult fare; and moderately mature crooners such as Andy Williams and Steve Lawrence. Meanwhile, Freddy Cannon and Dion DiMucci had retreated backward in time for "Way Down Yonder in New Orleans" and "Where or When." More than a few radio disc jockeys, who tended to be a half generation or more older than their teen audiences, were quietly admitting that they were relieved to be able to play songs they liked, such as "Theme From *A Summer Place*" or "Beyond the Sea" rather than pander to their adolescent audience.

Then, almost miraculously, as Brook Benton, Anita Bryant, and the Brothers Four seemed to be edging out the diminishing circle of rockers, Chubby Checker, a denizen of the row houses of South Philadelphia who had aspirations of leaving his dead-end job to become a full-time singer, was matched with a new dance song on Cameo-Parkway records, and "The Twist" breathed new life into a dying rock-and-roll genre. "The Twist" was essential to the eventual soundtrack of 1967, as the very simplicity of the dance enticed adults to enter a music transition in which 1950s rock and roll would morph into rock. Rock, in turn, expanded interest beyond its original intended teenage boundaries, as now even adults could dance to the tunes with absolutely no practice. Adults who would have been terrified to attempt to join the complex line dances of 1950s rock and roll, such as the Stroll, were now routinely ambling to the dance floor in clubs and at parties to twist, just as their younger counterparts were doing at high school dances and teen hops.

There is no exact moment at which rock and roll morphed into rock, but it was clear by the eve of 1967 that the thumping rhythm of original 1950s rock and roll was now morphing into what one music critic declared was "an electric cornucopia," a "music of today," which "makes the rock and rollers of the 1950s sound as if they were Neanderthals working it out on hollow trees" as "lyrics are upgraded from back seat passion to the joys and ills of the whole shaking world." By the time of the year of fire and ice, while a *Teen Age* magazine cover story asked if Peter Noone of Herman's Hermits was really a hermit, the editors of *Life* magazine were beginning work on an upcoming cover feature on "The New Rock Music That's Hooked the Whole Vibrating World."

The musical soundtrack of a memorable year would emanate from an American entertainment infrastructure that had just undergone two major transformations that would create a very different mode of transmitting popular music compared to the music of the decade before. Much of the first wave of rock and roll in the Elvis Presley–era 1950s version was enhanced by the emergence of local television stations opting to carry dance parties, in which local teens could exhibit their talents while performers seeking audiences appeared on the program. This medium reached its apex in 1957 when the local Philadelphia dance party, *Bandstand*, was selected by the ABC network to broadcast a national format, *American Bandstand*. In 1964, the arrival of the Beatles on the rock scene encouraged the national television networks to move rock music into prime time with ABC's *Shindig* and NBC's *Hullabaloo*, enhanced by syndicated versions such as *Shivaree, Hollywood A Go-Go,* and similar programs. However, despite the popularity of these shows among young audiences, they could not match the ratings of *Gomer Pyle* or *The Beverly Hillbillies*. They flickered out one by one with the last holdout, Dick Clark's daily thirty-minute *Where the Action Is*, surviving into 1967 before it too was canceled.

While these outlets were dying during 1966, rock music fans were compensated by a Federal Communications Commission ruling that any broadcasting company that owned both AM and FM radio stations in the same city had to cease their money-saving practice of simulcasting programs on both outlets, and instead provide different programs on the two stations as of January 1967. The results were that 1967 witnessed the bifurcation of rock music into traditional top 40 on AM and edgier, album-oriented fare on FM, especially in the evening. For example, when the Doors exploded onto the scene in the summer of 1967, the AM stations played the top 40, under-three-minute version of "Light My Fire" while FM stations played the multiple keyboard and guitar riffs of the six-minute, fifty-second "long" version, often paired with the monumental twelve-minute, thirty-five-second excursion into darkness that was "The End."

While American rock music fans gained much more radio access to pop music—while seeing video outlets diminish to occasional rock group performers on such family shows as *The Hollywood Palace*—their European counterparts experienced an almost mirror-image situation. While Britain's TV networks canceled the largely popular *Ready Steady Go* about the same time that *Hullabaloo* and *Shindig* exited American screens, the government-controlled BBC continued to regularly broadcast *Top of the Pops* on TV but cut back rock-oriented programs on BBC radio. At the same time, it launched a massive campaign to silence offshore "pirate" radio stations that were blasting rock music 24/7 beyond the immediate shores of Britain. Popular music fans in Germany spent 1967 with their two-year-old television program *Beat Club* luring increasing numbers of British and American rock bands to their Bremen studios. A rival program, *Beat Beat Beat,* accomplished much the same feat by using bilingual hosts for their mixed audience of German youths and American servicemen.

Although *Shindig, Hullabaloo*, and *Shivaree* were all history by New Year's Day 1967, the most popular group with the most popular song on that first day of the year was almost entirely a creation of television. From California beaches to the snowy hills of Maine, anyone near a radio could not avoid hearing three mop-headed Americans and one diminutive mop-headed Briton belt out an upbeat paean to the magic of adolescent romance. The quartet of Peter, Micky, Mike, and Davy of the Monkees intoned that when they saw her face, "I'm a Believer." Even if listeners were not quite sure which young man was actually living his fondest dream at this moment, everyone knew that collectively "Hey, hey, hey, they're the Monkees" and they were definitely not monkeying around. How the group came into being is a unique story.

For almost two years after John, Paul, George, and Ringo had arrived at Kennedy Airport to stun viewers of *The Ed Sullivan Show*, American music promoters had assured the public that they would discover an American version of this magical quartet. By autumn of 1966 they were at least 75 percent successful. As NBC officials filled in time slots for the 1966–1967 television schedule, they penciled in a program idea that almost defied a neat category for the Monday 7:00 to 7:30 p.m. slot.

Network officials wanted a youth-oriented program that could somehow combine the humor and music of the Beatles into a fast-paced mélange of stop-action gags, musical performances, and an at least semi-coherent comedy plotline. *Newsweek* magazine opined that they were searching for "the direct videological descendants of the Beatles" by discovering "four twenty-something young men who could be quirky, funny and could sing."

Two young NBC producers, Bert Schneider and Bob Raffelson, placed an ad in *Variety* magazine for "4 insane boys age 17–21 who have the courage to work." Four hundred and thirty-seven potential Monkees showed up for the tryout. These hopefuls were narrowed down to Micky Dolenz, who had been a child star on the 1950s show *Circus Boy*; two struggling folk singers, Mike Nesmith and Peter Tork; and a British jockey named Davy Jones, who was seeking new adventures in America.

Before the quartet was ever seen on television, the boys were closeted for several months with talented songwriters Tommy Boyce, Bobby Hart, and Neil Diamond and produced an album fronted by an instant number one hit, "Last Train to Clarksville." By New Year's Day, *The Monkees* television show was a top ten hit, and "I'm A Believer" had replaced "Clarksville" in the number one record slot. The hits would keep coming throughout the year, with "Daydream Believer," "A Little Bit Me, A Little Bit You," and "Pleasant Valley Sunday" all topping out at or near the top of weekly top 40 hit lists. That year, *Teen* magazine featured more cover stories about the Monkees than any other pop music act. *Teen Screen* featured an "exclusive" report on the Monkees in England with "Groovy Travel Pics" and "17 new Monkee pix in color." *Teen Life* featured full-page autographed photos of each member, insisting "they're cute, they're funny, they're really way out," while *Flip* magazine had an "exclusive" on "Davy's secrets" while "he talks about everything important to him and you in a 'most private' interview in London."

While the Monkees could be seen every Monday night on television and live in some concerts, the group on which the foursome was based was tantalizingly just out of reach in a personal sense. On August 29, 1966, the Beatles arrived in San Francisco for the last engagement in their American tour. The Fab Four had already encountered Ku Klux Klan pickets outside the Mid-South Coliseum in Memphis, encountered deluge-level rain at Cincinnati's Crosley Field, and feared electric shocks from their guitars at an equally rainy St. Louis Busch Stadium. After a date at Shea Stadium in Queens, New York, which featured a less-than-sellout attendance yet probably the most hysterical, emotional crowd of the tour, the group flew across the country to end up needing police rescue as they were trapped in their Dodger Stadium dressing room on the eve of their climatic finale at the archrival Giants' Candlestick Park.

A sea wind that had literally blown a pitcher off the mound in a Giants game swirled in from the bay and the seating configuration placed the group more than 200 feet away from their fans in one of the most isolated performances they ever encountered. On the first leg of their long trip back to Britain, Paul McCartney told a young reporter for *Teen Set* magazine that "we're not very good performers; we work better in a recording studio where we can control things and work on it until we are right." As they left an America where both "Yellow Submarine" and "Eleanor Rigby" were on the hit list, the Beatles were about to embark on a journey that would result in their most discussed music project while coincidentally dissolving the Fab Four as a tangible performing entity.

Several months later, in the spring of 1967, *Life* reporter Thomas Thompson, who had last seen the Beatles at their Shea Stadium set the previous summer, was invited one night to EMI studios in London to watch the group spend virtually the entire night with producer George Martin to produce a single song. Thompson noted that "in 1963 the Beatles took only twelve hours to cut their first slap-dash album. Now, they would spend almost that amount of time producing a song called "Lucy In The Sky With Diamonds"; part of an LP to be called *Sgt. Pepper's Lonely Hearts Club Band*." The correspondent admitted that he "pondered their droopy French mustaches," their "bookwormish" faces, and their "bizarre clothing" as they were taking "the enormous risk of stepping ahead of their audience, recording music so complex and so unlike the music that made them successful that they could very likely lose the foundation of their support."

As the Beatles ran through six takes of "Lucy," John began to read a volume of E. E. Cummings's poetry, George showed off a black French coat he bought in a Chelsea antique shop, Paul entered a near-trancelike state listening to a playback, and Ringo started wolfing down a plate of mashed potatoes and beans. Three years earlier, when they first performed on *The Ed Sullivan Show*, a camera focused on John with a note to the audience: SORRY GIRLS, HE'S MARRIED. Now only Paul was still single, and the "boys" were clearly men who were both incredibly wealthy and essentially no longer a group, but a loose confederation that occasionally would come together to record anything that interested them.

By 1967, John came the closest to appearing like a hippie with groovy glasses, eccentric clothing, quotes from Bertrand Russell and Allen Ginsberg, and a role in the antimilitary satire film *How I Won the War*. Yet it was the still somewhat cherubic Paul who was becoming the most vocal proponent of LSD use and the most vocal critic of the Vietnam War. George had developed into the point man for a budding relationship with Ravi Shankar and excursions into mysticism in India, while Ringo provided the most significant glimpse back to 1964 Beatlemania as he collected old swords and gathered materials for a planned Beatles museum. Yet as all the Beatles reminded correspondents who questioned their massive makeover, they had already shed some of their first generation of fans back in Liverpool when Brian Epstein convinced them to morph from black leather jackets and sideburns to suits and new hairstyles. Now the second major metamorphosis had turned the Fab Four into a quartet of social commentators. They were now more than just entertainers, and their music carried into American college dormitories and sometimes even into classroom psychology and sociology discussions. The *Sgt. Pepper* album rewrote the soundtrack of summer 1967, but the Beatles were not entering the brave new world of the new rock alone, as the two population and cultural centers of California would soon create an American response to the emerging "trippiness" of the Beatles.

In the Bay Area, a mixed-gender group both reflected and at times created the unique experience that became the "Summer of Love," which emanated from the cultural ground zero of Haight-Ashbury. The previous autumn, a young woman with a penetrating voice that far belied her size fronted a band, formed by her husband Jerry Slick and his brother, Darby, that was named the Great Society in mock tribute to Lyndon Johnson. While Grace Slick was already dominating every stage on which she performed, Darby and Jerry managed to alienate both Grace and producer Sly Stone with frequent mood swings and total lack of organization. On October 15, 1966, a rival Bay Area group, the Jefferson Airplane, found itself minus its lead singer, Signe Anderson. Grace quickly joined the Airplane. Now, paired off with male lead Marty Balin, she helped take the group to superstar status.

Grace Slick's small stature belied an intense, funny, and strong-willed young woman in her midtwenties who merged the casually unkempt look of the emerging hippie culture with a stunning physical attractiveness that would soon focus television cameras on her more than the rest of the band. As America warmed up to the super cool summer of 1967, Grace caught young Americans' attention with her insistence that relationships were both necessary and yet transitory, as loneliness seemed to be a sad but natural state for much of a person's youth as she intoned "Somebody to Love."

Later in the summer, Jefferson Airplane struck gold a second time with a song that epitomized the double entendre language of hippie/drug/youth culture, as Grace followed Alice down the rabbit hole to connect her neo-psychedelic nineteenth-century adventure with the more blatant version of the late 1960s. "White Rabbit" was both playful and biting as the band upped the intensity level each time Lewis Carroll's hookah-smoking caterpillar's commands to "feed your head" grew more insistent and moved ever closer to current real-life culture.

While Grace Slick and Marty Balin created anthems for Haight-Ashbury and the Summer of Love, two other major pop hits focused on the relationship of San Francisco as a location in this expected transition to a more conscience-achieving America and world. In June, frizzy-haired, mustachioed Scott McKenzie invited everyone in the nation to visit San Francisco, specifically Haight-Ashbury, and share the laid-back lifestyle of the flower children by adopting their emerging anthem of "San Francisco

(Be Sure to Wear Flowers in Your Hair)." McKenzie's ballad insisted that to be anywhere around San Francisco that summer was to partake of some cultural experiment that seemed to have no downside as "a whole generation has a new explanation" for just about anything bothering humankind. A few weeks later, Animals lead singer Eric Burdon essentially offered his fans a three-minute update on what happened to him during and after the Monterey music festival in "San Franciscan Nights." As Burdon was drawing away from the other lads in the group, he was developing a fascination for the California American lifestyle, and in the song, he encourages everyone of "European residence" to "save their bread" and fly "Trans Love Airlines" to San Francisco, USA. The song then shifts from blaring-rock background to a laid-back harpsichord/lute ballad extolling the joys of nocturnal Ashbury, where even initially menacing police "feel all right on a warm San Francisco night." He then insists that while he wasn't born there, perhaps he'll die there in some form of nirvana of an extended Summer of Love. While not everyone in Europe visited Burdon's newly discovered paradise, Beatle George Harrison and his wife, Pattie, did make a triumphal walkabout that gave a measure of Fab Four endorsement to the Bay Area as a special place to welcome in the age of Aquarius.

Yet while San Francisco offered laid-back peace and love that summer, a newly emerging group in rival city Los Angeles offered a much darker side of life. Recent University of Southern California student Jim Morrison, product of a hugely itinerant upbringing that went with his father's naval officer career, began turning his massive range of emotional experiences into an album centered around his favorite reading material, Aldous Huxley's *The Doors of Perception*.

Morrison had longer hair than an average American young man of the day, but dressed in a manner that was more oriented toward sex appeal than nondescript hippie fashion, as did his bandmates Ray Manzarek, Robby Krieger, and John Densmore. Morrison was a perfect fit for a poster boy of late sixties rock as much as an equally handsome/menacing Elvis Presley had been a decade earlier. However, while Elvis had largely concentrated on won love, lost love, and regained love in his repertoire, Morrison burst on the scene at an even higher level of intensity, evoked in songs that were often long for traditional rock single playlists. The song that would remain Morrison's signature effort in his short life was so loaded with double entendres that it ensured his first appearance on the iconic *Ed Sullivan Show* would be his last, as "Light My Fire" scintillated, angered, and perplexed kids and adults. Ironically, while Sullivan allowed the Jefferson Airplane to fill the stage with psychedelic visuals and invitations to leave middle-class conventions behind, Morrison gained huge notoriety when Sullivan secured a promise that "we couldn't get much higher" would be deleted from *Light My Fire*. The phrase was sung anyway and the Doors were banned for life from the show, which probably added to their reputation among their young audience. "Light My Fire" controlled the top spot in the top 40 right at the height of summer, but even more important, the three-minute 45 rpm single that was only the pared-down version of a much longer version, embedded with tripping guitar and keyboard riffs perfect for listening on FM album-oriented stations after dark.

The Doors album quickly jumped into contention with the Beatles *Sgt. Pepper's Lonely Hearts Club Band* as young listeners searched for every hidden meaning they could conjure. If the Beatles "A Day in the Life" reeked of depression about contemporary life, Morrison's eleven-minute-plus marathon "The End" was an odyssey into self destruction that made the British song seem lighthearted by comparison.

As even serious adult music scholars were attempting to interpret the Lennon/ McCartney/Morrison statements on youth issues, 40,000 mostly young people were converging on the resort town of Monterey, where 26,000 residents were about to host the first in a series of multiday concerts that would culminate two years later in Woodstock. The event was marketed as an attempt to create "Love, Flowers and Music" in "a spirit of peace and acceptance" at a venue surrounded by bright flags bearing astrological signs and frequented by vendors selling everything from paper dresses to jeweled crosses to macrobiotic food. Members of the Monterey Kiwanis club sold fresh corn on the cob, Congregation Beth El vendors offered pastrami sandwiches, and a governing board including Paul McCartney, Mick Jagger, and Donovan would determine which charities should receive the proceeds.

The initial card of performers, which might very well have outshone Woodstock two years later, was whittled down by a combination of bad luck and generation gap–era legal and social issues. Bob Dylan had been disabled by a traffic accident, while Dionne Warwick, who already had a bad cold, also felt reluctant to participate in what some African American groups labeled a "whitey festival"; two members of the Rolling Stones had been forced to surrender their passports as they faced drug charges in Britain; the Beach Boys sent their regrets as Carl Wilson was attempting to maintain a low profile as he stayed one step ahead of his draft board; and members of the Lovin' Spoonful were dodging marijuana charges.

Despite this substantial no-show list (most of whom would also skip Woodstock), there was enough residual talent to produce a truly memorable event. Otis Redding and Janis Joplin found themselves on the same stage and exhorted the audience to "shake, shake, shake" as, according to one reporter, "they blew the minds of the crowd." Another correspondent marveled at the rapport that the Mamas and Papas had with the audience as they "proved that interesting people could work in rock and roll" and create intelligent songs in a mood of laid-back euphoria. Country Joe and the Fish provided the only overt political commentary of the festival with songs like "Thought Dream" ("Don't drop that H-bomb on me, you can drop it on yourself"), while the Grateful Dead created a slightly different mood with their mixture of blues and acid rock.

Ravi Shankar set the festival record for longest single song when he sat cross-legged and barefoot and played a monumental three-hour set that demonstrated why the Beatles had adopted him as their music guru, while the lesser known guitarist Jimi Hendrix gave the audience a "guitarorial" with extended riffs that, like Shankar's, seemed to put time on hold. The final merger of fire and ice that flavored both 1967 and the most important concert of that year was the contrast between the smooth crooning of Lou Rawls, who reminded the audience of the hopes and dreams of romantic relationships, and the literal fire of The Who, as their rendition of "My Generation" included smoke bombs and Pete Townshend torching his guitar, wrecking part of the stage in the process.

The intensity of Jefferson Airplane, the Doors, much of the *Sgt. Pepper* album, and the Monterey Festival sometimes obscures the fact that a great deal of the popular music then was a throwback to possibly gentler, simpler times and places. This intriguing new trend began to become evident in the closing days of 1966 when, on Christmas Eve, a little-known British group called the New Vaudeville Band scored the number one slot in the *Billboard* charts with the blatantly retro song, "Winchester Cathedral." The group was a gaggle of quirky university types from Britain who produced a throwback to the 1920s and 1930s music of performers like Rudy Vallee. Dressed like college swells of the era, the band came equipped with a Vallee-like megaphone and a soft but insistent mind-set that the bells of the famous cathedral might somehow ring out a return of a lost love. Their smash hit was quickly followed by the almost equally catchy retro "Peek-A-Boo." Suddenly there was a transatlantic boom in a Cole Porter–like reversion to the prewar, preatomic age. One of the Vaudeville Band's major British rivals for this new, softer sound was soon dueling with them for top spot in the pop charts, as Donovan Leitch touched the same level of laid-back musical mood in "Mellow Yellow."

As 1967 began, the intensity of the emerging album rock was being challenged by a noticeable trend in many singles, which focused on the softer or sometimes even amusing side of life. "Winchester Cathedral" was quickly joined in the charts by Nancy Sinatra's mellow "Sugar Town," the Seekers' soft spin on relationships in "Georgy Girl," the Lovin' Spoonful's gentle satire on country music in "Nashville Cats," and the Royal Guardsmen's hilarious soundtrack of Charlie Brown and the Peanuts Gang in "Snoopy vs. the Red Baron." At a time when music critics were discussing the nuances of Grateful Dead tunes, many young Americans were still more interested in listening to the Buckinghams' "Kind of a Drag" and Johnny Rivers's cover of the Four Tops' "Baby I Need your Loving," while the closest thing to social satire was Sonny and Cher's "The Beat Goes On." Many pop music acts were new compared to the top hit makers of four or five years earlier, but that did not necessarily mean that political and drug issues pervaded most of the songs.

A representative sample of five new acts that fully emerged in 1967 demonstrated that consistent singles and non-themed albums could still dominate radio programming and record sales, even if gaining little attention by social or political critics. One member of this quintet was Nancy Sinatra, just emerging as a challenger to her father's perch at the top of pop music. Nancy had exploded to the top of the pop scene in 1966 with her feisty "These Boots Are Made for Walkin'," a less than subtle reminder to her estranged boyfriend that affairs on the side would trigger unpleasant consequences ranging from dissolving the relationship to a possible literal stomping with her brand-new footwear. By 1967, the much softer "Sugar Town" was topping charts, and her collaboration with writer, singer, and producer Lee Hazlewood was making pop music news. The gruff-voiced Oklahoman jumped from producer's booth to on-record frenemy as he was drugged and robbed by a frontier-like Nancy in "Summer Wine," cavorted in fields with a tripping Nancy in "Some Velvet Morning," and engaged in virtually assured relationship termination in "Jackson." When Nancy was not pairing with Hazlewood on record, she was belting out one of the most iconic James Bond themes in the series with the haunting, borderline Asian-sounding "You Only Live Twice" and finally pairing off with her father in the mega smash "Something Stupid." Nancy was a typical paradox of this year of fire and ice as she toured Vietnam and became a poster girl for lonely grunts while politically opposing the conflict, sometimes at odds with her father's position.

The emerging male equivalent of Nancy Sinatra was Neil Diamond, who also celebrated his first full year as a major hit maker. Diamond had turned 1966 into a prosperous debut with significant hits in "Solitary Man," a brooding litany of failed relationships, and the more upbeat "Cherry, Cherry," which hinted that he had finally met the right partner. By 1967, Diamond had emerged as a dependable hit producer with the fast- moving "You Got to Me" and "Thank the Lord for the Night Time," ballads such as "Girl, You'll Be A Woman Soon" and "Kentucky Woman," and ongoing songwriting for the popular Monkees. Diamond was now a major persona who drew in both teen and older listeners who wanted to enjoy rock music but spurned drug references and hidden agendas in the lyrics.

The British equivalent to Nancy Sinatra was a little more mature and had enjoyed an earlier debut to stardom, but was fully hitting her stride in this year. In 1967 Petula Clark was still nicknamed the "Downtown" girl after her smash hit of the same name in late 1964 and early 1965. Now a relatively mature thirty-three, Clark had sold five million singles, become a huge concert and nightclub star, and was about to enter the world of film in the lead role in *Finian's Rainbow*. Clark regularly knocked out hits in four different languages and had gained superstar status through her ability to attract both teens and over-thirties to her alternately bouncy and tear-jerking songs while dealing with two preschool daughters at home. Clark bridged the generation gap by not hiding her age, her children, or her husband, and by admitting she was too old for the beach party movies that appealed to teens. She turned the British invasion toward Europe as well as America when she recorded French versions of her songs and appeared regularly on Euro-rock television programs. Along with singing the twenty-three songs from *Finian's Rainbow*, she continued her personal hit list with "This is My Song," "Don't Sleep in the Subway," and "The Other Man's Grass is Always Greener." Clark's husband/manager also insisted on 60 percent of the gate from all concerts, which allowed them to buy two houses in France and one in Switzerland, as well as their home in Britain.

While Petula Clark spent much of the year alternating between pop stardom and child rearing, a young lady from New York City, barely old enough to babysit Clark's children, produced a far edgier view of late sixties life. Janis Ian, a four-foot-ten-inch junior at the New York School of Music and Art, alternated homework assignments with television appearances to promote probably the most controversial mainstream song of the day. As a singer, she explored touchy topics such as interracial dating and generational divisions in her huge hit single, "Society's Child (Baby I've Been Thinking)." Within a week the song sold 600,000 copies, even though many radio disc jockeys refused to play it. A *Life* magazine profile noted that Ian's repertoire was centered around "outbursts at squaredom, declarations of independence from contemporary society and assault on corrupted religion." By early fall, Ian had moved up from performances in Greenwich Village folk clubs to a nationally telecast special linked with composer/conductor Leonard Bernstein. While insisting that her relations with her parents were quite good and that she generally liked most adults, she became a key object of the generation gap debate.

While Janis Ian lambasted adult society while enjoying a positive relationship with her parents, the other newly emerging teenage sensation was, on the surface, a picture-perfect family that was able to hide a massive generational rift. A former sailor named Bud Cowsill turned his concern with the edginess of adult-teen relations into a huge payoff when he organized a family rock group centered around his four teen sons, preteen daughter, and middle-aged wife, all rolled into an ensemble not-so-cleverly named the Cowsills. As the Summer of Love reached its peak, pop music stations and television network shows featured "The Rain, The Park & Other Things," which peaked as the number two hit record as fall approached. The song was a plaintive hope to reconnect with a mysterious "flower girl" in a mix of traditional pop music and a hint of trippiness. On their many television appearances, the group presented a mix of modish but clean-cut teen boys, a young girl with a preteen miniskirt and boots, and a middle-aged mother with only slightly more conservative outfits. The group's unique demographics guaranteed widespread appearances that carried the band toward extreme edges of pop music, from the folksy "Silver Threads and Golden Needles" to the arch hippie anthem of "Hair." Unfortunately, Bud Cowsill's attempt to instill naval discipline into his musical crew doomed the group to a short window of success.

While Janis Ian used generational differences as a main topic and the Cowsills used them as a cute marketing ploy, the most spectacular new performer on the soul horizon used former connections in a more complex manner. Aretha Franklin in 1967 was a twenty-four-year-old Michigan resident who was blessed/cursed with a father who had made a small fortune as a dynamic preacher and musician. As she coped with the death of her mother when she was ten, this eventual first lady of soul fused the gospel of Mahalia Jackson with the emerging heat of rock and roll, and by 1961 had entered the charts with "Rock-a-Bye Your Baby with a

Dixie Melody." While backed by the powerful Columbia label, Franklin had moderate success and enough talent to edge onto the television scene in *Hollywood A Go-Go* and *Shindig*, but as late as 1966 she was still not a marquee performer. A new deal with Atlantic records turned to near magic when "I Never Loved a Man (The Way I Love You)" slipped into the top ten list at number nine. The real ride to superstar status began on April 29 when she rode the Otis Redding hit "Respect" to number one in early June. Follow-ups such as "(You Make Me Feel Like) A Natural Woman," "Baby Baby Baby," and "Chain of Fools" followed in rapid succession, and it was clear by the end of the year that Motown now had serious competition in the soul sound.

Each of these six individuals/groups could point to 1967 as a definitive year in their music careers, and yet they only counted as one major element in a hugely diverse and complex popular music soundtrack for a year that was equally complex. While 1968 would become the most emotionally challenging year of the decade and 1969 would provide the two mega stories of Apollo and Woodstock, 1967 probably had a "cooler" soundtrack in a nation that had somewhat recovered from the assassination of John F. Kennedy and had yet to face the crises of Tet, the assassinations of Martin Luther King and Robert Kennedy, the Chicago riots, and the take-no-prisoners 1968 election.

Beyond the acts and songs already discussed, the year's music was a fascinating mix of edgy and romantic, experimental and familiar, sunny and pessimistic. Listeners from national magazine music critics to young people listening to bedroom stereo sets tried to decipher the meaning of the British group Procol Harum's cool but sometimes confusing "A Whiter Shade of Pale." Motown entered the final year of many of its stars' strings of hits as the Supremes sang of memories past in "Reflections," Martha and the Vandellas reprised the snappy style of "Heatwave" in "Jimmy Mack," the Four Tops longed for "Bernadette," and the Temptations rejoiced in their new relationship, "You're My Everything." Early British Invasion groups still had one or two hits left in their repertoire, as Peter Noone led his Hermits in "Dandy" and "No Milk Today," while the Dave Clark Five raided earlier American songbooks for "You Got What It Takes" and

"You Must Have Been a Beautiful Baby." For their part, the Rolling Stones added "Ruby Tuesday" and "Let's Spend the Night Together" to their concert repertoire for future decades.

Nineteen sixty-seven would produce a renaissance for Frankie Valli and The Four Seasons with "C'mon Marianne" and "I Can't Take My Eyes Off You," while the hugely successful Lovin' Spoonful's cute satire of country music, "Nashville Cats," would largely be the end of the road for that quartet. Yet if the Spoonful was finished, three mixed male-female groups would enjoy sensational years.

The Mamas and the Papas would continue their sensational string of hits for a few more months with the Shirelles hit "Dedicated to the One I Love" and the autobiographical "Creeque Alley," but as they slipped, the 5th Dimension, a five-member group fronted by Marilyn McCoo and Billy Davis, would combine elements of pop, soul, and later psychedelia with "Up, Up and Away" and "Go Where You Wanna Go," which would later turn the group into the most recognizable minstrels of *Hair* and land McCoo in choice television roles opposite major stars such as Robert Wagner. While the 5th Dimension mixed pop and soul, Spanky McFarlane and her male backups fused soft rock with an occasional touch of psychedelia so that Spanky and Our Gang became television favorites on every network with "Sunday Will Never Be the Same," "Making Every Minute Count," and "Lazy Day."

Three mainstream male bands would supply much of the soundtrack for boys or young men entering the world of romance and its myriad complications. The previous year a quartet of young men dressed in the knickers, paperboy caps, and suspenders of tough urban street kids circa 1910 began exploding on the scene from *American Bandstand* to *Hullabaloo*. Initially promoted as the Young Rascals, by 1967 they had softened their image just a bit and rebranded as the Rascals. The leader of the group was keyboardist and vocalist Felix Cavaliere, who wrote most of their songs and led the group with blockbusters "You Better Run" and "Good Lovin'," which were rapid-fire dares to young ladies to take on a new relationship. The 1967 version of their repertoire produced a peak of stardom built around a far softer side of relationships in "Groovin'," "A Girl Like You," and "How Can I Be Sure," which all produced an atmosphere of mellow yearning that evoked so much of that year.

One of the major rivals to the Rascals for network program television exposure was another group that had recently emerged with the top ten hit "Hanky Panky." While the name "The Rascals" gave no clue to the identity of the group's leader, Tommy James and the Shondells left little doubt who was the front man. Like the Rascals, James and his group seemed to be everywhere on television, backed by increasingly psychedelic backdrops as they sang "I Think We're Alone Now," a kind of updated version of Del Shannon's "Keep Searchin'" format of young lovers on the run; "Mirage," which posits a downbeat side of a relationship; and "Gettin' Together," which produces a happy outcome for the trilogy. Tommy James and his band were emerging superstars, to be confirmed the following year with the garage sound of "Mony Mony" and the clearly psychedelic "Crimson and Clover."

The third male band that was able to score coveted spots on all of the major network variety outlets was also new to the national scene. Only the previous summer, the Association premiered with the enigmatic "Along Comes Mary," which produced an argument among fans, disc jockeys, and even the national media as to whether or not the song was a cover for some relationship with marijuana (Mary Jane). Yet the band wore conservative suits and ties and seemed quite articulate. After scoring a number one hit with "Cherish" in the last weeks of 1966, the band continued a major run in 1967 with "No Fair At All," a modest hit, and two major successes, "Windy" and "Never My Love," the first song filled with enigmas about who or what "Windy" really is, the second an extremely traditional love song worthy of numerous wedding receptions.

While this trio of male groups scored enormous television exposure, a band of young Chicago-area kids was matching this trio in record sales even though many listeners had little idea what they looked like. The Buckinghams shocked much of the music industry during Valentine's week of 1967 when their first hit, "Kind of a Drag," pushed aside the Rolling Stones and Monkees for the number one spot on the charts. They proved to be far beyond a one-hit wonder with "Don't You Care," "Mercy,

Mercy, Mercy," "Hey Baby (They're Playing Our Song)," and "Susan," guaranteeing the band a spot on the upper tier of the charts almost every week of the year in what might be termed "The Revenge of the Garage Bands." The band essentially transformed early 1960s doo-wop into a contemporary late 1960s sound with more complex arrangements, more background instruments, and just a tinge of the "trippy" sound of this new era.

While male groups were as popular in 1967 as 1962 or 1963, one of the most astonishing aspects of the soundtrack of 1967 was the near disappearance of the girl groups that formed a vital element of early sixties rock music. Mixed-gender groups such as the 5th Dimension, Spanky and Our Gang, and the Mamas and the Papas were huge in the year of fire and ice, and in each of these groups the female members Marilyn McCoo, Spanky McFarlene, and Mama Cass Elliot were more famous than their male counterparts. Yet as traditional girl groups like the Angels, the Crystals, and the Ronettes faded, few new groups moved in to replace them. Even single female artists such as Lesley Gore and Peggy March were moving on, as Gore was continuing her college studies and March was emerging as a top ten star in Germany, 3,000 miles from her Lansdale, Pennsylvania, home. The traditional girl group sound of the early 1960s would not fully come back until two decades later, with the MTV-inspired emergence of the Go-Go's, Bananarama, and the Bangles.

Yet if girl groups in their traditional sense were fading, the music culture that had nourished them was producing an exploding subgenre of American pop increasingly identified as "soul." The most appropriate anthem for this element of pop music is probably Arthur Conley's frantic "Sweet Soul Music," which in rapid-fire succession lists everyone who is anyone in that segment of pop music. Soul music was all over the charts of 1967, from Stevie Wonder's "I Was Made to Love Her" to Aaron Neville's "Tell It Like It Is." Sometimes soul was evoked by mixed-race groups like Allentown, Pennsylvania's, Jay and the Techniques' "Apples, Peaches, Pumpkin Pie" or even all-white groups like the Music Explosion's "Little Bit O' Soul" or Steve Winwood's Spencer Davis Group in "Gimme Some Lovin'." Motown had been a major innovator of the 1960s, but now that sound had become so popular that it was becoming difficult to define its parameters. Arthur Conley's song is an open invitation to join the fun of belonging to an expanding universe, and if it was fun to try to figure out what Bobbie Gentry's character was actually doing on the Tallahatchie Bridge in "Ode To Billy Joe" or outrage at Janis Ian's character in "Society's Child," 1967 still provided plenty of music for junior proms, fraternity parties, and wedding celebrations. Determining which year in the 1960s had the best musical soundtrack is an exercise in personal tastes, but 1967 can easily hold its own in providing special musical memories for anyone who cared about the beat in that year.

CHAPTER VI

Vietnam: The Battle for the Borderlands

On a sunny April afternoon in 1967, a young Radcliffe student making her way across the Harvard campus was surprised to stumble across a number of her classmates building a fire on the lawn. Shock set in as she realized that they were burning an effigy, and that the crude mannequin was a representation of her father. The young lady was Stevie Westmoreland, and while her father had actually studied at Harvard a generation earlier, he was now one of the most powerful and controversial men in the world: General William Westmoreland, commander of all American troops in the Republic of South Vietnam.

At the moment of her chance encounter with that burning effigy, Stevie Westmoreland was preparing to drive to New York City to join her father for an eagerly awaited press conference on the war, to be followed by an address to a Joint Session of Congress concerning the state of the war roughly eighteen months after American forces had entered full-scale combat. Her worries about telling her father about the Harvard demonstration were quickly subsumed by the far larger number of demonstrations ringing the Waldorf-Astoria hotel as they confronted the army general with shouts of "Hell no, we won't go" and "Westmoreland is a war criminal."

Yet unlike the experience of many American leaders the following spring and summer, the marchers were still relatively polite and the general was warmly applauded during the ensuing press conference.

The generally warm welcome for Westmoreland continued as he journeyed southward toward the national capital, and on April 28 he delivered his address to Congress—an address that was interrupted sixteen times with cheers and applause. At the time of Westmoreland's address, and for a few months afterwards, a majority of Americans still expected a moderately favorable outcome to the conflict in Vietnam. On this special day, even those lawmakers who felt otherwise were far too polite to intrude on the general's historic moment. Few members of Congress winced at his bold assertion that the American force in Vietnam was "the finest army ever fielded in our nation's history."

Even relatively skeptical Congress members admitted that Westmoreland was a great general who gave a fine presentation and applauded him for telling the truth about the war. Countering that were some increasingly skeptical critics of Lyndon Johnson's war aims who wondered why the president virtually demanded that Westmoreland return home to present the administration's case when he was so badly needed at the center of the conflict. By late April, heavily publicized American offensives such as Operation Cedar Falls and Operation Junction City had petered out with massive hauls of enemy weapons and supplies but surprisingly small enemy body counts. At the time, the Communists fielded an army of over 300,000 men and were augmenting their forces by 12,000 personnel a month.

The quandary for Westmoreland and his field commanders was that the American army, trained to deflect a massive Soviet westward drive across the open plains of Germany, was now being deployed in a totally alien environment in which armored forces were almost impossible to mass and air squadrons seldom detected massive enemy formations. While South Vietnam was not a particularly small landmass, the nation featured only a very narrow strip of habitable coastal plain stretching down from the demilitarized zone toward the northern suburbs of Saigon. Only then did it open up and widen into a vast, flat plain that was crisscrossed by thousands of canals, waterways, bays, and assorted outlets of the central feature of the region, the Mekong River.

By that spring, almost every Communist fighting unit in South Vietnam was ten miles or less from some type of wilderness refuge where thousands of men could hide and choose the time to launch an attack. From the uninhabited rain forests of the central highlands to the almost deserted salt sands of the coast to the seemingly endless mangrove swamps of the Mekong River Delta, Ho Chi Minh's forces had established base camps that had not been detected, much less attacked, by American forces. At the time of General Westmoreland's congressional address, American forces had actually done quite well in defeating enemy units that chose to defend relatively major bases, and the mostly one-sided casualty counts in favor of the Americans were relatively accurate. Yet despite some success, American casualties were indeed soaring, escalating from 142 in 1964, 1,369 in 1965, and 5,008 in 1966 to a projected 7,000–8,000 in 1967. Meanwhile, the tally of 1,038 American wounded in 1964 had soared to 30,093 in 1966 and was expected to push toward 50,000 in 1967.

While the growing number of congressional doves, who were becoming more skeptical about the whole Vietnam enterprise, were still complimentary to the general, they became considerably less enthused as information leaked out concerning Westmoreland's overnight visit to the White House. President Johnson had just made an arduous journey to Guam a few weeks earlier to follow up his previous Pacific inspection tour in October 1966. Now, only a few weeks later, his commanding general began calling for massive additional reinforcements, without which the conflict would most likely devolve into a long-term quagmire.

In essence, the general asked the president for a quarter of a million men in addition to the 415,000 already in country, and suggested that such an augmentation of forces could smother the enemy by expanding the war in Laos, closing down the Ho Chi Minh trail supply route, and expanding the air war on North Vietnam to include more permitted targets. Walt Rostow, Johnson's national security advisor, readily agreed with the reinforcement plan, but suggested that they should commit to significantly shortening the war by making an amphibious landing in the demilitarized zone (DMZ) between North and South Vietnam. While risky, such a move could emulate some of the most successful trap-and-destroy operations of World War II.

General Westmoreland began the long flight back to Saigon genuinely moved by the reception from Congress and moderately optimistic that his commander in chief would at least seriously consider significant reinforcements to take the war north of the DMZ. Yet as Westmoreland was discussing a potential strike north of the DMZ, the American commander on the scene was preparing to fight a potential major enemy thrust in exactly the opposite direction.

William Westmoreland's commander on the scene at the DMZ was Lieutenant General Lewis Walt, the man responsible for the pivotal I Corps region, the northernmost segment of the four military zones that constituted the American presence in South Vietnam. Walt was a burly, cantankerous marine who rode herd over one of the most volatile areas in the American intervention, the far northern region that stretched along a 170-mile coastline, home to two million Vietnamese, many of whom would die to bring down the South Vietnamese "puppet" government. The sheriff in this expansive "Dodge City" environment commanded 80,000 marines and an army infantry division poised to repel an invasion over the 17th parallel, while at the same time attempting to frustrate North Vietnamese efforts to funnel their regular soldiers south in support of their guerrilla brothers. Action on this front ranged from artillery duels across the DMZ to forays along the paths, tracks, and roads known collectively as the Ho Chi Minh trail.

When Lewis Walt was not dodging enemy artillery fire or giving pep talks to his officers and men, he was logging 10,000 miles a month flying low-altitude helicopter runs, carefully searching for ambush sites to keep the enemy off balance. Between aerial scouting missions, the general came under a military and press microscope for his initiation of Combined Action Company operations, in which small units of marines lived in South Vietnamese villages and trained civilians to become part-time soldiers capable of defending their hamlets when they were not farming. Yet now, nearing the end of his two-year tour of duty in the I

Corps hothouse, Lew Walt and his men were about to encounter a new wave of challenges.

As combat raged from the Mekong Delta to the DMZ in early spring, the boldest Communist gamble of the war was taking shape in Hanoi. Responding to the massive infusion of American forces since the 13th Communist Party Plenum had been convened in December 1965, the party leaders accepted the prospect of a prolonged war. It was their view that the will of the American fighting forces and home front would be sapped by escalating casualties and an inability to exploit battle gains in a conflict that appeared to have no main battlefront and few tangible physical objectives.

Now, almost a year and a half later, Chairman of the Communist Party Ho Chi Minh was increasingly coming to grips with his own impending mortality, a reality that heightened his desire to see the unification of Vietnam before his death. The 13th Plenum obliged their leader's wishes and, in a major change in strategy, decided to change the tempo of war in the south. The largely hit and run guerrilla tactics would give way to a conventional assault involving nearly 90,000 Vietcong and North Vietnamese regulars. The "General Offensive General Uprising" would be launched under the cover of the annual Tet New Year's truce, in which both sides tacitly scaled back operations to allow their men to celebrate this most important of Vietnamese holidays.

The chief architect of the uprising was General Nguyen Chi Thanh, who, as head of the Central Office for South Vietnam, was the senior commander of all Viet Cong forces. His basic plan was to spend the remainder of 1967 drawing the bulk of American forces toward the northern highlands and the DMZ, while key cities such as Saigon, Hue, and Da Nang would be left garrisoned primarily by South Vietnam troops whom he viewed as second-rate puppet forces. Thanh insisted that "America is wealthy but not resolute," so if the Communists could seize the major cities and in turn "squeeze tight to the American chest and attack," the United States might accept terms that allowed for the safe evacuation of the American army in return for reunification under Ho Chi Minh.

The Tet Offensive was actually expected to be the middle stage of a three-stage campaign to win the war sometime in 1968. The first phase would extend through the rest of 1967 and would draw American and allied forces out of the cities and into the countryside, especially the border regions such as the DMZ. Finally, there would be some version of Dien Bien Phu, in which the now unsupported Americans would be surrounded and offered free passage out of the country or in turn captured and released after American concession of unification under the Communist Party.

On the other hand, the South Vietnam to which General William Westmoreland returned from his New York and Washington activities was, according to one highly placed American newsman, "slow, tough but coming along." Hedley Donovan, editor in chief of Time Life, informed readers of *Life* magazine that "Saigon is shabbier, smellier and noisier by the day; it will not be the dream city of American tourists in 1987." Yet he marveled at the World War II–like power that the United State military had assembled during the past eighteen months. "The vast allied force now numbers more than 1.1 million men—US, ARVN, Korean, and a few thousand Australians, New Zealanders, Filipinos, and Thais. American military engineering and architecture is heavily imprinted on the countryside the blunt geometry of jet air strips, radars, piers; the endless ranks of barracks, hangers, sheds of fatigue green, olive drab, and blazing corrugated metal; the concrete, tar, sand and newly scarred clay."

South Vietnam in spring and summer was a world of contrasts, a "fire and ice" dichotomy of both environment and human activity. Anyone riding a helicopter in that period—and the helicopter was becoming the icon of the Vietnam War—could see vast white beaches packed with bathers, and then fly over the roads of the vast Mekong Delta and see streams of cars, motorcycles, and bicycles out on errands or pleasure trips in a countryside seemingly at peace. Yet cities, towns, and beaches gave way to jungle canopies in the south and massive hills and mountains in the north, and the passengers and crews of a disabled chopper landing in these places might find themselves aided or shot at depending on who controlled that site at that moment.

Both Communist and American planners were attempting to shift the balance of forces decisively in their favor and battles were erupting from the outer edges of Saigon to the border with North Vietnam. Each side was using new tactics and war weapons, which in some cases harkened back to earlier wars and earlier times. One of those increasingly intricate battles occurred near Saigon in June.

One of the new weapons in the growing American arsenal was a "back to the future" reversion to the river war force of the nation's Civil War. When the American buildup in the wake of the near Viet Cong victory in 1965 resulted in the reactivation of the 9th Infantry Division, General Westmoreland authorized units of this new force to be trained "to utilize the extensive waterways of the Mekong Delta to get at the Viet Cong." The plan was to deny them the ability to rapidly transport supplies and men via the extensive river system.

This new Mobile Riverine Force took on the look of General Ulysses S. Grant's strike forces that pushed the Confederate army from the gates of Ohio all the way back down the Mississippi in 1862. *Newsweek* magazine marveled at the willingness of the American military to reach back to the nineteenth century to parry enemy threats, as "not since the Mississippi flotilla was deployed to fight Shiloh and Vicksburg has river warfare been as important as Mekong Delta river assault forces." "Craft that look strikingly like Civil War ironclads are part of the river assault flotilla designed to root out the Vietcong from the rivers and swamps near Saigon."

This rooting-out process often uncovered enemy hornet nests, and in June a series of engagements less than twenty miles from downtown Saigon gained national media attention. American intelligence units began receiving information that enemy forces were developing a staging area near the Soài Rap River in possible preparations for an operation in the Saigon area. On the morning of June 19, American war craft landed the 4th battalion of the 47th Infantry regiment along beaches on the outskirts of the town of Cần Giuộc.

The American assault force plodded through sodden rice fields until they halted at a waterway lined with mangrove trees. As they moved along the edge of the water into an open field, Viet Cong machine guns sputtered into life. Alpha and Charlie companies now shifted from patrol to combat mode while enemy fire quickly destroyed two of the supporting river craft. More than fifty members of the assault forces were wounded or killed almost immediately. As an American gunboat let loose with cannon fire that would have impressed Ulysses Grant, helicopters swirled overhead like angry falcons protecting their endangered young. Navy gunners sent shells skipping off the surface of the water in order to drop their deadly contents on enemy positions.

The combination of air, ground, and naval firepower ultimately pushed the Viet Cong from the waterlogged battleground, where they left 250 of their comrades dead or dying. However, the engagement left Alpha company nearly incapable of immediate operations and Charlie company badly mauled. The tally soared to forty-eight dead and 143 wounded Americans. The carcasses of two wrecked helicopters littered the field like two winged dinosaurs that had lost their final duel. Yet the Communist dream of annihilating a substantial American unit had not occurred, and a few days later the river craft and their passengers would resume operations to push the enemy farther away from Saigon. Meanwhile, far to the north, other American forces contended with a new threat that would become the opening gambit of what would soon emerge as the Tet Offensive.

While American sailors and soldiers dueled with the Viet Cong around the swamps and rivers that dotted the greater Saigon area, General Westmoreland was also preparing to parry the growing threat of a North Vietnamese invasion across the DMZ into the northern provinces of South Vietnam. By spring the Communist high command had mobilized a crack force of three divisions of North Vietnamese regulars, about thirty-five thousand men, to threaten Quang Tri province, the area abutting the DMZ. In response, General Westmoreland had rushed 10,000 marines to fend off any enemy incursions across the zone.

In April, Radio Hanoi issued warnings (or promises) that Quang Tri City was about to be "liberated." Soon after, a Communist assault force of 1,500 men poured into the city of 20,000, occupied a number of key government buildings, rescued 250 of their comrades from the local jail, and destroyed dozens of South Vietnamese (ARVN) combat vehicles. The South Vietnamese garrison counted over 300 dead, with many more wounded, while ten members of the small American screening force also died. American headquarters belatedly rushed a reinforcement of a marine battalion and two battalions of army artillery to construct a stronger defense perimeter against a possible enemy attempt to capture the provincial capital.

This eventuality seemed increasingly likely when Communist frogmen blew up a bridge network that connected Quang Tri with the vital Danang air base, while a massive mortar attack demolished another highway bridge and two railroad bridges vital to keeping the lines of communication to the south open for ARVN forces.

A *Time* magazine narrative of the Communist invasion of Quang Tri gave an eerie preview to the events of the Tet Offensive the following year. "The Communists have never managed to take over a provincial capital, and their success in Quang Tri might be a heavy psychological blow that will reverberate throughout South Vietnam." The presence of the civilian population would preclude the use of American air and artillery, making the city's recapture a difficult operation of house-to-house fighting more akin to World War II than to the Vietnam War.

As engineers began repairing the damage to Quang Tri City, American marines and South Vietnamese soldiers began piling sandbags around key buildings, digging hundreds of foxholes, setting up minefields and barbed-wire obstructions, and preparing for a renewed assault. At the same time, Premier Nguyen Cao Ky flew north to inspect the damage, hinted at some form of civilian evacuation, and echoed American Secretary of Defense Robert McNamara's assertion that some form of physical barrier might be necessary to prevent a full-scale invasion across the DMZ. Even the marines, who generally opposed McNamara's plan as too defense oriented, were now manning dozens of bulldozers and erecting massive new supports around camps in a tacit admission that the war might morph into a more conventional set-piece battle. Ironically, one of the events that nudged those leathernecks to take such a mundane task so seriously was a crisis that could eventually have long-term benefits for the United States: the growing schism between the two giants of the Communist world.

One of the issues that prompted the United States to provide huge financial and military assistance to South Vietnam was the belief that the Marxist ideology anchored around the world's largest nation, the Soviet Union, and the world's most populous nation, the People's Republic of China, was a definitive struggle between democracy and totalitarianism. Too many American retreats from Communist aggression would force the United States into being an isolated island in a Communist sea. When Lyndon Johnson dispatched the first major combat forces to South Vietnam, he made it clear that failure to act then might eventually push the American front lines all the way back to the Golden Gate Bridge.

In 1966, Chairman Mao Tse-tung of China stirred the pot of Marxism by launching his nation into a Cultural Revolution to get rid of the last vestiges of "bourgeoisie" lifestyles. Through most of 1966 and all of 1967, Western television screens and magazines were emblazoned by alternately brutal and unbelievable images of distinguished Chinese professors made to wear dunce caps or carry placards that they were "capitalist roaders," all the while being harassed by young fanatics of the Red Guard. An upheaval that seemed to be a witch's brew of totalitarianism and insanity spread wildly and resulted in even Soviet and Eastern European diplomats in China being harassed, beaten up, and threatened with death. A great schism had erupted, with the USSR and China vying for the role of the "true" guardian of the legacies of Marx and Lenin. Russian diplomats and visitors in China, who had become accustomed to moderate luxuries such as televisions, stylish clothes, and even a chance to own an automobile, were harassed by Red Guards as "turncoats." Soviet leaders and citizens in turn viewed the Chinese, including Chairman Mao, as insane.

In the not too distant future, President Richard Nixon would use this schism to enhance American foreign policy, but in 1967 the Soviet and Chinese governments were attempting to outdo one another in their aid to their "fraternal ally," North Vietnam.

The Soviet Union demonstrated its loyalty to the freedom fighters of North Vietnam by supplying most of the nation's petroleum needs; fleets of trucks, tanks, and armored vehicles; nearly 10,000 antiaircraft guns; surface-to-air missile batteries; scores of jet fighters and helicopters; plus two dozen naval patrol boats. China responded with about 50,000 tons of rice a month and a huge supply of AK-47 assault rifles that outgunned ARVN forces, as well as mortars, mines, and pistols. By the spring and summer, the cornucopia of fraternal aid meant that Hanoi could begin planning a serious campaign to win the war, the first major part of which entailed fixing American attention on South Vietnam's borders while Communist forces prepared a massive uprising in the relatively undefended cities at Tet in 1968. The Communists had begun this complex operation by attacking Quang Tri City and its primarily ARVN garrison; now they would shift their attention to the American marines in the narrow northern neck of South Vietnam, with powerful North Vietnamese regulars just above them, mixed guerrillas and regulars on the border with Laos to the west, and the South China Sea at their backs.

For the remainder of 1967 and well into 1968, one of the most iconic places on American television news was a nondescript fortification complex named Khe Sanh. This strongpoint, originally a French fort only four miles from Laos and ten miles from the DMZ, had first seen American use as a camp for the famous Green Berets. By late April, major elements of the 325th North Vietnamese Division were attempting to surround the base, held at the time by a small marine garrison of two rifle companies and an artillery battery. On April 24, a marine scouting party was ambushed by the enemy, and while it was forced to pull back to base after suffering more than thirty casualties, the engagement revealed the strength of the North Vietnamese presence and initiated relief plans. In a multiday struggle to gain or keep command of the highest points around Khe Sanh base, a series of engagements known as the "Hill Fights" swirled over the undulating battleground. Meanwhile, another kind of battle began to escalate as combat widened. The marines had just begun to receive the new M16 rifles, which replaced their 1950s-era M14 weapons. More than a few leathernecks viewed the M16 as an "army" weapon and insisted that its largely plastic construction made it more of a toy than a real combat instrument. Jokes circulated, comparing the weapon to the Mattel toy company television slogan "if it's Mattel, it's swell," an attitude that would eventually lead to a congressional investigation in which charges were made that many dead marines were found with jammed rifles in their hands or near their bodies.

By the late summer, Khe Sanh was becoming a magnet drawing both North Vietnamese and American attention toward what would eventually be the last major military news story on the eve of the Tet Offensive in 1968. The approaching autumn would produce increasingly bloody battles in Vietnam and a massive surge of politic opposition in the United States and around the world. Yet in the late spring and summer of 1967, Vietnam was not the only center of conflict over what America was, and what it would become.

CHAPTER VII

Storm over Sinai, Summit at Hollybush

In the warm predawn hours of May 24, 1967, just over a week after the celebration of Israel's nineteenth anniversary as a nation, a dapper gentleman with the upper-class British accent of his Cambridge University background boarded an El Al 707 jet airliner and prepared for takeoff. In an eerie scene reminiscent of Rod Sterling's hit television show *The Twilight Zone*, Israeli Ambassador Abba Eban settled in for takeoff in the cabin of an airliner on which he was the only passenger. The purpose of his mission was to present the case of an Israeli nation that was about to be economically strangled.

By 1967, Israel was the most modern, Western-oriented society in the Middle East. For many Americans, Eban was the face of the still-adolescent Jewish state. He had grown up in the British colony of South Africa, received undergraduate and advanced degrees from Cambridge University, served as an officer in the British army during World War II, and held an important position in the British Foreign Office before emigrating to Israel and becoming that nation's ambassador to the United Nations. Now Israel was facing economic strangulation as Egyptian dictator Gamal Nasser had barred Israeli ships from the Straits of Tiran, the choke point of the Suez Canal system, and had dispatched thousands of troops into the officially demilitarized Sinai desert, the scene of a brief, brutal conflict a decade earlier. Nasser's moves effectively ended an eleven-year truce cobbled together after Israel, France, and Great Britain routed Egyptian forces in a brief 1956 conflict that ended with the stationing of UN peacekeepers as a buffer between Egypt and Israel.

During the ensuing decade, American policy in the Middle East was complicated by a desire to develop a profitable relationship with the almost exclusively nondemocratic Arab states that controlled much of the world's petroleum production, while at the same time admiring the pluck of the Israelis who had managed to cobble together the only Western-style democracy in the region. President Johnson was also extremely aware of the fact that the majority of American Jews were Democrats, and that many of them had close relations in Israel. He was also aware that the small Jewish enclave was in some places little more than a few miles wide, with hostile Arabs peering down from imposing heights.

Despite this, Johnson was now almost obsessive about the escalating conflict in Vietnam; he limited his attention to the Middle East crisis to vague concepts of an international peacekeeping mission that would keep the Arabs and Israelis at arm's length. Eban himself was using his personal jetliner to reach France and the Elysee Palace, the domain of the first citizen of the nation, President Charles de Gaulle.

In the late spring, most Israeli leaders viewed France as one of their most steadfast allies. They had been heavily involved in the 1956 Sinai War and were now the primary suppliers to the Israeli defense array. Thus the Israeli minister was shocked when de Gaulle largely dismissed Eban's pleas for aid and insisted, "it would be catastrophic if Israel were to attack." The French president backed up his rhetoric with an order to delay delivery of weapons already paid for by the Jewish state and refused to sign a Freedom of Shipping declaration that was proposed by the United States. A cross-channel flight to Britain brought an invitation to Prime Minister Harold Wilson's Downing Street office where, amid clouds of foul-smelling smoke from Wilson's pipe, the British leader agreed that Nasser's blockade could not be allowed to stand. This led to vague promises of British cooperation "with other nations" to open the Straits of Tiran as part of an international (probably mostly American) task force.

Eban's jetliner then crossed the Atlantic Ocean to Washington, DC, where the minister checked into the Mayflower hotel. While there, he received a telegram from his ambassador to the United States, informing him that an Egyptian-Syrian attack on Israel was imminent. When he delivered this intelligence to Secretary of State Dean Rusk and Undersecretary for Foreign Affairs Eugene Rostow, the American officials insisted that their intelligence sources could detect almost no evidence that Arab forces were ready to escalate from economic to military warfare. They promptly advised Eban to discuss the matter with President Johnson.

When the Israeli foreign minister was ushered into the Oval Office, he was opening a conversation with a deeply distracted president. Eban was eloquent, persuasive, and able to compare Israel's plight as a small, endangered democracy surrounded by a sea of autocratic Arab states with the danger facing the infant American republic in the early years of its independent existence. Johnson stated that the United States was committed to keeping all Middle East waterways open to all traffic and offered to explore the idea of forming an international armada to pass through the Straits in defiance of Nasser's closure. He did this without volunteering to actually take the lead role in the expedition. Ironically, a president who reveled in his ability to use his power to bend Congress to his will told Eban that he was powerless to help Israel without the approval of that legislature.

On the other hand, that legislature and much of the American public had developed a far more positive impression of Israel and its people from the Sinai War of a decade earlier. Much of this sympathy for the Jewish state had begun to emerge with Leon Uris's smash bestselling book, *Exodus*, which compared the tiny Jewish population of postwar Palestine to the patriots of the American Revolution. Uris's book was followed by an even more successful film starring first-tier actors Paul Newman, Eva Marie Saint, and Sal Mineo. At one point in the action, the Jewish freedom fighter Newman reminds the Midwestern Protestant visitor Saint of the tiny force of minutemen who started a revolution on Lexington

Green, and stesses that the small band of Jews in Palestine are attempting
to accomplish the same thing.

The film version of *Exodus* was followed by another War of Independence
movie, *Cast A Giant Shadow*, which centered around the role of American
World War II colonel Mickey Marcus, who brought his military organiza-
tional magic to newly formed Israel and died before returning to America.
A Hollywood A-list cast, with Kirk Douglas as Marcus being supported by
John Wayne, Frank Sinatra, Yul Brynner, and Angie Dickinson, depicted
the birth of Israel in sweeping Panavision format while hinting that much
of the Arab support in the War of Independence seemed to be coming
from Nazi advisors to Arab military forces. As a growing segment of the
American population was beginning to see the Israelis as counterparts to
the embattled American republic of the Revolutionary and early national
period, Arab nations such as Egypt and Syria seemed to be drifting into
the fringes of the Communist camp as the region edged toward becoming
a key element in the chessboard of the Cold War. Lyndon Johnson could
still keep Israel security issues at arm's length by insisting "come sundown,
I'm the one who's got to put the bell on the cat," but the president's range
of options was about to narrow considerably on June 5, 1967.

At 7:45 on that Monday morning, the sultry silence hanging over the
Middle East was pierced by the whine of jet engines firing to life across the
chain of Israeli airfields that provided the front line of defense against the
more powerful forces of the Arab nations, which were increasingly committed to driving the inhabitants of the Jewish state into the sea. General
Mordechai Hod, commander of the Israeli Air Force, had ordered an
aerial armada of primarily French-built fighter-bombers to fly across the
arid countryside, level out over the the sea, and then fly in just above the
sand dunes of the Egyptian desert to strike a vast array of enemy planes
that hopefully were still tethered to the ground.

As the planes flew over the lush farming country of the delta, local
Egyptian farmers waved at what they thought were friendly aircraft as the
pilots maintained rigid radio silence. At many Egyptian airfields, pilots
were sitting in the cockpits of their planes waiting for their own morning
patrols. At the moment before the attacks began, the Egyptian air force

outnumbered the Israelis by more than two to one, but that ratio was about to change significantly.

As Israeli pilots swept over the enemy airfield network, millions of dollars in high-tech planes turned into burning junk piles as bombs and missiles hit targets with deadly precision. Defensive antiaircraft guns shot down nine Israeli planes and six of their pilots would never return home, but 304 Egyptian planes had been destroyed. Whatever battles the Egyptian army fought would now be contested largely without air cover.

Despite the tensions within the Arab world, Syria, Jordan, and Iraq dutifully fulfilled their pacts with Egypt and followed President Nasser's forces into war. While the pilots made good on their leaders' pledges to retaliate against Israel, many of the pilots focused on largely undefended targets such as farms, nursing homes, and beach resort facilities, which created Israeli civilian casualties but hardly changed the calculus of the war. Israel squadrons that had been held back for follow-up strikes on Egypt were quickly redirected to these new threats and shot down a host of Arab planes. Parachuting pilots were crisscrossing the countryside in a tableau that looked like the Battle of Britain in 1940.

Unlike American forces contending with the canopy jungles of Vietnam, the third Arab-Israeli war was the ultimate open-ground contest, where cover was virtually nonexistent. As the Israeli air force cleared the skies of hostile aircraft, ground forces could move with an ability to call in air strikes if enemy barriers appeared. Israel was now fighting a three-dimensional war against a two-dimensional adversary.

Israeli leaders kept hoping to limit the war to a conflict with Egypt, but much of the Arab world, including small states such as tiny Kuwait, felt obliged to back Nasser's plans. Those nations now became legitimate military targets. One benefit to Israel in fighting a multifront war emerged when Syria began bombarding the country from its towering Golan Heights positions. Now those artillery batteries became prime targets for an Israeli offensive, as Sherman tanks led a thrust into Syria in a frontal assault against ridges as high as 3,000 feet above the Israeli farmlands below. The Syrians had regularly turned the kibbutz communities below into a virtual shooting arcade as they periodically shelled farms below the heights. Now Israeli armor lurched up the hills and dueled with defenders who were deployed behind Soviet-designed earthworks that were difficult to penetrate. Yet one by one the Syrian strongpoints were overrun, and the Golan Heights would soon become incorporated into the Israeli state.

Unlike the American combat experience in Vietnam, where total control of the airspace above battle zones produced mixed benefits in a largely jungle environment, the open spaces of the Middle East war provided enormous offensive possibilities for the Israeli military once the skies were cleared of Arab aerial threats. The battlefield on the ground began to take on the appearance of France in 1940 after the German blitzkrieg had cleared the skies of Allied aircraft and unleashed Panzer units that could move at will without worrying about a threat from above. June 1967 was providing the Israelis with a similar scenario.

The mostly French-made Israeli planes seemed to be everywhere as the forces of the Jewish state fought a battle that one American correspondent insisted was "still suspended between nightmare and a dream, relishing a moment of ecstasy in which legends are being born that fathers will tell children to tell their children after them." However, the biggest prize of the war had not even been a target at the beginning of the week. The major reason for the initiation of hostilities was to reopen Israeli access to the sea, and there was every expectation that the relatively moderate Arab state of Jordan would see fit to sit out this particular conflict. However, Israeli advice to young King Hussein to essentially sit out the war was overridden by bellicose boasts of victory by Nasser and his allies. Somewhat grudgingly, Jordan entered the conflict.

Jordanian artillery duly opened fire on the Jewish half of the partitioned city of Jerusalem, and with those shells came the glimmer of an Israeli dream. No flag of Zion had floated over a united Jerusalem since the Romans had vaporized the city nearly 2,000 years earlier, but now the fortress walls of Jordanian-occupied East Jerusalem and the Old City were on offer to the strongest combatant. During a sixty-hour period that would become a legendary epic for the Jewish state, the unimaginable became reality. On Monday morning of the Six-Day War, Israeli gunners raked Jordanian positions on the Mount of Olives while covering jets knocked out several battalions of Jordanian tanks that were poised for their own offensive. By Tuesday morning, as Israeli artillery began firing into the Old City, soldiers were able to hoist the Israeli flag on the roof of the Palestine Archaeological Museum. On Wednesday morning, a column of a dozen Israeli tanks lumbered up the Mount of Olives road as supporting artillery blasted Jordanian positions on Mount Scopus. Meanwhile, planes dropped napalm canisters around a heavily wooded glade that surrounded Augusta Victoria Hospital with pine trees.

As Israeli Prime Minister Levi Eshkol and members of his cabinet listened to reports in their command center, a last burst of Jordanian mortar fire was parried by Israeli armored forces. As the last shots sputtered out, ecstatic Jewish soldiers rushed to pray at the Wailing Wall, the surviving piece of Solomon's Second Temple that was the holiest single spot in the Jewish religion. Now, finally, it had been repatriated to the descendants of the people that had built the structure 3,000 years earlier. At the moment, the damage or destruction of perhaps 600 buildings in Jerusalem took a backseat to what would only be seen as a miracle a week earlier.

Less than a week after the first Israeli air attack on Egyptian air bases, the Jewish state seemed to be the new colossus in the Middle East. American news magazines and television networks showed spectacular color images of triumphant Israeli warriors celebrating a multifront victory, from cooling off in the Suez Canal to praying at the Wailing Wall. A tiny nation had become a David against the Arab Goliath. At a cost of roughly 700 dead and 2,600 wounded, Israel now controlled the entire Sinai Peninsula to the Suez Canal, the Gulf of Aqaba, and the missing half of a Jerusalem that had up to now been a tantalizing mirage beyond the reach of their citizens.

In the United States, the almost frenzied celebration of many Jewish Americans was joined by more than a few gentiles who saw the Six-Day War as a victory of a beleaguered democracy over an Arab world that at the least had a spotty relationship with America and, in the case of Egypt, seemed destined to become an extended member of the Soviet Bloc. Yet the universal celebrations of Israeli Jews were not fully mirrored in the US, for two reasons.

First, Americans who were becoming increasingly hostile to the Vietnam enterprise openly wondered how the Israelis had annihilated several modern armies in less than a week while the United States seemed semipermanently bogged down in Southeast Asia. Many people who were opposing the Vietnam commitment could now demonstrate that they were not actual passivists by enthusiastically celebrating the Israeli triumph.

Second, while many Americans celebrated a vicarious victory for democratic forces in the Middle East, they also mourned a shocking loss of American life in a collateral aspect of the Six-Day War that still remains largely without closure a half century later. The tragedy occurred on the fourth day of the war as an American communications vessel, the USS *Liberty*, hovered twelve miles from the coast of the Sinai desert, processing the massive information stream coming from the nearby war.

Just after 2:00 p.m., the shimmering heat emanating from the desert now included three specks that proved to be a trio of Israeli warplanes. The ship's crew initially felt at ease under a fluttering American flag, but then, to their utter shock, the planes opened fire with machine guns and cannons while shooting down the flag from its visible perch. One of the six strafing runs badly wounded the ship's master, Commander William McGonagle, who ordered the flag run up again as he was carried to sick bay. The gesture proved useless. Three Israeli torpedo boats joined the assault, letting loose their deadly fish, which began exploding along the side of the *Liberty*. Then, as quickly as it began, the planes and vessels veered off, leaving behind almost 110 American injured, including thirty-four fatalities.

Almost immediately, Israeli authorities offered an apology, including compensation to families of the injured and dead, and insisted that the *Liberty* was simply mistaken for an Egyptian ship. While the United States accepted the apology, a generally pro-Israeli American public was shocked that now Vietnam was not the only place where Americans were dying in a conflict. A wide spectrum of theories about the incident emerged, varying from the Israeli belief that *Liberty* was an Egyptian ship under false colors to hints that the communications ship was gathering far too much sensitive military information to be allowed to continue its mission.

The *Liberty*'s commander in chief, Lyndon Johnson, now found himself facing three crises in rapid succession: the Middle East conflict, which many Arab leaders insisted was secretly abetted by the United States; the *Liberty* tragedy, which some Americans believed was a deliberate attack to warn the United States from attempting to blunt the Israeli military; and the war in Vietnam, which was continuing to escalate rapidly, with 11,153 Americans destined to die in Southeast Asia during 1967. On the other hand, the multiple June crises created a feeding frenzy for the American news media, and network television commentators and journalists detected in the White House "the exhilarating crucible of crisis," as one reporter insisted. "Crisis, in a bizarre way, fascinates strong men, this time creates a brilliant arena for this in this age in the White House. The people in the White House are completely gripped by it, enthused not only by the peril but the exercise of raw and instantaneous power in the purest sense."

President Johnson may or may not have agreed with that analysis, but the president and Soviet Prime Minister Alexei Kosygin were in constant touch over the relatively new "hotline" system. As one journalist observed, "each single word spelled out more than all the ambassadorial conversations of the last year." Presidential advisor McGeorge Bundy described the impact of the Six-Day War linked with the Vietnam conflict as "a high wire act in which a man and his methods are put to a test." Johnson felt that he had handled the Middle East crisis well, but more than one pundit insisted that the Texan was so preoccupied by Vietnam that he was allowing the Middle East to become an "orphan," especially since the role of the assistant Secretary of State for the Near East had remained unfilled for the previous five months and there had been no ambassador resident in Egypt since late winter.

In many respects, the Six-Day War had created the most massive shift of the global power balance since Nikita Khrushchev had introduced nuclear missiles to Cuba in the autumn of 1962, an event that had a special meaning for Lyndon Johnson. The then vice president had sat in on the dramatic meetings of John Kennedy's Ex-Com crisis team, but had exercised almost no impact on one of the most dramatic moments in American history. In fact, in perhaps the most iconic film about the crisis, *Thirteen Days*, Lyndon Johnson is largely noticeable as being physically present in the deliberations but never uttering a word through several segments of extended dialogue. The Cuban Missile Crisis was John Kennedy's crisis, but now the confluence of Vietnam and war in the Middle East and the emerging ideological rift between the Soviet Union and China was presenting the president with an opportunity to create a legacy beyond the Great Society.

The road to what would become the most productive summit between American and Soviet leaders in the entire decade of the 1960s had actually begun well before the shock of the Six-Day War nudged Lyndon Johnson and Alexei Kosygin toward meeting in Glassboro, a small college town in southern New Jersey. The brush with Armageddon during the Cuban Missile Crisis of 1962 had occurred in a Cold War at its iciest depths, as Francis Gary Powers's U-2 spying mission, the rise of the Berlin Wall, and regular air-raid drills in the schools of America and Russia offered stark evidence. This was a late 1950s/early 1960s era, in which it seemed that every other episode of *The Twilight Zone* dealt with some aspect of nuclear war, ranging from Burgess Meredith sitting in a pile of post-nuclear rubble as he prepares to read the contents of a badly damaged library to Charles Bronson and Elizabeth Montgomery discussing the fact that they are the only survivors of a massive nuclear war. Theater audiences watched the end of the world on a large screen from *On the Beach* to *Dr. Strangelove* and then went home to read magazine instructions on how to build a fallout shelter in their basement.

Ironically, the American–Soviet face-off had cooled considerably by 1967 as the United States hoped for Russian assistance in escaping the morass in Southeast Asia and the Soviet Union watched in horror as Mao's Red Guard "scouts from hell" threatened to unleash their extremist contagion into Soviet satellite states. During the period preceding the Glassboro summit, American theatergoers were laughing at the parody of Cold War tension in *The Russians Are Coming, The Russians Are Coming*, in which residents of a small coastal community help Alan Arkin and his Soviet submarine crew refloat their beached vessel before the American military arrives to capture them. In other movies of the day, James Bond finds a Chinese plot to force Russia and America into a war neither wants in *You Only Live Twice*, while presidential psychiatrist James Coburn is befriended by a high-ranking Soviet agent as he is chased by frantic government officials in *The President's Analyst*. The most popular television spy drama, *The Man from U.N.C.L.E.*, pairs American Napoleon Solo with Russian partner Illya Kuryakin against the evil multinational organization known as THRUSH.

At the same time, in the real world, the leaders of the Soviet Union were genuinely shocked at the ease with which Israel tore through their Arab surrogates during the Six-Day War, and Kosygin attempted to salvage something from the fiasco by making a speech at the United Nations. Kosygin arrived in New York with a sixty-six-person entourage, including his daughter, and quickly denounced Israeli imperialism at the General Assembly. The Soviet leader lambasted the Jewish state as a modern version of Japan in 1941, "launching an attack of unprecedented perfidy" only hours after the government had "spread profuse assurances of its peaceful intentions." In a supreme irony, Kosygin linked Israeli "atrocities and malice" to the heinous crime perpetrated by the Nazis in World War II, citing premeditated attacks on hospitals and orphanages, murder of prisoners of war, and burning of villages, and called for "restitution in full" for damage suffered by the Arabs.

While the Soviet leader made ridiculous peace demands on an Israel that had won one of the most stupendous victories in military history, Lyndon Johnson suggested to his advisors that Kosygin might be as anxious to sit down and talk face to face as the president was. Since the United States as yet provided only minimal direct military aid to Israel, the Six-Day War had not been a surrogate for a Soviet-American confrontation, and perhaps this was a good opportunity for the two leaders to meet. Neither leader would be required to travel any great distance, and a summit meeting could hardly hurt the president's sagging poll numbers.

The two leaders agreed to meet, but the location of the meeting caused some initial disagreement. Johnson believed that the informal atmosphere of Camp David in the Maryland mountains would be an ideal venue where the two leaders could conduct serious business against a relaxing backdrop. However, Kosygin preferred meeting on the neutral ground of the UN building, as he feared that newly defeated Arab leaders, North Vietnamese allies, and the Chinese would gloat that the leader of the powerful Soviet Union was going "hat in hand" to the "imperialist lair," much like the French and British leaders had done in 1938 when they met with Hitler and Mussolini in Munich. Johnson balked at the UN venue, as he expected to have to push his way through mobs of anti-Western or anti-Vietnam War protestors, and a jostled president would hardly appear as a dynamic world leader. Several Johnson aides suggested Maguire Air Force Base in New Jersey, a rough middle ground between the UN and the White House, but Kosygin aides responded that photos of the leader of the Socialist world arriving at an American military base would make it appear that he was somehow surrendering to the capitalist victors of the Cold War.

As the venue impasse escalated to the point of a probable cancellation of the whole summit, one of Johnson's political allies, Governor Richard Hughes of New Jersey, suggested that the leaders could convene at one of New Jersey's state colleges, most of which had ample sleeping and dining facilities due to most students being home for summer vacation. Ultimately the staff personnel accepted Hughes's offer and chose the campus closest to a roughly halfway point between New York City and Washington. The selected campus, Glassboro State College (now Rowan University), was in a town of 14,000 residents sixteen miles from Philadelphia and easily accessible from highways and airports in either direction. The town was also home to a bottle-cap manufacturing plant, seven taverns, fifteen churches, a single movie theater (which, at the time, was showing *Hot Rods to Hell*), and a Little League team that had won the state championships in 1956. Most important, the college president was more than willing to temporarily vacate his campus home, a two-story Victorian house with enormous amounts of nineteenth-century charm and no twentieth-century air-conditioning system.

In the early morning of June 23, the owner of the movie theater changed the *Hot Rods to Hell* heading on the marquee to *The Russians are Coming*;

technicians retrofitted the college president's home, Hollybush, with air-conditioning; phone company personnel installed 200 new telephone lines; and thousands of curious locals, reinforced by a growing crowd of outsiders, began lining the street. These witnesses to history were dressed in summer casual wear of T-shirts, shorts, sneakers, and sunglasses, while many of the younger people in the crowd carried transistor radios fitted with earplugs to maintain contact with the music, news, and sports of their world. They waved American flags, posed confidently for news photographers, and bought ice cream from a growing array of perspiring vendors.

President Johnson arrived at Hollybush at 10:30 a.m. on what was developing into a hot, humid, typical early summer day in the American Northeast. The president greeted Premier Kosygin as he left his car, thanked the Russian for his congratulations on the birth of Johnson's first grandchild forty-eight hours earlier, and jocularly accepted his counterpart's teasing that he had already been a grandfather for eighteen years even though only five years separated their births. Johnson led his guest into the house, supplied him with ice water, and directed him to a rocking chair while the president dropped onto a sofa opposite the Russian.

In terms of ideological discussions, the Glassboro summit was light-years apart from the Gorbachev-Reagan summits two decades later. Those meetings began as frosty recitations of vastly different agendas and gradually morphed into genuine mutual affection as the Soviet leader ultimately admitted that Russia would immediately come to the aid of the United Sates if America faced an invasion from an alien planet. On the other hand, Glassboro was equally distant from the only other full-scale summit of the 1960s when, in 1961, Nikita Khrushchev threatened America so blatantly with possible nuclear attack that John F. Kennedy left the meetings visibly shaken. Glassboro featured two canny, hard-bargaining men who saw little value in their counterparts' political systems but realized that neither nation could win an all-out war with the other. Both men employed a hard edge to all of their dealings and, at best, generally "agreed to disagree." Yet unlike the Munich summit of 1938, when the best possible outcome was only a temporary delay to an inevitable war, both of the men at Glassboro agreed that neither nation wanted a war with the other. Disputes about which side caused the Six-Day War were sprinkled with more lighthearted banter about grandparenting. Both leaders also agreed that China relished the thought of an American–Soviet war and that it was up to these two men to ensure that this outcome did not occur.

Alexei Kosygin wanted to leave Glassboro with some level of American admission that the Soviet Union was an equal superpower to the United States, and the American president generally conceded this point. A dramatic moment occurred when, after the two men shook hands and the Russian leader climbed into his limousine, Kosygin ordered the driver to stop, jumped out of the car, and told the slightly startled crowd, "I can assure you we want nothing but peace with the American people," which provoked massive applause and cheering.

After Kosygin's car headed north to New York, Lyndon Johnson, beaming at the knowledge that what was supposed to be a two-hour summit meeting had edged well over five hours, began shaking hands with the Glassboro residents while accepting congratulations on the recent birth of his grandson, Patrick Lyndon Nugent. The surprise summit at Glassboro had been a polar opposite of its 1961 predecessor, when Nikita Khrushchev had bullied newly inaugurated John F. Kennedy and insisted on Western evacuation of West Berlin with no hint of compromise. Kennedy had returned to Washington amid National Guard call-ups, distribution of pamphlets instructing Americans on the construction of home fallout shelters, and a feeling that nuclear war was increasingly imminent. Now, after Glassboro, a president embattled in the Vietnam conflict could tell the American people that all-out war with the Soviet Union was far less likely, as "Mr. Kosygin and I agree that we want a world peace for our grandchildren." If the Munich summit of 1938 was the opening act of World War II, a leisurely lunch of Russian rice pilaf and American roast beef between two guests of a college president may very well have been the first small step toward the end of the Cold War.

CHAPTER VIII

Summer Dreams, Autumn Thrills

As UCLA, the Philadelphia 76ers, and the Toronto Maple Leafs were moving toward the championships of the three major winter spectator sports, a hugely exciting baseball season was emerging for the fans of the twenty franchises that constituted Major League Baseball. The biggest surprise of the 1966 season was the ability of the Baltimore Orioles to supplant the Minnesota Twins as the lords of the American League and then stage a four-game sweep of a glamorous and powerful Los Angeles Dodgers squad that was heavily favored win the World Series.

The Orioles' relatively short history in Baltimore since they morphed from the St. Louis Browns twelve years earlier had provided more futility than excitement as they matched the neighboring Washington Senators in their inability to field a winning team. However, while the Senators wallowed in the mediocrity of a 71–88 eighth-place finish in 1966, Orioles manager Hank Bauer imposed marine-like discipline that ignited a season-long run that ended with the men in black and orange nine games ahead of the Twins at the end of the season.

Now, in 1967, the Orioles looked even more powerful as they paired All-Star infielder Brooks Robinson with former Cincinnati Reds outfielder

Frank Robinson, who had won a Triple Crown in his first year with the Orioles with forty-nine home runs, 122 runs batted in, and a gaudy .316 batting average. As teams reported to spring training, one baseball preview magazine insisted, "when a team wins a baseball pennant by nine games and accomplishes a World Series victory in a four-game sweep, it doesn't seem to make much sense for it to make sweeping changes. The Orioles played it cool and like a card player holding an ace-high flush, remained with a pat hand."

Most baseball writers predicted that the American League pennant race would devolve into a duel between the Orioles and the Twins, with Minnesota countering Baltimore's immense talent with its own trio of stars: potential home run king Harmon Killebrew, potential batting champion Tony Oliva, and twenty-five-game-winner Jim Kaat. While the Orioles and Twins were expected to duel for the pennant, the most shocking aspect of American League baseball in 1967 was the fact that the New York Yankees were expected to duel the atrocious Boston Red Sox for ownership of the league cellar in the upcoming season. One preseason magazine featured a major feature on "They're Breaking Up the Bronx Bombers," as the piece related the sad tale of the baseball's iconic team engaging in a free fall toward last place. The Yankees were "a sad tale of a far from promising infield backed up by an equally inept outfield, where the power duo of Mickey Mantle and Roger Maris romped to new records, are now replaced by Tom Tresh and Steve Whitaker, hardly the premier goals for a kid's baseball card collection." Roger Maris had been traded to St. Louis and Mantle had acquired a first baseman's glove, and the brightest spot in the Yankees' future seemed to be that television giant CBS had purchased the team and might infuse just enough energy to move the team out of the cellar.

More than a few sportswriters believed that if the Bronx Bombers could actually climb out of the league cellar, the dubious last-place slot would then be occupied by the equally flawed Boston Red Sox. The Red Sox ninth-place finish in a ten-team league in 1966 seemed to put the relatively recent heroics of Ted Williams into the ancient history category, and the current team was supposed to be so bad that new manager Dick

Williams "would become as popular as Ted Williams if he could lead the team all the way up to a seventh-place finish in 1967."

Many baseball experts believed that the Red Sox had the worst pitching staff in the American League, as they allowed over four runs a game, listed nearly a dozen candidates for their starting rotation, and featured a staff ace in Jim Lonborg who was coming off a mediocre 10–10 season with one of the highest earned run averages among starting pitchers in the league. Manager Williams, a thirty-seven-year-old career utility player, hoped that his questionable pitching staff could be counterbalanced by a trio of fine batters, George Scott, Tony Conigliaro, and Rico Petrocelli, and a pair of prized rookies, Mike Andrews and Reggie Smith. Yet even if all of the hitters produced, the most optimistic expectation was something approaching a .500 season.

Over in the National League, most sports analysts believed that despite their shocking defeat in the World Series, the team to beat was still the Dodgers, even though their best pitcher for the entire decade was now doing guest appearances on television. Sandy Koufax had been virtually unhittable for most of the sixties, but an early onset of arthritis had ended his career the previous October. Now sports magazines featured articles such as "Can Don Drysdale Do It Alone" and "Who Will Be the Next Koufax?" One article insisted, "the pedestal is vacant and applications are being accepted for prospective successors to Sandy Koufax. Ever since 1961, he was the top pitcher in baseball. He dominated the game as no hurler since the days of Walter Johnson and Cy Young. He was, without a doubt, the best in the business."

Sandy Koufax had spent the first half of the 1960s marrying actor Richard Widmark's daughter, appearing regularly in cameo roles on television, pitching a perfect game and three no-hitters, striking out 382 batters in one season, leading the league in earned run average for five consecutive years, and winning the Cy Young Award three times. Now the Los Angeles Dodgers would be forced to defend the pennant without their best pitcher and without Maury Wills, the spark plug of their offense. While Koufax was setting pitching records, shortstop Wills was setting equally impressive offensive records for base stealing and forming the glue that held the Dodgers' defensive infield together. But Wills had been traded to Pittsburgh and other National League teams began eyeing that elusive pennant.

The team that seemed poised to upset the hopes of the Dodgers repeating as National League Champions was the equally iconic franchise from St. Louis. The Cardinals had been in the thick of the pennant race in early August 1966, but then the talent-laden club had swooned back into the middle of the pack. Yet now manager Red Schoendienst's team seemed poised to challenge the Dodgers behind staff ace Bob Gibson, a twenty-one-game winner in 1966, and one of the most daunting batting orders in all of baseball. The Cardinals had brought in slugging first basemen Orlando Cepeda from the Giants, home run record holder Roger Maris from the Yankees, and speedster Lou Brock from the Cubs and paired them with homegrown outfielder Curt Flood, infielder Mike Shannon, and catcher Tim McCarver to produce a lineup that could challenge the Dodgers at every position.

The season began with the Cardinals going undefeated for opening week. General Manager Stan Musial had gone under the radar to provide pitching depth behind Bob Gibson, and for a time the Redbirds appeared unbeatable. The Cincinnati Reds, picked to wallow in the second division all season, caught fire in May as sluggers Pete Rose, Vada Pinson, and Tommy Harper all started hitting at once. The team won fourteen of eighteen games and soared into first place as Memorial Day approached. Then star shortstop Leo Cardenas went down with a broken hand as the Cardinals seemed poised to make their move. Yet, in one of the many shocks of the season, it was not the Redbirds but the lowly Chicago Cubs who suddenly sprinted toward first place. The Cubs had ended 1966 in last place and were generally expected to maintain their residence in that spot in 1967. A team that lost 103 games received an unexpected emotional boost from the presence of fiery, controversial Leo Durocher, who was beginning his second season as manager of the Cubs. "Leo the Lip" had earlier made news from Gotham to Hollywood as he managed the Dodgers and Giants, cavorted with Hollywood starlets, commuted between divorce courts and baseball dugouts, and staged verbal duels with an army of sportswriters.

Now Durocher began to receive outstanding offense from young batters Billy Williams, Ron Santo, and Don Kessinger; spurred aging icon Ernie Banks to new heights; and centered his pitching staff around young Canadian phenom Ferguson Jenkins. By July 4, residents of the Windy City opened their newspapers to see their poor, lovable Cubs sitting in a first-place tie with the Cardinals. Three weeks later, the Cubs traveled to St. Louis for a crucial three-game series. Chicago fans staged wild celebrations when their team won the series opener 3–1.

Then manager Schoendienst began to work some magic of his own as young starters Ray Washburn and Nelson Briles pitched the Cards to 4–2 and 4–3 victories. The stage was now set for a return engagement in the Chicago, where Cubs fans felt that Durocher would again work his magic in Wrigley Field. The magic was certainly there on Lake Michigan, but it was the Redbirds who supplied it as they swept a three-game series and left stunned Cubs fans wondering what had gone wrong.

The Cardinals had to endure one more minor swoon on the road to the pennant as they dropped two out of three games to the struggling Dodgers and then promptly lost a series opener against the Giants. However, as Cubs fans held out new hopes, the Redbirds simply cut a swath through the rest of the league winning by winning 22 of the next twenty-seven games, which gave them a comfortable cushion of a 10- to 13-game lead on all contenders for the remainder of the regular season.

Meanwhile, the American League race continued to intensify. While the Cardinals spent at least half of the season reasonably confident that they would be appearing in the World Series come fall, there was no such feeling among the contenders for the American League pennant. If the Redbirds expected to be a good to a great baseball team that year, their eventual World Series opponent, the Boston Red Sox, were listed as a 100 to 1 shot to win the pennant as of opening day. Their path to the postseason was not assured until several hours after their seemingly magical regular season ended.

The American League pennant race was a wild tag-team match among the White Sox, Tigers, Twins, and Red Sox, in which each team seemed to unravel the moment they climbed into first place. Boston fans, initially suspicious that they were cheering for a near-last-place team, seemed to dare the Red Sox to prove them wrong as 1.7 million people crammed every nook and cranny of Fenway Park over the course of the season, with no one quite sure whether they were experiencing reality or a realistic dream. Controversial manager Dick Williams admitted later that his swaggering, sarcastic, brawling style was at least partially staged in order to turn his team into a modern version of the St. Louis Cardinals' successful "Gashouse Gang" of three decades earlier. That mixture of reality and myth won him Manager of the Year and his team a highly unlikely pennant.

The Red Sox had entered the season with one proven superstar in Carl Yastrzemski. The Red Sox outfielder turned a very good 1966 season into a 1967 Triple Crown experience, chalking up a sensational forty-four home runs, 121 runs batted in, and a .326 batting average. Jim Lonborg attained the same level of excellence in pitching, turning a stellar 22–9 and 246 strikeouts into a Cy Young Award as the outstanding American League pitcher of the year. Using the popularity of the current Broadway hit musical *Man of La Mancha*, the Red Sox developed as their theme song "The Impossible Dream," combining a gaudy home record with the only winning road record in the American League.

As Williams's charges continued to overperform during the season, the manager realized that they still were saddled with potentially crippling weaknesses, including a mediocre pitching staff beyond Lonborg, a pair of inexperienced, light-hitting catchers, and little depth in the outfield. The manager partially alleviated the catching problem by acquiring aging Elston Howard from the Yankees and juggled his shaky pitching rotation to get as many starts as possible for Lonborg. Yet when star outfielder Tony Conigliaro was struck on the face by a wild pitch and nearly killed, the Red Sox magic season seemed to be turning into a nightmare.

As Conigliaro's injury threatened to derail the team's momentum, another seemingly preseason also-ran, the Chicago White Sox, began a determined run on the Boston lead. White Sox manager Eddie Stanky was as much a firebrand as Williams, but while the Red Sox were loaded with hitters and short of pitchers, the Chicago squad faced the opposite dilemma. Staff ace Tommy John, who would later supply his name to a famous form of reconstructive surgery, was breezing past American League hitters with a spectacular 2.48 earned run average, but had so little hitting support that he was limping toward a 10–13 season record. Yet despite a horrendous team batting average of .225, John and other staff aces Joel Horlen and Gary Peters seldom allowed many runs, and the team kept winning. Manager Stanky, in the meantime, managed to receive multiple ejections from the umpires for arguing, while achieving special notoriety in Boston for insisting that team icon Carl Yastrzemski "is an All-Star only from the neck down."

As the Red Sox and White Sox exchanged insults and rolled up the score of pitchers hitting opposing batters, the Detroit Tigers and Minnesota Twins started nudging back into the pennant race. Sportswriters in newspapers outside of Boston hinted that the Red Sox were about ready to slump back toward the second division, while the Minnesota management replaced field manager Sam Mele with virtual unknown Cal Ermer (it appeared that Mele was losing control of his team). The change of managers produced immediate results as the Twins swept the White Sox in a three-game series and arrived in Boston for a two-game season-ending finale, only one game out of first place. At the same time, the still very much contending Detroit Tigers went home for a four-game set against the Angels.

The last weekend of the baseball season saw the Red Sox, Twins, and Tigers all in contention to win the pennant. If the Tigers could sweep the Angels in all four games, the pennant was theirs, although Los Angeles manager Bill Rigney confidently told the news media "there is no way the Tigers can beat us four straight." Now thousands of Boston fans became temporary Angels fans as their hometown team came from behind on two consecutive days to beat the Twins in Fenway. If Rigney's team could beat the Tigers in Detroit on that same final day, the pennant flag would be raised in Boston. As fans filed out of Fenway, the crackle of transistor radios permeated the air as the Angels turned back Tiger rallies. Then Tiger shortstop Dick McAuliffe hit into a ninth-inning double play and the game was over. Thousands of fans poured out into the streets of Boston in the ultimate night of celebration.

Now, in a series of crisp autumn afternoons, at a time in which the World Series was not played after dark, one of the most exciting matchups in baseball history played out in two baseball-mad cities. The Cardinals entered the Series as substantial favorites with a pitching staff that centered on star Bob Gibson and fell off only a bit with the other three starters. Boston's pitching staff beyond ace Jim Lonborg was erratic and unpredictable, but the Sox did have Carl Yastrzemski and his new Triple Crown award. The first two games would be played in Fenway, where Redbird pitchers would have to contend with the looming outfield wall called the Green Monster, which hovered only 315 feet beyond homeplate.

One national magazine insisted that although the Cardinals seemed to have the edge in talent, "not since the fictitious Joe Hardy, the outfielder who took the lowly Washington Senators to a pennant in *Damn Yankees*, has a single player carried a team so far with a bat and glove than Carl Yastrzemski, who has admitted 'if I live to be 100, nothing can top these games.'"

The Red Sox outfielder may have been eager to get the series under way, but he and the other Boston players hit a buzz saw named Bob Gibson, who held the Sox to only six hits, none of them by Yaz. Cardinals speedster Lou Brock went four for four and stole two bases, with the only Red Sox counterpunch coming from losing pitcher Jose Santiago's unlikely home run.

The opening loss at Fenway nullified Boston's home field advantage, but Jim Lonborg proved just as dominating as Gibson during Game 2 as he hurled nearly seven innings of perfect basball before walking Curt Flood. When the game was over, Lonborg had tallied the fourth one-hit World Series game in history while Yastrzemski atoned for his dismal opening game performance by swatting two home runs in a 5–0 Sox win.

Tensions heated up as the teams flew to St. Louis, especially when Cardinals starter Nelson Briles plunked Yastrzemski in the first inning of Game 3. Yet even before some of the St. Louis fans had located their seats, Lou Brock swatted a lead-off triple and scampered home on Curt Flood's single off of relatively unheralded Sox pitcher Gary Bell, who secured an early shower the next inning when catcher Tim McCarver opened with a single and came home just ahead of Mike Shannon on his two-run blast. In a move that would stun modern baseball fans, Red Schoendienst played out the entire game using only nine players in a turbocharged two hours and fifteen minutes, little more than half of the playing time of a World Series games of the 2017 era.

The next day, the Red Sox were in serious trouble as, under gun-metal skies and cold 50-degree temperatures, the Gibson-Santiago pitching matchup of the opening game fizzled into a near blowout as the Cardinals batted around in the first inning. In that inning, Roger Maris's line-drive double provided a 4–0 cushion as the fireballing Gibson upped his already startling intensity by allowing only five hits and an early trip to the showers for both teams in a final 6–0 blowout that would have been even more one-sided if a fan had not grabbled Lou Brock's screaming line drive that was downgraded from home run to double on an interference call.

Jim Lonborg had no room for error in his next start, and the St. Louis fans were eagerly anticipating a victory parade the following afternoon. It wasn't to be, however, as the Redbirds' bats went silent for almost an entire game. The Red Sox didn't exactly tear the cover off the balls, with a meager six hits allowed by Steve Carlton, but Lonborg was even better as he threw a three-hit game in a 3–1 victory that sent the Series back to Boston.

When the Red Sox returned to Boston on October 11, they clearly had their backs to the wall, as a single Cardinal victory would secure the World Series title. On the other hand, the team would be playing in a ballpark that fit their strengths and would enjoy the support of rabid fans. The relative lack of offense in recent games quickly evaporated as 35,188 fans savored a four–home run barrage while rookie hurler Dick Hughes, one of the Cardinals' most exciting pitching prospects, threw away an early 2–1 lead as Yastrzemski, Reggie Smith, and Rico Petrocelli set a World Series record in the fourth inning with three balls flying into the stands. Once the scoring gate was opened, twelve men crossed the plate. Before the final pitch had been thrown, both managers were making plans for game seven.

The finale of one of the most discussed World Series in baseball history was set against the dramatic backdrop of a third titanic Gibson-Lonborg duel. The Red Sox seemed to have momentum on their side, and clearly enjoyed a home field advantage, but Gibson had enjoyed a day's more rest than Lonborg. The seventh and deciding game was tagged as "The Great Confrontation," and Gibson hoped to repeat his feat of winning the crucial Game 7 against the Yankees in the 1964 World Series.

The two pitchers locked into a scoreless duel for the first two innings, but trouble loomed for the Red Sox when light-hitting Dal Maxvill, the Redbirds' number eight hitter, tripled off the wall and Gibson followed with a 400-foot home run. Lonborg never fully recovered his composure as he allowed ten hits in six innings while his opponent had given up only fourteen hits in three games. Red Sox pitchers had largely nullified two of the Cardinals' most potent hitters as Orlando Cepeda wound up the Series hitting an anemic .103 while Tim McCarver was little better at .125. However, Roger Maris contributed an impressive .385 and Lou Brock ripped the cover off the ball at .414 with five hits between them in the 7–2 win in Game 7. Only Carl Yastrzemski's sizzling .400 average and five runs batted in matched the Cardinals' duo, and no Red Sox player came close to matching Brock's record-tying seven stolen bases for the Series. The Boys of Summer had provided an exciting season and a scintillating World Series. Now sports fan attention would shift to the gridiron.

CHAPTER IX

The Silver Screen

The decision of the major television networks to begin broadcasting exclusively in color for the 1967 season was potentially the most dramatic threat to the American film industry since television broadcasting emerged two decades earlier. Between 1946 and 1966, despite the closure of numerous theaters and the pared-back quantity of films produced, the motion picture industry had remained a viable force in American entertainment as Technicolor and large screens offered a viable alternative to a black-and-white situation comedy on a twelve-inch television screen. Yet now color and larger screens were entering the American living room and Hollywood producers were urged by the motion picture companies to develop plotlines and scripts that could not be easily attempted on network television. Just as the film industry lured first-generation television viewers to periodically leave the comfort of home to view film noir, lush Broadway musicals, and the panoramic vistas of the frontier west, a new generation of cinema producers and directors attempted to parry the threat of color television with themes and story lines that the networks simply could not or would not duplicate. This process was often enhanced by the simple demographic reality that America now had tens of millions of teens and young adults who were constantly looking for reasons to escape the oversight of adult authority, and who found a darkened cinema an ideal alternative to the family living room or recreation room. One sure way to entice this huge young audience into theaters was to ramp up the level of violence and rebellion against authority. As such, a hugely profitable trio of action films ventured into new territory, garnering both enormous public attention and legions of young theatergoers that guaranteed a healthy bottom line for the projects.

The first of these groundbreaking films was actually the fifth installment of perhaps the most iconic action series of the past half century. The production team of Albert "Cubby" Broccoli and Harry Saltzman, who brought Ian Fleming's James Bond character to the screen in *Dr. No*, secured the services of famed writer Roald Dahl and premier musical score creator John Barry to maintain the stunning momentum of the Bond series in what critic Pauline Kael noted was "the best package of entertainment that skill and ingenuity and money can provide." While no entry in the 007 series would ever knock the third installment, *Goldfinger*, from its perch as the most iconic Bond film, with its memorable characters such as Pussy Galore and Auric Goldfinger and its climactic assault on Fort Knox, *You Only Live Twice* would ultimately give that 1964 film a solid run in fan favorite lists. The film was both exotic and visually stunning as Broccoli and Saltzman decided to forgo the mock-up of Fort Knox on a back lot in Britain for on-location filming in Japan. Nancy Sinatra was the first actual pop/rock singer to perform a Bond movie theme that hit top forty charts, as Matt Monroe and Shirley Bassey were adult-oriented singers and Tom Jones's "Thunderball" never really emerged as a rock hit, even if the artist himself was popular with young listeners.

In an exceptionally daring move, the producers centered *You Only Live Twice* around a single (albeit hugely popular) Western star and teamed him up with a trio of unknown (in the west) Japanese actors, Tetsuro Tamba, Mie Hama, and Akiko Wakabayashi to play his two love interests and the head of the Japanese secret service, respectively. For younger Americans who had grown up on World War II films portraying the Japanese as brutal enemies, and for their elders who viewed the Nipponese as virtually inhuman during World War II, *You Only Live Twice* created a major revision. In this latest Bond thriller, the lovely female agent, "Tiger" Tanaka, and a hundred ninja warriors are all that stands between the non-Communist world and nuclear annihilation plotted by an alliance between SPECTRE's chief operator Ernst Blofeld and Mr. Osato, a Japanese affiliate.

Many American film viewers watching *You Only Live Twice* had their first full-scale look at Japan two decades after World War II, and in some respects they saw a Nipponese version of *The Jetsons* laced with futuristic devices such as television-equipped superfast cars, fleets of nimble helicopters flying through the skies, and other marvels.

While *You Only Live Twice* combined James Bond's individualism and resistance to follow orders with a futuristic vista of 1967 Japan, a major rival in the box office contest that year was an even more violent confrontation between World War II–era American convicts and the state-sponsored violence of the Third Reich. Recently popular World War II films of the 1960s, such as *The Longest Day* and *The Battle of the Bulge*, offered viewers an extended panoramic sweep of dramatized real events, in which large numbers of combatants had died but with little emphasis on truly graphic violence. In 1967, director Robert Aldrich took World War II action in a very different direction that was funny, disturbing, and more violent than its predecessors.

The plotline of *The Dirty Dozen* is straightforward and enormously enticing. An American army major (Lee Marvin) has been threatened with court-martial for his consistent violation of almost every regulation in the army manual. His superior (Ernest Borgnine) secretly admires Marvin's individualism and, when forced to prosecute, offers the major a final chance to clear his record. He is ordered to pick a dozen "volunteers" from a maximum-security military prison and offer amnesty for anyone who survives a near-suicidal mission. They are ordered to parachute behind enemy lines on the night before D-day and attack a French resort center known to be entertaining a contingent of high-ranking Nazi officers with a mandate to simply kill as many as possible and then attempt to escape to American lines.

The first half of *The Dirty Dozen* is essentially a military comedy merging aspects of pre-Pearl Harbor films staring Abbott and Costello and Laurel and Hardy, which focus on the comic elements of basic training, and a simulated war game with the 1960s antiauthority shenanigans of *McHale's Navy* and *Gomer Pyle*. The men, given one final chance to escape the firing squad or hangman's noose, were basically a 1960s multimedia all-star team with television's Clint Walker and Charles Bronson, pop singer Trini Lopez, NFL All-Star Jim Brown, and actor/director John Cassavetes. After failing in mission training, they are given a final chance if they can defeat a huge mock enemy force in a simulated war game. The Dozen simply break all of the rules of the game, capture the opposing team's general, and are granted the "honor" of going on the nearly suicidal mission.

While the first half of *The Dirty Dozen* linked the squad's issues with authority to 1967 counterparts, the actual assault on the rest center, in which almost all of the Nazi generals, most of their female companions, and all but one of the twelve convicts are killed, is replete with the graphic violence that was emerging in films at that time. Five years earlier, in the semidocumentary *The Longest Day*, hundreds or even thousands of Axis and Allied soldiers are killed, but on a monochrome backdrop with little personal graphic violence. *The Dirty Dozen* depicts far smaller numbers but far more graphic violence. Psychotic misfit Telly Savalas gleefully strangles the mistress of a German general just to clear the way for his assault on that officer. Lee Marvin drops hand grenades down ventilation holes to blast officers and women who are trapped below. A review of the film in *Life* magazine wondered about the glorification of an (admittedly fictional) operation that blatantly disregarded the rules of "civilized warfare."

The themes of confrontation with authority and graphic violence suggested in *You Only Live Twice* and amplified in *The Dirty Dozen* took on an even more distinct counterculture ambience in the landmark film *Bonnie and Clyde*. Despite the violence of the first two films, the perpetrators at least have government sanction for their actions and the people killed are fictional characters, not real human beings. In *Bonnie and Clyde*, Arthur Penn moved back from World War II to the gangster-laden decade of the Depression era. Penn used the hugely photogenic talents of Warren Beatty and Faye Dunaway in a melding of violence, comedy, and social messages that related the tale of very real robbers and murderers, Clyde Barrow and Bonnie Parker. Only a few years earlier, television viewers had viewed the crime scene of the Depression era from the lens of heroic Elliot Ness and the men of *The Untouchables* as they confronted and usually killed an all-star team of notorious 1930s mobsters and psychopaths.

Only four years after *The Untouchables* entered the world of reruns, viewers of the silver screen met eminently human, physically attractive gangsters who nonchalantly admit to acquaintances that they rob banks, as if this equated to managing a drugstore. The relatively bloodless, black-and-white deaths of gangsters and victims on *The Untouchables* of the early 1960s now gave way to graphic, slow motion, Technicolor demises of law enforcement officials, innocent bystanders, and ultimately Bonnie and Clyde themselves. The film spurred a whole retro-1930s mood in late 1960s America—from slouch hats and vests for men, cloche hats for women, to a popular record hit from British rocker George Fame—while some scholars viewed the couple as early insurgents against capitalist American greed.

While authority-defying secret agents, misfit World War II soldiers, and glamorous young 1930s gangsters transfixed many of America's youthful viewing audience, the seemingly endangered species of the western film seemed able to beat a hasty retreat from getting the boot. Unfortunately for the genre, the most expensive, star-studded film of the year almost proved that the genre was indeed on life support when *The Way West* scored underwhelming box office returns. This film version of A. B. Guthrie Jr.'s epic novel followed in the multiple plot tradition of *How the West Was Won* and *Cheyenne Autumn*. Kirk Douglas, Robert Mitchum, and Richard Widmark knew how to belt on a holster and saddle a horse, but they became so enmeshed in subplots of natural disasters, stampedes, hostile native Americans, and murderous outlaws that many viewers felt they could not keep up with the action.

On the other hand, the more modestly budgeted *The War Wagon* had just as much action but a more linear plot and much more fun. While John Wayne's foray into the Vietnam War with *The Green Berets* the following year produced decidedly mixed results, when the Duke put on his cowboy hat there was still magic in the air. Aiming to settle the score with villainous land baron Bruce Cabot, Wayne partners with Kirk Douglas and a small gang of misfits to attack Cabot's gold shipments carried on a vehicle that morphs from glorified stagecoach to proto-twentieth-century tank as Wayne and the gang concoct ever more clever ways of separating the villain from his spoils.

In a sense, the tongue-in-cheek mayhem of *The War Wagon* was a transatlantic cousin to the far more discussed birth of the spaghetti western being concocted in Europe by Sergio Leone. In 1964, Leone decided to utilize the huge popularity of the American western on the old continent to hire *Rawhide* television series star Clint Eastwood to film the genre on his side of the Atlantic. Armed with the pulsing, haunting backbeat of Ennio Morricone's music, Eastwood, who was cast enigmatically as the Man with No Name, drifted from range wars to battles for control of a frontier city to locating caches of stolen gold in an uneasy alliance with frenemy Lee Van Cleef, who usually played a villain in American television westerns, and finally Eli Wallach, who was the leader of the small army terrorizing the Mexican peasants in *The Magnificent Seven.* While Leone filmed three movies over a relatively leisurely three-year pace between 1964 and 1966, the trilogy was force-fed to American audiences with *A Fistful of Dollars* released in January 1967, *For a Few Dollars More* in May, and *The Good, the Bad and the Ugly* in December, taking the Man with No Name from frontier towns to a Civil War battlefield all in a single year. This trilogy essentially created a parallel world of westerns to a sometimes amused, sometimes shocked, and often confused American audience that saw their Rowdy Yates of *Rawhide* seemingly stripped of most feelings and morality.

While the Man with No Name trilogy dramatically expanded the parameters of what could be defined as a western movie, a pair of wickedly funny satires took direct aim at the romantic comedy genre that had been a mainstay of Hollywood from Fay Wray to Doris Day. Bud Yorkin and Norman Lear, who would open the seventies with their groundbreaking *All in the Family* and its multiple television offshoots, concentrated on the approaching end of a marriage in *Divorce American Style.* While Archie

Bunker's world was acted out with a cast of rather second-tier Hollywood personnel, the Lear-Yorkin team went to the all-star roster for a film *Life* magazine critic Richard Schickel insisted was a "hard, funny look at Splitsville USA." Television situation comedy king Dick Van Dyke and movie and song sweetheart Debbie Reynolds, both usually portrayed as bedrocks of the American family, were cast as a couple morphing from martial skirmishing to all-out nuclear war. Alternating between banal marriage counselors and door-banging home fights, the couple brings in attorneys who largely conspire to "give her the stock in the uranium mine and him the shaft." As Van Dyke crams into a bachelor apartment and Reynolds gets her first whiff of single loneliness, the estranged husband begins plotting to find a new husband for his ex-wife who will in turn eliminate much of his financial stress.

When Van Dyke convinces self-absorbed used-car salesman Van Johnson to enter the lists for Reynolds's hand, it appears that the future holds little more than a basic standoff of alimony and child custody disputes that were becoming a real part of late 1960s American society. Yet just as the Bunkers never really split in the 1970s, Reynolds and Van Dyke drift toward an ambiguous, less-than-heartwarming possible reconciliation that left the audience wondering what might come after the end of the film.

While *Divorce American Style* was satire bordering on marital drama, *A Guide for the Married Man* was satire bordering on slapstick. Gene Kelly's take on late-1960s marriage and family centered around fumbling but generally good-hearted money manager Walter Matthau, who is pushed toward adultery by his neighbor and office mate, attorney Robert Morse. Despite a beautiful, adoring wife and children, Morse lives for the excitement of extramarital excursions. The centerpiece of the film is Morse's "tutorials" of the do's and don'ts of philandering, with each topic illustrated by guest stars such as Art Carney, Lucille Ball, Jack Benny, and Jayne Mansfield. Each "lesson" is replete with sight gags as the cameos demonstrate "right" and "wrong" strategies for adultery. The main running gag of *Guide* is that Matthau is happily married to gorgeous, attentive Inger Stevens, who is literally a perfect wife and mother, while her husband is targeting far less attractive or considerate women in his quest. While the ending of *Divorce American Style* is ambiguous, the climax of *A Guide for the Married Man* is far more concrete as Matthau, who sneaks a female client to an out-of-the-way motel, is about to back out of the affair when Morse's wife and a camera-wielding detective catch Morse with a neighbor's wife in the next room in a sequence that sends Matthau back to his family with a new realization of the value of marital fidelity.

While Lear and Yorkin satirized sixties divorce and Kelly spoofed issues of marital fidelity, probably the most discussed family relationship film of 1967 was director Stanley Kramer's widely acclaimed *Guess Who's Coming to Dinner*. The film received huge attention even before it was released, as it was the final role for Spencer Tracy, who played opposite Katharine Hepburn for the eighth time in their long film careers. The film was an excellent vehicle for the discussion of a 1967 American roiling in both generational and social upheavals as it centered on the response of the actors' husband and wife characters to the announcement by their daughter (played by Hepburn's real-life niece, Katharine Houghton) that she is engaged to an African American man (Sidney Poitier), who is as opinionated and argumentative as Tracy. In a riff on mothers of that time dreaming that their daughter will marry a doctor, Hepburn gets her wish, but with obvious complications. In an interesting plot twist, not only does Tracy initially reject his daughter's intended, but Poitier's father rejects Houghton just as vehemently. Since the film was a comedy, or at least a dramedy, Kramer interjects a Catholic priest as a sort of relationship referee and all ends well in this final Hepburn/Tracy film, several decades after their partnership started.

While Kramer successfully mixed elements of drama and comedy in a film about relationships, young director Roman Polanski fused horror and comedy in his brilliant and erratic *The Fearless Vampire Killers* (or *Pardon Me, But Your Teeth Are in My Neck*). Polanski both directed and starred in an alternately terrifying and hilarious romp through the whole classic vampire trope as he paired his character Alfred, an apprentice vampire hunter, with innocent and often clueless Sharon Tate, who is kidnapped by an offshoot of Dracula but doesn't really realize she has been abducted.

Polanski mixed elements of the iconic 1930s Universal horror films, 1940s Abbott and Costello comedy knockoffs of those films, 1950s Hammer Horror, and, without yet knowing it, 1980s music videos such as Michael Jackson's "Thriller." At a time when classic horror seemed to be giving way to psychological thrillers, Polanski revived and previewed the supernatural side of the genre while unintentionally creating an enormous irony, as the Sharon Tate character is largely saved from a horrendous death in the film only to suffer an equally hideous demise two years later at the hands of the real-life Manson Family.

Two excellent examples of the more common 1960s psychological thrillers competed with Polanski's film for critical acclaim. The more claustrophobic of this duo was set almost entirely in a cozy New York City apartment occupied by an upscale young couple played by Efrem Zimbalist Jr. and Audrey Hepburn. The film, *Wait Until Dark*, was based on Frederick Knott's Broadway play and focused on a blind Hepburn left alone by her husband just long enough to be terrorized by Alan Arkin and a gang of psychotic underlings.

While *Wait Until Dark* was based on a play, *In Cold Blood* was a film version of Truman Capote's bestselling book about a pair of psychotic youths who massacred an entire innocent family in the American heartland. Director Richard Brooks shot the film in a black-and-white documentary style that portrayed the killers, played by Robert Blake and Scott Wilson, as almost soulless entities without any trace of humanity in a real-life version of Michael Myers in the *Halloween* series that would begin a decade later.

The psychotic energy of Arkin and his henchmen in *Wait Until Dark* and Blake and Wilson's unemotional killing machines in the *Cold Blood* film bookended the lead character in the third major crime film of the year, *Cool Hand Luke*. Director Suart Rosenberg scored a major coup in signing Paul Newman for the lead role after the actor's run of hits in *The Hustler, Harper*, and *Hud,* as he consigned the actor to a Florida chain gang. Rosenberg's sweat-drenched hopelessness of his coterie of convicts was given added veracity by the fact that the original novel had been written by Donn Pearce, who had actually spent two years on a real chain gang. As Newman engages in an endless game of escape and capture with his arch nemesis Strother Martin, his character becomes so likeable that the audience sometimes forgets who are the convicts and who are the law enforcers. George Kennedy scored an Oscar as Luke's pal Dragline, but it becomes clear that Newman is in a no-win game even before his death in a boiling Florida sun.

If Paul Newman's Luke was cheered by young audiences as an antihero who died among losing elements of American society, Dustin Hoffman was emerging as an even bigger hero while circumnavigating an elite environment in suburbia. *The Graduate*'s theater run ensured that more people saw the movie in 1968 than the previous year, but director Mike Nichols was actually filming in the less divisive, less supercharged 1967, which allowed him to almost totally avoid political messages that would have been more obligatory only a few months later.

The Graduate was the ultimate "cool" movie of late 1967, backed by a Simon and Garfunkel sound track loaded with hits such as "Scarborough Fair" and "Mrs. Robinson" and the emergence of Dustin Hoffman and Katharine Ross as topflight young stars. The film is actually set in late spring of 1967 as Hoffman's character, Benjamin Braddock, is graduating from college and perusing career and/or graduate school options. Hoffman has supportive parents, a cool sports car, no pressing financial obligations, yet finds himself confused and disturbed by his seduction by his middle-aged neighbor and his growing love for her soon-to-be married daughter. While Paul Newman's Luke plots his next, probably doomed escape from a sweltering bunkhouse, Hoffman's Benjamin plots his future romantic life from an outdoor pool. Newman suffers a last-minute death through capture, but Hoffman enjoys last-minute success by eloping with Ross only seconds before she says "I do" to Benjamin's rival.

While Mike Nichols won professional plaudits and eager young fans because of the irony and relative self-centeredness of his characters in *The Graduate*, Robert Mulligan gained significant attention by chronicling the adventures of another new college graduate who spurns swimming pools and sports cars for public transit buses and the questionable ambience of an inner-city classroom.

Mulligan traded the lush audience of upper-class suburban California for the gritty streets and classrooms of New York City that become the environment for Sandy Dennis to work her very uncertain magic in *Up the Down Staircase*. Based on Bel Kaufman's bestseller about surviving urban high school teaching and student experiences, Dennis traded her supporting role kudos from the 1966 *Who's Afraid of Virginia Woolf?* for the thrust and parry of teaching *A Tale of Two Cities* to overcrowded classrooms of at-risk urban teenagers. While Dustin Hoffman confronts Mrs. Robinson's advances and pines for her engaged daughter, Sandy Dennis's rookie teacher is dealing with a three-sided dilemma of forging a relationship with the handsome young male teacher who will never schedule their first date; a classroom of forty-two students who couldn't care less about Charles Dickens; and a micromanaging assistant principal who chastises her for going "up the down staircase" when she tries to force her way through the mob of students surrounding her.

Dustin Hoffman's character appears to have rescued Katharine Ross's character from her nuptial mistake at the end of *The Graduate,* but Mike Nichols never really tells the audience whether Benjamin actually follows the "plastics" career path suggested by a family neighbor; Sandy Dennis's teacher character Sylvia Barrett gains more vocational resolution in *Up the Down Staircase* as the climax shows her ripping up a resignation letter and forming at least a truce with her most exasperating student. Yet Dennis's main romantic love interest, Patrick Bedford, disappears from the school and her life as he leaves the school, and her, in the middle of a class period.

A third film centered around young people and their choices in 1967 achieved a resolution of both career and romantic issues, even if the action took place well east of either California or New York. Director James Clavell's *To Sir, with Love*, like *Staircase*, was a memoir of a new teacher surviving in a somewhat hostile learning environment. Sidney Poitier, who experienced a hectic, transatlantic shooting schedule in 1967, plays the real-life character of E. R. Braithwaite, a Royal Air Force veteran of African descent who fell back on teaching when his engineering qualifications were seemingly dismissed by British employers. Usually referred to by students only with his official title, "Sir," Poitier finds himself in the

London equivalent of the South Bronx with a class cobbled together with the least promising students in an otherwise below-average school. As in *Up the Down Staircase*, these school students are aware that they are at the bottom of the educational food chain and were allowed to leave earlier than their American counterparts, able to gang up on Poitier even faster than Dennis's miscreant charges. While Dennis plods along with *A Tale of Two Cities*, "Sir" junks the prescribed curriculum and begins to win the class over with a combination of discussions of what "real life" holds for them and "cool" excursions to cultural sights of "Swinging London" at its peak.

In an American society where nearly half the population was under twenty-one, school films were bound to be popular. Even if the British accents were a bit tough to comprehend, *To Sir, with Love* featured pop star Lulu as both student and rock singer, hip London fashions, and a young cast that was relatable to American students. Both *Staircase* and *To Sir, with Love* featured a faculty resignation letter and a makeover of student attitudes to convince the teacher to stay. Yet the British film offered a bit more background on the students' home lives, a more rewarding and optimistic romantic relationship for the teacher, and a more startling ending. While Dennis's character merely goes back to class after she decides to forgo resignation, Poitier attends the graduation party of his charges and returns to discover the next batch of students proclaiming that they are even worse than the predecessors and daring him to make it through the following school year with them.

While the teacher-student relationships in *Up the Down Staircase* and *To Sir, with Love* produced a strong commonality despite the Cockney accents that had to be deciphered by Americans in the latter film, Richard Lester's satirical vision of the British experience in World War II, *How I Won the War*, brought nowhere near the connection among American audiences that his mega hits, *A Hard Day's Night* and *Help*, had enjoyed only two to three years earlier. The major tie-in among the three Lester films was that John Lennon appeared in all of them, with his role as the Cockney soldier Gripweed giving a rare glimpse of his acting ability. However, more than a few American Beatles fans were shocked when their hero died a horrible death in the film.

Public reaction to *How I Won the War* reflected the huge division in America over the Vietnam War in the same way that *The Green Berets* split audiences in two the following year. Lester's film satirized the concept of falsely heroic war movies, but the same type of nonlinear plotline that made the two Beatles films so much fun gained mixed reviews in this more cynical feature.

While Lester's view of a recent British conflict produced mixed reactions among American audiences, director Joshua Logan's treatment of a far older, almost mystical confrontation in ancient Britain managed to create the same mixed level of critical and popular acceptance. The Broadway musical *Camelot* was one of John and Jacqueline Kennedy's favorite shows, one that was increasingly compared to the Kennedy White House soon after the tragedy in Dallas.

Logan centered his film around three actors not particularly well-known for their singing abilities—Richard Harris, Vanessa Redgrave, and Franco Nero—and plunged them into the semi-mythical world of sixth-century Britain. *Camelot* had a huge budget and a phenomenal set, and middle-aged Americans were excited to see a film version of one of the iconic Broadway shows of the era. Jack Warner's last production was powered by a $15 million budget that was reported as producing "an unstinting commitment to detail" to capture every aspect of T. H. White's bestselling book, *The Once and Future King*. Unfortunately, some of the mood of this distant and magic time was frayed by publicity shots of Harris (who played King Arthur) cavorting in the Malibu surf wearing a T-shirt and a crown while Vanessa Redgrave alternated her scenes as Guenevere with attacks on American foreign policy and the Vietnam War.

Camelot came off well as a period drama carried out with good non-musical actors. However, none of the trio had spectacular singing talent, and the sunny, warm California backdrop hardly brought visions of gloomy, damp early Britain to life. The producers had to settle for Oscars in minor areas such as costumes and art direction rather than any of the really important trophies, as much of the middle-aged audience left the theaters perhaps wondering when *The Sound of Music* or *My Fair Lady* would be rereleased.

While neither of these seminal films were due back out anytime soon, movie fans who wished for a more entertaining period drama had one alternative, while those determined to find a musical where the leading actors could actually sing had another option.

The period drama option centered around the reuniting of Richard Burton and Elizabeth Taylor after their controversial roles in the previous year's *Who's Afraid of Virginia Woolf?* Director Franco Zeffirelli, who would stun audiences in 1968 with his adroit use of real teenagers in his version of *Romeo and Juliet*, set the stage for that critically acclaimed project by using Burton and Taylor in another hit from the Bard, *The Taming of the Shrew*. The film was essentially a nonstop romp of what the couple's home life might actually have been, but this time with period costumes. Zeffirelli chose to produce an actual film instead of a stage play that happened to be turned into a movie, which produced splashy interior and exterior scenes backdropping the ultimate battle of the sexes. Great second-tier stars such as Michael Hordern and Michael York seemed made for costume drama and comedy as the action never seemed to slow for a moment.

Fans who wanted a good period musical comedy instead of the tragedy that enveloped *Camelot* were generally satisfied with one of the queens of the genre, Julie Andrews, in the 1920s farce *Thoroughly Modern Millie*. Director George Roy Hill, who actually leaned toward action movies, created what film critic Bruce Williamson admitted was "one of the season's nicest surprises" as Hill jettisoned the sixties for a romp through a 1922 world of rumble seats and vamping, as the critics insisted, "Julie as Millie is back where she belongs, up to her dimpled knees in mischief." The film was set against almost every silent movie gimmick the script writers could concoct, from automobile chases to cliff-hanging stunts, but Andrews and her pals Mary Tyler Moore, Carol Channing, and John Gavin kept the action moving for almost two and a half hours while Elmer Bernstein walked away with an Oscar for the musical score.

Warner Brothers' musical bath in red ink with *Camelot* was actually exceeded by Twentieth Century Fox's excursion into the family/musical arena when *Doctor Dolittle* was released. The film, based on a series of stories by Hugh Lofting, secured great media attention and seemed like a sure hit when Fox tapped musical comedy superstar Rex Harrison for the lead role. Director Richard Fleischer supported Harrison's male lead with young actress Samantha Eggar and high-profile troupers such as Anthony Newley and Richard Attenborough, backed by a musical score by James Bond theme creator Leslie Bricusse. The film won an Oscar for the pop hit "Talk to the Animals," and the animated/live action connection generally worked well. However, a 152-minute running time was asking the impossible of non-adult viewers, and some critics insisted that the film was designed to induce sleep among unruly children.

While rumors of the film pushing Fox into bankruptcy trailed this film all the way to the Academy Award presentation, the all-animated Disney counterpart to *Dolittle*, *The Jungle Book*, proved a far safer financial investment. Like *Dolittle*, *Jungle Book* was adapted from children's stories by a famous writer, in this case Rudyard Kipling, but Disney studios kept the action strictly animated, while using familiar movie voices such as Sebastian Cabot, Phil Harris, Louis Prima, George Sanders, Sterling Holloway, and Verna Felton. The animated characters generally matched up perfectly with the corresponding voices and the film was another in a series of Disney-animated hits, one that could theoretically be rereleased in multiple successive generations.

While *Dr. Dolittle* assumed that size, length, and a big budget would create a smash hit, the expansive special effects often seemed too mechanical, the book's plump physician became Rex Harrison's lean figure that seemed out of place for a magical story, and the director's insistence on a love interest for the good doctor tended to bore children. In contrast, *Jungle Book* captured a magic that would transcend the time of its release.

If *Jungle Book* was relatively timeless, several significant films of this year of fire and ice were very much products of the "trippiness" that was now infiltrating much of popular culture. Four very different films, two British and two American, received wildly different reviews and box office returns, but each one, for better or worse, depicted an aspect of modern society that was moving toward a climactic cultural and generational confrontation as the end of the decade neared.

The first British entry rated numerous American magazine cover stories due to its context and controversial cast. *Blow-Up* was director Michelangelo Antonioni's paean to a "Swinging London" that threatened to turn a dowdy, postwar culture of endless rationing, austerity budgets, and attempts to contain an exploding youth rebellion into the "cool Britannia" of the Beatles, Twiggy, and *The Avengers*. David Hemmings plays a somewhat intense photographer who, while preparing a book compilation of his best violent and sexually suggestive photos, discovers young Vanessa Redgrave engaged in a relatively innocent banter with an older man on a park bench. Redgrave notices Hemmings's activities, demands surrender of the exposed film, and meets with a rebuff that sets off a slow fuse in which Hemmings returns to his studio to enlarge every minor detail of the photos toward an eventual obsession with this London bird.

Backed by the blasting soundtrack of the hit group the Yardbirds, Hemmings takes his audience on a tour of mod London, from a riot in a discotheque to a pot party to experiments with other hallucinogens that gradually consume Hemmings's waking moments. Still, he never gives closure on just what this hip culture is really about.

At about the same time in America, director Mark Robson was tasked with turning young author Jacqueline Susann's hugely successful book *Valley of the Dolls* into a major film. Susann's book spent most of 1966 at the number one position on bestseller lists as almost 10,000 people a week paid $5.95 to read the adventures of Anne Welles, Neely O'Hara, and Jennifer North, who use "dolls," or pills, to wake up and cope with the never-never-land of Hollywood, while alternately stealing from one another's boyfriends and husbands. Susann's book was a nonstop happening that Twentieth Century Fox paid $35 million to turn into a film while giving the author a bit role as a reporter. *Dolls* introduced Sharon Tate, Patty Duke, and Barbara Parkins, who never seemed to mesh, in a feature that was panned as terribly written, acted, and directed. Yet *Dolls* did demonstrate how the trippiness of young people was rapidly spilling over to adult fashion, language, and social outlooks in a 1967 that seemed decades away from the America of even 1962.

While these two films suggested that large numbers of adults were joining the kids in that era's emerging social and cultural revolution, *Privilege* and *The President's Analyst* provide two possible outcomes of the revolution in the near future. *Privilege* is set in the near future of 1970 and chronicles the emergence of pop singer Steve Shorter as a super-Beatle for the new seventies decade. However, instead of being managed by the generally ethical Brian Epstein (who had just died in real-world Britain), he is pushed toward stardom by a nebulous management group that plans to make him "the biggest star in five hundred years," all the while planning a fascist takeover of Britain.

Director Peter Watkins scored a pop-culture coup by signing former lead singer of Manfred Mann ("Do Wah Diddy Diddy") Paul Jones, perhaps the closest rival to Paul McCartney on teen pinup photos, and Jean Shrimpton, the stunningly attractive supermodel rival to Twiggy in Swinging London. As Jones belts out 1970 hits, he becomes a pied piper for the forces of evil until their leaders decide to make him a martyr in a torch-lit stadium that would do Hitler proud. In a 1967 of "peace, love, and understanding," Watkins suggested that pop music could entice youthful masses to do some very non-loving things, and even the near future of the seventies might be a very different world.

Back on the other side of the Atlantic, director Theodore Flicker used a much funnier plotline to suggest in *The President's Analyst* that the surrender of American freedoms might not require swastikas and torchlight parades but only their own telephones. While Peter Watkins utilized a highly recognizable pop star, Flicker chose just-below-superstar-status James Coburn to become the target of a massive plot by The Phone Company (TPC) to insert tiny transistors into every American, which will replace the expensive telephone hardware and allow surveillance at all times.

Coburn had scored well in *Our Man Flint* and *In Like Flint*, the fast-paced, hilarious takeoffs on the James Bond films, and he reprised much of the role to play the "Chief Shrink" of the American president. During a brilliant series of high-energy sight-gagged confrontations, the exasperated Coburn resigns his position and is then pursued by every American, allied,

and Communist spy agency, all eager to discover the president's intentions. In a fit of self preservation and emerging détente, Coburn teams up
with a sympathetic KGB agent to foil the TPC plot in a series of violent
but hilarious shoot-outs where ammunition magazines never seem to go
empty. The final scene moves to a Christmas in the future with Coburn
and his initially kidnapped girlfriend now sitting in domestic tranquility
in their new home; yet as the camera pulls back, the audience sees phone
company agents watching every move on a video feed, nodding in satisfac-
tion that TPC can now keep surveillance on just about anyone.

By 1967, the film industry had almost, but not quite, recovered the
profitability of its golden age. However, the box office gross was rising at a
steady 11 percent a year and passed the billion-dollar mark late in that year
with a 22 percent jump in pictures produced, which pushed the industry
back over the 200-film-a-year level. Film critics were accepting the fact
that the violence levels, now at far higher levels than a decade earlier, were
not about to disappear, but there was still a feeling that gratuitous violence might eventually destroy the film industry. Despite this, Hollywood
would never go back to the innocence of a decade or a generation earlier.

CHAPTER X

Youth Quake

During much of 1967, visitors to Washington, DC, could enter the headquarters of the United States Commerce Department and take part in a giant national guessing game. The centerpiece of the Commerce Department lobby was an enormous proto-digital clock that listed the estimated population of the United States and clicked upward by one person each eight seconds. American television and radio stations, magazines, newspapers, and other news outlets touted the "Great United States Population Sweepstakes" as people attempted to guess who would become the newborn baby that would be counted as the 200-millionth American. Relatively simple calculations revealed that the event would occur around 11:00 a.m. on Monday, November 20, 1967, and Lyndon Johnson, never one to walk away from a public relations coup, duly showed up in the Commerce Department lobby on that day and began speaking. The president was quickly interrupted when newsmen, census personnel, and visitors saw the huge clock click to a single number two followed by eight zeroes at precisely 11:03 a.m. Personnel scoured incoming hospital notices from across the nation. For a brief moment newborn Josh Bagley, son of two Harvard students, seemed to be the most likely candidate to be the 200-millionth American, until further calculations around the nation revealed that Sally Woo, an engineering student at Georgia Tech, had delivered a son, Robert Jr., half a minute earlier and had won the "200 millionth sweepstakes." Mrs. Woo was a refugee from the chaos of China's Cultural Revolution and had herself been born during a Japanese bombing raid in her hometown in Canton. Robert Woo Jr. became the 200-millionth resident of a nation that had spent the past two decades in a frenzied birth spurt that was just now beginning a slight trailing off that was largely unnoticed as youth culture and its impact on society dominated much of the nation's analysis of itself. Nearly half of the population was considered "young," and they lived in a society that owned more than 302 million record players, radios, and television sets and were growing up a time in which television viewers had risen—in two decades—from only sixteen thousand to 94 percent of the current population. These citizens, called merely "The Kids," were riding a demographic wave that made authors, film producers, and television network executives sit up and take notice, while scholars were beginning to study an emerging age divide that they were labeling the "Generation Gap." Many of these young people could name heroes from Mickey Mantle to the Beatles to John Kennedy, but Lyndon Johnson seldom made the short list. They were enrolled in an educational system that graduated nearly 90 percent of them from high school, the highest rate either before or after their generation. However, they had to deal with overcrowded classrooms, severe teacher shortages, and outdated textbooks, and then had to fight to be accepted by colleges that would reject large numbers of them and then flunk out many who actually were accepted.

A decade earlier, many adults had believed that they were confronting the most rebellious, challenging adolescents in American history, as they coped with boys in black leather jackets, girls in poodle skirts, films that stoked generational tension such as *Blackboard Jungle* and *Rebel Without a Cause,* and strange vocabulary such as "daddy-o" and "see you later, alligator!" Now, in 1967, the social threat posed by 1950s teens seemed almost quaint, as the demographics of youthful rebellion dropped down in age to include increasing numbers of preteens and lurched upward to include college students and even students at graduate schools. The somewhat limited forces of beatniks in 1957 had exploded into a hippie invasion of

1967 that carried an agenda far beyond the beat poetry and dialectic jazz of their predecessors.

A cover story carried by *U.S. News and World Report* in October 1967, titled "Worried About Today's Young People," described "campus protests, anti-war demonstrations, dope raids . . . of a loud mouth arrogant, unkempt and idle, if not rioting (generation) . . . that's the picture of American youth today that millions get in news headlines and photos, especially from college campuses." The report noted that in the autumn of 1967, 1,388,000 new freshmen had entered a higher education system that now cost America more than 18 billion dollars a year and yet, according to one college dean, was also "the most exciting group we've had in years." However, an advantage of having "exciting" students was often nullified by the reality that colleges were becoming hugely overcrowded with increasingly politically active and socially frustrated young people. A *Time* magazine cover story of State University of New York Chancellor Samuel Gould noted that the SUNY system had exploded from 47,600 students in 1960 to 139,000 in 1967 and was expected to reach 290,000 in 1974, with similar growth rates across the nation.

While *Time* focused on college expansion, overcrowding, and tension from the perspective of the top administration of a massive state university system, the magazine's sister publication, *Life*, dispatched a twenty-something staff journalist to the Midwest to return to college for six weeks and report on events from the student perspective. Gerald Moore became a resident of North Wing, McNutt Quadrangle, room 314 at the University of Indiana, Bloomington. Moore marveled at the continuity with his own collegiate experience, noting the institutional yellow paint of dorm corridors, decorations from girlie magazines posted on the bulletin boards of male dorms, and the throbbing pulse of rock music, even if the Doors and Supremes had replaced the Elvis Presley and Bill Haley of his student days.

The campus was a riot of color, with a rainbow of madras men's shirts and women's blouses often paired with multicolored nylon Windbreakers for both genders. The author noted that, like Alice in Wonderland, he had "tumbled into the Generation Gap" but, if this world contained hints of the hippie culture around the edges, the center included a politically conservative student body president and liberal vice president who were not only friends, but could also find common ground. It was their belief that most of the student body was more interested in soap operas on TV than political and racial issues. In effect, far more students followed the adventures of Barnabas Collins the vampire and governess Victoria Winters at Collinwood in the popular gothic soap opera *Dark Shadows* than political trends in the nation. Both leaders insisted that Greek life and passionate support for the powerful Hoosiers basketball team would dominate the scene—unless Selective Service began eliminating some or all student draft deferments, the Vietnam War entered a massive escalation period, or the upcoming presidential campaign took turns not yet predicted.

While Indiana University was more fixated on soap operas and college hoops that fall, one of their Big Ten rivals was experiencing far more political turmoil on its massive tree-lined campus.

On October 16, a recruiter for the Dow Chemical Company checked into the Ivy Inn, ten blocks from the University of Wisconsin campus in Madison. The employee signed in with an assumed name, as his employers were beginning to experience opposition on college campuses due to the controversial issue of their napalm agent in attacks on suspected Viet Cong positions in Vietnam. Dow offered excellent pay and benefits and welcomed applications from both business and science fields, but a company that had recently been best known for plastic wraps to preserve sandwiches and leftovers was now pilloried for its continued manufacture of a chemical that had been initially used against Imperial Japanese forces in World War II.

The state of Wisconsin's status as a center of the progressive movement in earlier decades had attracted a significant faculty and student presence from cities such as San Francisco and New York and created a hint of Cal-Berkeley and Columbia in this heartland institution.

While much of the student body still welcomed the first year, in which the football games featured a sixteen-member pom-pom squad and lamented the team's horrendous winless record, a thriving counterculture produced a visit by Allard Lowenstein, the director of the "Dump Johnson" movement, and offered an Anti-Military Ball as an alternative to the annual ROTC dance. Membership in the campus Young Republicans still far exceeded that of Students for a Democratic Society, but on such an enormous campus it was not difficult to recruit a respectable turnout for just about any cause or event.

The "Battle of Madison" began on the morning of October 17 when, after the reading of poems in honor of the recently killed Che Guevara, a cry of "Down with Dow" initiated a demonstration initially fronted by the "guerrilla theater" of the San Francisco Mime Troupe. Protestors self-divided into students and faculty who would picket the Business School's Commerce Building when the Dow recruiting began, and others who would attempt to obstruct the interviews through a sit-in.

These events imitated a choreography that would define much of the late sixties/early seventies protest movement. Students who were eager to secure a well-paying job from a targeted corporation or agency would push between phalanxes of students who agreed with their position, and against another mass of individuals who were picketing, chanting, or shouting but not willing to go further. Just outside the Commerce Building, and in the corridors, were young people sitting in halls and outside entrances, waiting to see what the authorities would actually do.

On this gray, cool morning, University Chancellor William Sewell's hope for a relatively amicable outcome ended when student leaders demanded a permanent expulsion of Dow recruiters from the campus as nonnegotiable. Sewell had voted against inviting Dow recruiters when he was a faculty member, but he also insisted that the effective takeover of the building was an illegal assembly that could not be condoned. Students who refused to leave were now threatened with expulsion.

By early afternoon, the stalemate had turned into violence, as university officials turned the crisis over to the Madison police department. A usually quiet academic building turned into a battlefield, as paddy wagons lined up outside and police dragged out mostly limp but occasionally fist-swinging students who populated a casualty list on both sides. The smell of tear gas, the crunch of broken glass, and the sirens of police vehicles became the backdrop for a confrontation that would climax in the fatalities at Kent State and Jackson State thirty months later.

The "Battle of Madison" had ended with the administration as the tactical victor and the students who organized the sit-in wondering how much they had accomplished. However, only hours later a contingent of students boarded three buses near the campus and headed toward the ultimate student "Youth Quake" of 1967, the March on Washington. If the hundreds of students at Wisconsin had set their sights on discouraging the producer of napalm from recruiting students to join them, a major national organization intended that same week to confront the government that was conducting the conflict in the first place.

While large numbers of college students across the nation intended to spend the weekend of October 21–22 watching football games, attending homecoming events, or simply catching up on assignments, busloads of students and other young people were making their way toward the nation's capital in the ultimate version of generational action: a massive protest of the Vietnam War. As early as October 2, Lyndon Johnson was meeting with congressional leaders about the rally being planned for Washington in three weeks. While some congressional leaders suggested that the weekend might be a good time for the president to head to his Texas ranch, Johnson curtly insisted, "They are not going to run me out of town." True to his word, the president was very much present in the capital as the first buses began rumbling into town, the advance guard of what Attorney General Ramsey Clark predicted would draw 100,000 people, most of them young protestors. The umbrella organization for this March on Washington was called the New Mobilization Committee to End the War, better known as the "New Mobe." The most notable leaders of this mostly youth-oriented peaceful invasion were Reverend William Sloane Coffin, chaplain at Yale University; the famous baby doctor and author Dr. Benjamin Spock; and bestselling author Norman Mailer, who already sniffed a book emerging from the weekend activities.

While the event organizers promised demonstrators that they would be part of a more than a 200,000-person contingent and government officials made very selective counts that topped out at 30,000, the March on Washington was probably about midway between the two figures. The opening act, which infuriated Lyndon Johnson, began when Coffin went up the steps of the Department of Justice building and attempted to deliver about 1,000 draft cards turned in by young potential conscripts. Clark sent one of his assistants, who refused to receive the bag that the champlain dropped on the floor.

Eventually, the marchers made their way across the river to the Pentagon, where they were confined primarily to the building's parking lot and a large field nearby. Occasional forays of two or three thousand marchers lurched toward the Pentagon building and then drifted backward as tear gas containers exploded in a mélange of songs, curses, and taunts. Soldiers and federal marshals dueled with the kids, and the two dozen injuries incurred by the authorities were perhaps quadrupled by the protestors, while another seven hundred found themselves under arrest.

While Norman Mailer seemed to be everywhere on this weekend of confrontation, the younger Abbie Hoffman, apparently high on LSD and wearing an Uncle Sam hat, "attacked" the Pentagon twice, once by attempting to "levitate" the structure through his "psychic powers" and the second time by simply urinating toward the structure. Mailer would win a Pulitzer Prize for his account, *Armies of the Night*, while Hoffman would get new ideas for confronting authorities the next summer amid the tear gas explosions of Chicago's Democratic Convention.

While the March on Washington featured a cast largely composed of college students, adult Americans were fascinated and concerned about the exploding demographic tidal wave of teenagers in America. A decade after rock and roll and Sputnik had fueled a perceived crisis in American high schools, new reports on teen sexuality, drug use, study habits, and viewing and listening activities fueled reports on the college scene. If the relatively small cohort of 1950s teens could wreak havoc on the adults of that decade, current adolescents could form a generational tsunami crashing against adult values of the late-sixties era.

By 1967, almost every aspect of teen life in America was a subject for print and visual media, and numerous articles and network specials displayed a "class picture" of young people attempting to navigate across the bridge from childhood to adulthood. Reporters, producers, and commentators openly worried about what was actually behind the "photography" of this young America entering a great transition. One national magazine had just a bit earlier run a series on teenagers with the obligatory pictures of seas of smiling adolescent faces. "There they stared for their class picture, a crop of high school seniors, earnest, brash, and vulnerable, trying to choose a face to show the camera. Someday, much later, they will find this picture with a small smile and an ache on how young they looked then and back will come this special time when life keeps changing and changing and everything both good and bad is supercharged." By 1967 the "supercharged" generation seemed on the brink of running amok to more than a few American adults.

Surveys of teens and their sometimes mysterious habits pervaded newspapers, magazines, and television special reports throughout the year, and they often proved disturbing or contradictory to adults. The revelation that more than 40 percent of teens smoked, about five times the rate fifty years later, was hardly a sensation in a society still largely accepting of tobacco use, but the fact that three out of four teens seemed to dismiss the links between smoking and cancer boded ill for successfully reducing these numbers. Adults were also bewildered when they contrasted the admission of almost three of five underage teens to drinking alcoholic beverages, yet seven in ten felt that their parents and other adults should not serve teens alcohol at home parties.

In a late sixties, replete with sexually charged books, films, and to a lesser extent television programs, it was hardly shocking that more than half of teen girls and two thirds of boys now believed sexual relations before marriage were acceptable and that 90 percent of high school students desired far more comprehensive sex education in schools than they currently received. Unlike their counterparts five decades later, a startling number of teens saw what is now known as the "digital revolution" as an enormously mixed blessing, as many believed that the newly emerging computer industry might create a soulless punch-card culture where machines would as likely cause conformity and vast unemployment as they would a dazzling future of ease and entertainment.

Much of the high school population of America viewed the "groovy" element of the sixties as a lifestyle for young adults more than a "happening" to which they were invited. In many cases, this attitude produced a running guerrilla war between teen fashion statements and seemingly implacable school officials. At Oyster Bay High School on Long Island, students carried protest signs proclaiming "better flowing locks than throwing rocks," after the school principal banished five "mop top" boys to a separate classroom after they refused to visit a barber. The duel ended relatively amicably when the quintet visited a hair stylist for a modification of their locks. A suburban Detroit high school suspended more than 150 students who walked out after a school official cracked down on long hair, as the perplexed superintendent insisted that "those kids are staging a mini version of social unrest they read about elsewhere."

Yet generational confrontation was not always the order of the day. Students at many private high schools were simply called to the office and encouraged to cut their hair to a moderate degree, while the principal of Santa Monica High School in California staged a combined picnic and fashion show for the students, featuring student models demonstrating what could or could not be worn.

Even the over-twenty-one world of the discotheque was partially opened to teen audiences when a nightclub owner franchised a string of more than thirty Hullabaloo dance centers that packed in teenagers almost every night of the week. One news magazine ran an extended feature on the Conshohocken, Pennsylvania, location just outside of Philadelphia and described "music so loud it blocks your ears." Interviewed teens relished the idea that "the smoke fills your head. You forget it and just dance" in an "adult" environment that included a high decibel level to compensate for the absence of alcohol.

During the summer, the energy and curiosity of teen runaways, idealistic college students, and curious but sometimes skeptical adults all began interacting within the few square blocks of San Francisco that was Haight-Ashbury. By May, the Summer of Love was fully underway in what was alternately called Hashbury and Psychodelphia, with perhaps an unofficial inauguration when Beatle George Harrison and his wife Pattie walked, danced, and romped through the neighborhood as the troubadour from

Liverpool, dressed in authentic hippie garb, informally gave his blessing to all that this hippie kingdom stood for.

As Scott McKenzie's "San Francisco (Be Sure to Wear Flowers in Your Hair)" and Eric Burdon and the Animals' "San Franciscan Nights" dueled for ownership of the theme song of the Summer of Love, tour buses were filled with camera-laden middle-aged and older tourists who gawked at the native flora and fauna, as if Haight-Ashbury had become the newest American theme park. In this case, one could feed the animals, as the hippies often accepted cash to have their photos taken by the squares. Tourists snapped up authentic hippie crafts and artifacts, which many of the denizens viewed as a small price to pay in order to otherwise maintain their lifestyle.

Tourists who actually stepped out of the buses might very well have noticed numerous signs such as STP USERS DO NOT TAKE THORAZINE, SECONAL, OR OTHER DOWNERS FOR BAD TRIPS.

One ugly truth of the Summer of Love was that Hashbury was plagued by new, potent hallucinogens that were far more dangerous than LSD, which were at best inflicting bad-trip hell on the users and in some cases making the Summer of Love their last season on earth. A major destination for hippies—not on the tourist map—was the Haight-Ashbury equivalent of a MASH unit, a crisis center where locals could go to "a cool place where you can see a cool doctor without getting busted." The building featured "groovy" orange, purple, and black décor with piped-in music by the Grateful Dead and Jefferson Airplane, while over 200 "trippers," almost 90 percent teens, dealt with hepatitis from dirty needles and crashed in "meditation" rooms as they endured a three- or four-day private hell that emanated from roughly 10,000 "bad doses" of various hallucinogens that always seemed to be in ample supply that summer.

While many American adults viewed the youth antics in Haight-Ashbury as something between humorous and bizarre, at almost the same time another form of "quake" largely involving American youths was turning dozens of cities into virtual war zones. The cool of the Summer of Love contrasted sharply with the fire belching from a wide spectrum of American cities, from Newark, New Jersey, to Long Beach, California.

Four years before the greatest urban firestorm in American memory, Reverend Martin Luther King had addressed the largest gathering of civil rights supporters on a sweltering late-August day in 1963. Set against speeches and entertainment by such luminaries as Charlton Heston, Peter, Paul and Mary, and Bob Dylan, King articulated his dream of a common table at which Americans of all races could come together in a spirit of harmony and equality. Despite long hot summers of riot and violence from New York City to Watts in California, the momentum of Lyndon Johnson's Great Society allowed for the passage of moderately successful civil rights and voting legislation that partially curbed the most outrageous of laws designed to keep African Americans at the lower ends of the economic and political spectrums.

By 1967, King's "common table" of a multiracial American experience was still largely an unfinished dream within the confines of private homes, as only 7 percent of white respondents in polls admitted that they would be comfortable if their son or daughter brought a "Negro" home for dinner. Yet a clear majority of these same people admitted that sitting next to racial minorities in movie theaters, public facilities, or restaurants, or using the same dressing rooms in department stores, were no longer significant issues.

Another hopeful sign of greater racial inclusiveness was beginning to emerge against the backdrop of the sports arenas and stadiums of high-profile southern universities. At the end of the 1966 college basketball season, the all-white squad of powerhouse University of Kentucky entered the championship game against a mostly black team of almost unknown Texas Western University (now University of Texas at El Paso). The Kentucky Wildcats were largely favored over the Texas Western Miners, yet Don Haskins's team nearly annihilated Adolph Rupp's squad in a game that was never close. Subsequently Rupp, and much of the football and basketball coaching fraternity in the region, began opening the gates to African American players who could improve or secure the fortunes of the southern schools. One by one, teams and power conferences such as the Atlantic Coast Conference and Southeastern Conference began integrating teams, while most—although not all—of the fans gradually accepted integration as a more tolerable situation than a constantly losing team that had refused to move in that direction.

Yet these notable gains, from public bus terminals to sports arenas, were to some extent counteracted in 1967 by the most violent of the long, hot summers that punctuated much of the 1960s urban experience. Headlined by back-to-back riots in Newark, New Jersey, and Detroit, Michigan, youthful residents of urban areas escalated urban violence into something little short of outright insurrection. Compared to the previous decade's direct conflict between two groups of rival ethnic, religious, racial, or even geographical groups, as in *West Side Story*, the inter-youth violence of the Sharks and the Jets gave way to a guerrilla war against the system, ranging from setting fire to and looting the shops of local merchants to active resistance to police and military forces sent to restore order.

Only days after a massive riot in Newark, New Jersey, claimed twenty-six deaths, 1,200 injuries, and $15 million in property losses, a minor police raid on an after-hours club in a largely black Detroit neighborhood turned the Motor City into what one national newsweekly called "Battlefield USA." Largely young rioters set fire to stores and public buildings and then skirmished with police and army paratroopers, who were often about the same age. As the nation's fifth largest city began to resemble a battle area in Vietnam, the casualty toll climbed to forty dead, 2,300 injured, 4,000 arrested, and $250 million in property damage. In a strange preview of the street fighting that would rock Saigon and Hue six months later, the president dispatched Task Force Detroit, 5,000 paratroppers from Fort Bragg and Fort Campbell, to suppress what was in many ways an urban insurrection. Now nineteen-year-old paratroopers were dueling with nineteen-year-old Detroit residents against the backdrop of burning buildings as they moved from neighborhood to neighborhood in almost textbook urban fighting.

Lt. Gen. John Throckmorton, formerly William Westmoreland's deputy in Vietnam, divided the city into zones and sent units armed with M16s, tear-gas launchers, and light armored support to track down rioters who were advancing from the business district into the affluent Grosse Point neighborhood. Reports coming from police and army headquarters began to sound like Vietnam communiques while some members of the African Ameircan community began sliding into a generational conflict, for while Bayard Rustin condemned the riots as a "threat to all civil liberties" and Congressman John Conyers drove through neighborhoods urging rioters to "cool it," H. Rap Brown invited young African Americans to spread the violence further into white communities.

Soon after the upheavels of the Long Hot Summer of 1967 began to diminish, at least until the next year, over 300 student leaders from across the nation convened at the University of Maryland. They had gathered for the annual congress of the National Student Association (NSA), and President Ed Schwarz of Oberlin College articulated the need for students to borrow techniques from the civil rights and anti-war movements to force administrators to either yield to student power or force a year of unprecedented upheaval. From this relatively small band of representatives came demands for the students to take control of their lives outside the boundaries of strict academic areas. An increasing number of students wanted to set their own dormitory rules, including decisions on when visitors of either sex would be allowed to visit, all based on the feeling that college administrators were too far removed from student issues to make valid decisions.

The buzzword of late 1960s student speak was "relevance," as many students began the fall semester with deep concerns that what they were being taught was not relevant to either their current or later adult lives. Students were now demanding joint student-faculty control over such previously untouchable areas as course requirements, grading polices, admissions standards, the topics taught in courses, and the hiring and dismissal of the faculty members who taught those courses.

One of the NSA officers insisted that "the quest for student power will end only when students feel they, as members of the academic community, are represented in shaping their own lives, from choice of courses they may take to eliminating administration control over whether they could drink in their rooms or choose to bring their dates inside with them." As the 1967–1968 academic year began, the gauntlet was being dropped in more than a few colleges in a student revolt that would expand rapidly in the spring 1968 semester, from Columbia to Berkeley and even from Mexico to France. The Youth Quake of 1967 was now forcing teachers, deans, presidents, and trustees to hear the demands of a new generation. The tension underlying the generation gap was about to achieve critical mass in 1968.

CHAPTER XI

The War Comes Home

As Americans engaged in their annual rituals of summer vacation, a strange assortment of Jeeps, buses, motor scooters, and automobiles made its way up and down the roads of Vietnam, somewhat like a traveling circus. Crowds of people from many of the 13,000 hamlets that constituted the core population of the Republic of South Vietnam gathered to listen to the promises and opinions of a multitude of candidates running for office, from local assemblies to president of the Republic. Most of the adults had grown up under French rule, where Gallic overlords routinely slapped rickshaw drivers, servants, and farmers as if they were naughty children, and only provided educational opportunities to the tiny number of natives who might make themselves useful to stable management of the colony.

American correspondents noted ongoing attempts by US officials to "hot house" a new generation of native-born leaders, as within the past six years the number of university students had soared from 13,000 to 32,000 and elementary school attendance had risen from 1.2 million to 1.8 million students. Now the expanded educational opportunities and relative security provided by over 400,000 American troops were expected to end the seemingly endless rounds of coups and countercoups and produce a stable government that could allow South Vietnam to function as a real

country. Time was of the essence, as each monthly poll of American opinion about the Vietnam War showed an increase in opposition to Lyndon
Johnson's overall military plan for Southeast Asia. Yet even as officials in
Washington analyzed the significant drop in support for current military
policies, other officials in Hanoi were using that same information to initi-
ate the most daring Communist initiative since the capture of Dien Bien
Phu had ended the French presence in the region thirteen years earlier.

The massive American escalation of the Vietnam conflict in late 1965
prevented an almost certain Communist unification of Vietnam, but two
years later an increasingly physically challenged Ho Chi Minh was more
determined than ever to unify the country before his seemingly imminent passing. The Communist dictator and his ranking generals had been
shocked at the ability of American forces to move rapidly and employ
massive firepower against the insurgents on a level far greater than anything the fading French empire was able to accomplish.

General William Westmoreland's aggressive search-and-destroy operations had pulled the Republic back from the brink of destruction and
guaranteed that South Vietnam would survive as long as a major American
military presence remained. However, unlike Operation Desert Storm a
quarter century later, the forces opposing the Americans were not arrayed
across an open desert, but operating largely in a jungle environment that
nullified much of the American firepower advantage.

The result was that by the late summer, the Vietnam War had evolved
into a giant chess match, in which the Americans were attempting to
destroy COSVN, the Communist headquarters for the South, while the
Communist forces were attempting to inflict enough casualties on the
Americans to erode American public support for the conflict. During the
spring, one of the major objectives of Operation Junction City was to
find and destroy COSVN headquarters, and two American divisions had
forced the enemy to abandon hospitals, staff schools, arms factories, and
thousands of documents as they retreated out of range. However, COSVN
was a sort of mobile capital that was always on the move, and once clear of
the immediate danger, they reinstituted a mobile reign of terror, moving
from village to village, extorting money, impressing less-than-enthusiastic

recruits, and liquidating over 12,000 "enemies of the people" who didn't demonstrate revolutionary fervor. This traveling horror show met some stiff resistance whenever American forces happened to be close enough to engage the Viet Cong, but Communist leaders were carefully following American opinion polls in 1967 and plans were emerging in Hanoi to create an environment in which the Americans no longer had a South Vietnam to save.

As American search-and-destroy missions racked up increasingly significant tallies of enemy casualties, General Nyguyen Chi Thanh, senior military commander of COSVN, began formulating a plan for a spectacular Communist offensive early the next year. Called "General Offensive, General Uprising," it was fully expected to be the decisive battle of the war. The operation would begin with a series of North Vietnamese and Viet Cong offensives all around the borders of South Vietnam. The plan was to draw American forces out of the cities while leaving the urban areas largely garrisoned by South Vietnam forces. The Communists would then overrun the cities, make the upcoming South Vietnamese elections irrelevant, and force the Americans out of the newly united Vietnam People's Republic.

While the Communists planned their border campaign and their New Year's offensive, a modern version of nineteenth-century American political barnstorming was working its way up and down the roads of South Vietnam. In what one American correspondent termed "a touring political carnival," representatives of multiple South Vietnamese political parties shared the same buses, cars, and occasionally planes, addressed residents in the same villages and towns, and promised to create various versions of a South Vietnamese dream. The most prominent campaign team was formed around two former political enemies, General Nguyen Van Thieu and General Nguyen Cao Ky. Three years earlier, both of these men had been colonels in the ill-fated Diem government, but after an American-approved coup removed and executed Diem, the wealthy Catholic Thieu and lower-middle-class Ky had alternately feuded and allied during a bewildering succession of coups that opened the gates for a Communist takeover. Among the multitude of candidates vying for election, the most serious outsider challenge came from Tran Van Huong, a former primary school principal who was two decades older than most of his opponents. He had gone from mayor of Saigon under Diem to a clerk/typist for the Vietnamese Dentist Association as he made a symbolic exit from that doomed government. Now dozens of candidates vied for the votes of people who barely knew how to vote and included large numbers who secretly, or not so secretly, pledged themselves to Ho Chi Minh and the Viet Cong. The whole process of conducting an election campaign was effectively riding on nearly half a million Americans who would spend most of the rest of the year parrying Communist operations designed to clear the board for the Tet Offensive. Yet in one of the supreme ironies of a conflict that had no shortage of paradoxes, the person most responsible for promoting the General Uprising, General Offensive was no longer alive to oversee his plan.

The field commander of COSVN, the Communist forces south of the DMZ, was General Nguyen Chi Thanh, the archrival of General Vo Nguyen Giap, the mastermind of the battle of Dien Bien Phu, the siege that ended French power in Indochina. While Giap directed operations from an office in Hanoi, Thanh set up shop in the triple canopy jungles of South Vietnam and viewed himself as an archetypal guerrilla leader. The COSVN commander ducked and weaved through American ground and air attacks until his luck ran out during a B-52 bomber raid in July, when he was apparently seriously wounded and conveyed to an East European hospital, where he officially died of a heart attack.

Giap had now lost his major rival and was clearly Ho Chi Minh's chief enforcer, sealing his power with the arrest of over 200 senior officials for "counterrevolutionary crimes," meaning they had been too close to Thanh. Giap promptly appropriated Thanh's Tet plan and initiated a fall offensive designed to pull the American forces away from target cities while also inflicting enough casualties to "keep American coffins going home," a sure way to incite rising opposition to the conflict back in the United States. To ensure that those coffins kept heading stateside, Giap was willing to accept heavy casualties among his North Vietnamese and Viet Cong regulars, as he fully expected the Tet uprising to end the war and allow Vietnam's burgeoning birthrate to make good any losses in a unified country.

General Giap had a good sense of the rising home-front opposition to the war in the United States, but far less appreciation for the mobility and firepower of American forces that would allow William Westmoreland to rush powerful reinforcements to any of Giap's targets.

The run-up to the Tet Offensive began in September in a desolate patch of American-held hills just south of the DMZ. Con Thien, named the Hill of Angels by French missionaries, was one of six major strongpoints designed to deflect or at least delay any North Vietnamese incursions across the boundary between the two Vietnamese states. Relatively near the sea, the hills were garrisoned by a battalion of 1,200 marines of the 3rd Marine Division. The monotony of coping with nearly hundred-degree temperatures alternating with torrential downpours was suddenly broken when General Giap's mammoth inventory of 100 mm, 130 mm, and huge 152 mm guns launched a barrage that quickly turned the base into a moonscape of water-filled shell holes and mud-spattered marines sprinting through the jungle.

Photos and film footage of Americans looking far older than their years evoked images of Guadalcanal and the Chosin Reservoir as the marines endured nearly a thousand rounds a day from Soviet-supplied artillery enhanced by rockets and mortars. As monsoon rains arrived, more and more defenders were whisked away by medical-evacuation helicopters. The more fortunate headed to hospitals, the less fortunate to morgues.

Yet Con Thien was not about to become a 1960s version of the Alamo. Marine and army gunners were firing 6,000 rounds a day at the enemy, while just offshore, Seventh Fleet cruisers added another 3,000 shells to the daily barrage. American air units dropped napalm and high explosives on the north side of the DMZ and the drone of helicopter gunships was always part of the background noise of a contest that was now dominating the news back home.

Despite this array of firepower, the Communist forces were digging in for a siege, hoping for a Dien Bien Phu sequel that would end American involvement in Vietnam. On the other hand, William Westmoreland viewed the semi-siege of Con Thien more as a poker game. Unlike the French in 1954, he had large stacks of chips to play. Marines called the earsplitting sounds of B-52 bomb runs "the most beautiful noise on the earth," as the Americans had control of both the air and sea. General Giap had assumed that he would force Westmoreland to rush far more ground forces to Con Thien than he actually did. Regardless, the Communist commander saw this confrontation as merely the first in a series of attacks. The focus of attention would soon shift to the west, near the Cambodian border.

While the struggle for Con Thien played out, Giap's next major target was Loc Ninh, a bustling city of 10,000 people at the center of a vast array of rubber plantations stretched along low, rolling hills near the Cambodian border. The city was a riot of color, as the red tile roofs of French-style villas contrasted with stunningly green lawns and the exotic ambience of tropical flowers. Much of the city's business was conducted at the local country club, which featured a huge swimming pool, tennis courts, and an air of tranquility that seemed to blot out the conflict going in other parts of the nation.

Communist military planners were particularly attracted to the prospect of seizing an important district capital that featured a remarkably puny garrison of only four militia companies with no regular forces readily available. In the early hours of October 29, two assault regiments, the Viet Cong regulars of the 272nd and 273rd Regiments, poured into the city and Viet Cong flags were soon waving over important buildings. The initially spectacular victory was somewhat marred by a lack of clarity as to whether this operation was a raid or a short-term occupation of a relatively important South Vietnamese population center. The picture was further complicated when Viet Cong troops who had been assigned to move through the towering trees of the rubber plantations ran headlong into a scouting force from a nearby US Special Forces compound. As the battle surged through the heavily wooded landscape, the Green Berets were able to call in "Puff the Magic Dragon" gunships that began spraying the woods with Gatling guns.

Almost as soon as the Special Forces command bunker began issuing radio alerts of the assault, Major General John Hay, commander of the 1st Infantry Division, began cobbling together a four-battalion relief force from his own units and the 25th Infantry Division. As daylight returned to Loc Ninh, a 1960s battle with Civil War overtones emerged as the mixed open country and tree groves of the rubber plantations at times resembled a contest between Yankees and Rebels in the fields and trees of the plantations of Dixie. The Viet Cong grudgingly ceded ground to Americans supported by armor and airplanes, but the Communists turned the battle back to the twentieth century as they doggedly fought for a 3,200-foot airstrip just outside of town and set up defense lines around the grounds of the country club.

As General Hay positioned newly arriving units, the Viet Cong forces washed their clothes in the club's swimming pool, raided the large wine cellar, then gradually backpedaled out of town. The Viet Cong took most of their dead comrades back toward Cambodia with them, so American commanders could only estimate the enemy loss at about 1,000 compared to twenty Americans and thirty South Vietnamese killed and several dozen wounded.

Only days after the Viet Cong were driven out of the lush grounds of the Loc Ninh country club, American intelligence reported another border thrust in the highland border region where Vietnam, Laos, and Cambodia all converged. General Giap had dispatched four regiments of North Vietnamese regulars to assault the town of Dak To. As seven thousand well-equipped Communist regulars started fanning out along highland trails on November 3, General Creighton Abrams, in temporary command as Westmoreland was on his way to Washington, deployed nine American battalions to check the enemy advance. In a series of battles that Westmoreland later described as fiercer than the bloody encounter at Ia Drang Valley two years earlier, the two sides rolled up and down the hills and valleys of the border country against a backdrop that might have looked familiar to federal and Confederate soldiers in the Virginia campaigns of 1862. Nineteen days of continuous combat produced several minor instances of temporarily cut-off American units that often survived due to massive American air strikes on the besiegers. The American 173rd Airborne Brigade suffered a 27 percent casualty rate during the Dak To battles, while the entire operation produced nearly 400 dead and over

1,400 wounded in return for an "official" count of enemy dead at 1,644 with perhaps 2,000 North Vietnamese wounded.

As the "Battle of the Borders" raged along the periphery of South Vietnam, in downtown Saigon 25,000 ARVN troopers lined the streets of the capital city as representatives of twenty-three nations, including Vice President Hubert Humphrey, converged on the whitewashed Assembly building to participate in the inauguration of President Nguygen Van Thieu and Vice President Nguyen Cao Ky as the leaders of the first electorate-based government in South Vietnamese history.

The two military officers, dressed in civilian business suits, emerged from limousines to a twenty-one-gun salute. Thieu lit a symbolic flame of liberty in an urn and then mounted the carpeted steps to recite an oath of office that was accompanied by the release of thousands of colored balloons, which rose into the air front of a six-foot red-and-yellow cake. As South Vietnamese jets flew over the palace, the new president inspected an honor guard made up of the rather compact alliance that Lyndon Johnson had cobbled together to counter charges of this contest being exclusively an American war. Military personnel from Thailand, Taiwan, South Korea, Australia, New Zealand, and the Philippines saluted the now officially recognized head of the South Vietnamese government. In the background, the sound of celebratory firecrackers, mixed with the eruption of Viet Cong explosives, reminded all those present that South Vietnam was a nation at war.

This festive inauguration day was most likely the last pure day of celebration during the relatively brief history of the Republic of South Vietnam, in a nation that only thirteen years earlier was a French colony and in a capital city that eight years later would be named for the man who even now was plotting the destruction of their government and way of life. For just a little while, the archrivals Thieu and Ky had melded into a single elected team that promised deliverance from both the dictatorial rule of the Diem family and the chaos of serial military coups and countercoups that were ripping South Vietnam apart. On this celebratory day, however, the seeds of the Republic's destruction were already being planted from the quarters of Ho Chi Minh and Vo Nguyen Giap several hundred miles to the north in Hanoi, and from the streets of America to the halls of Congress thousands of miles distant.

The most recent American experience with a conflict that featured relatively limited objectives had occurred during the previous decade, when North Korean dictator Kim Il-sung's armies crashed across the demilitarized zone separating that nation from its southern neighbor and threatened to unify the Korean peninsula under Communist rule. President Harry Truman had dispatched massive American aid, which resulted in an eventual allied counterattack that had driven the invaders back to the Yalu River. When Mao Tse-tung committed the massive power of the People's Army of China to smash an intruder that had moved too close to the "Celestial Kingdom," however, the war degenerated into a bloody stalemate that congealed on the border between the two Koreas, an event that largely convinced Harry Truman to forgo seeking the 1952 presidential nomination from his party.

The American intervention in Vietnam had been gradual, but by the autumn of 1967 American deployment in Vietnam was approaching the half-million mark and the broad political consensus that had supported the war was beginning to unravel. A significant part of the mythology of the American experience in Vietnam centers around the Tet Offensive of early 1968. The attendant coverage on television turned many Americans against the war, with perhaps the iconic moment occurring when CBS anchor Walter Cronkite, probably the most respected correspondent in middle America, returned from a post-Tet trip to Vietnam and informed viewers, at the end of a prime-time special, that the United States could not reasonably expect victory in Southeast Asia.

However, the reality of the Vietnam experience was that by the autumn of 1967, weeks or even months before the General Offensive, General Uprising, opinion polls confirmed that a majority of Americans no longer supported Lyndon Johnson's policies in Vietnam. A majority of adult Americans were old enough to have experienced World War II as either adults, adolescents, or preteens, and they knew that, with some major setbacks, the Allied forces had moved ever forward toward ultimate victory. However, by the autumn of 1967, an increasing number of Americans were becoming exasperated at the extreme fluidity of the Vietnam conflict and could see no visual evidence that the United States was closing on the enemy. The only certainty was that the casualties were edging upwards, draft calls were coming closer to home, and many of those in authority, up to and including the president, could not seem to even define "victory" if and when it came. In the year of fire and ice, the Vietnam War sometimes pushed the two elements together more than is realized a half century later. For example, among the sometimes not clearly defined commentary of young men being called "war resisters" were Americans who thought the conflict was immoral and were seeking ways to avoid service. More politically conservative resisters also had little reason to "die for a tie" and urged the Johnson administration to either go all-out or get out. The Young Americans For Freedom and the Students for a Democratic Society may have had few points of agreement, but both organizations did call on the government to end the draft. Media interviews of young men who had fled to Canada to avoid conscription revealed a surprising mix of political beliefs.

The dissent among young people was gradually spreading to more adult voters who were clearly impatient with Lyndon Johnson's failure to gain any closure on the war. The president was shocked when future Speaker of the House Thomas "Tip" O'Neill, who only a year earlier had led fellow House members in a vote of confidence for the president's Vietnam policy, now insisted that the war was probably unwinnable and felt that American involvement was a losing proposition. O'Neill seemed quite in line with many constituents as October polls revealed only 28 percent of Americans approved of the president's handling of the war. The remaining respondents split between de-escalation or expansion of military operations. One Gallup poll showed 70 percent of Americans supporting a United Nations takeover of Vietnam operations by replacing American forces or turning combat responsibility over to South Vietnamese in the relatively near future.

This expanding opposition to the war almost literally came to Lyndon Johnson's front door on the weekend of October 21–22 as the "new mobilization against the war," an umbrella organization of anti-war groups, descended on Washington with roughly 100,000 participants. In one of the most visually iconic protests of the sixties decade, protestors attempted to "levitate" the Pentagon while alternately urinating on that building's lawn, attempting to drop flowers down the barrels of soldiers' rifles, and wildly cheering the 256 daring members of the march who burned their draft cards. Meanwhile, prize-winning author Norman Mailer combed the gathering for stories that would eventually result in *Armies of the Night*. Since no one took attendance, some security officials quickly inflated the march numbers to 200,000. "Mobe" leaders hardly complained at the extra publicity, although they had mixed feelings that an arrest total of fewer than 700 marchers hardly gave evidence of a massive government carnival of violence. While William Westmoreland temporarily left the battle of the borders to fly home and give Congress a report that "we are confident we are winning this war; we are grinding the enemy down," *Look* magazine was publishing excerpts from Robert Kennedy's new book, *To Seek a Newer World*, which tore into Johnson's Vietnam policies. Senator Kennedy focused on "what we can do to end the ongoing agony of Vietnam" by calling for immediate negotiations as the only way out of the growing morass. He argued the point that successive South Vietnamese governments had failed to win the allegiance of the people and were not likely to improve in the future. He went on to state that "the South Vietnamese army rarely fights except for elite units and suffers from a ten percent desertion rate—more men than we will add to our forces in 1967," while insisting that the newly installed government was "a military ticket with legitimate rivals excluded from the contest who won only 34 percent of three fifths of the nation." The senior remaining representative of the Camelot era of the Kennedys accused the president of "casting away what may well have been the last best chance to go to the negotiating table" and hinted that a new face in the White House in 1968 might be the best hope for peace in Southeast Asia.

On the last day of November, as the 325th North Vietnamese Army Division probed the marine base at Khe Sanh, which would be the site of the most spectacular battle of the border engagements, a tall, intellectual former seminarian and amateur hockey player gave a press conference at the Senate and announced that he intended to contest Lyndon Johnson's reelection nomination. Eugene McCarthy was handsome, aloof, and erudite, as the former St. Johns economics professor used more than a few words that reporters were forced to check in pocket dictionaries. McCarthy's major issue was the Vietnam War, and he called especially on America's huge youth population to rally to him and turn the nation away from war. General Giap's battle of the borders had cost his army far more casualties than the American forces, which had largely deflected each thrust. However, McCarthy's entry into the presidential race demonstrated that if Americans no longer sensed imminent disaster, neither did they feel that the war was nearing any kind of positive resolution. Tet was now only weeks away and the eagerly anticipated 1968 presidential campaign was now more than ever connected to the Vietnam War.

CHAPTER XII

Gridiron Gladiators

As the Boys of Summer dueled that fall in Boston and St Louis, the sport that now dominated autumn prepared for its second season as a merged entity on the professional level and as a disparate collection of regional leagues on the collegiate end. A decade earlier, college football had held the upper hand over its professional counterpart, as nearly 100 major universities fielded teams in every corner of the nation, while a dozen professional franchises had no representation at all in New England, the Southeast, the Southwest, and the Northwestern states. Now, in 1967, the emergence of the American Football League and the initiation of a carefully planned expansion of the National Football League placed the professional game in virtually every region of the nation. As a symbol of that growth, most of the sports magazine publishers that had traditionally carried only a combined collegiate/professional annual created two separate issues for the college and professional versions of the sport. At the same time, while football themes were beginning to emerge on network television series, NFL stars were also garnering cameo roles in some programs. A few former players, such as Jim Brown, were even cast in moderately important film roles. Despite this, the sport was still hampered by a three-network system that mostly limited exposure to Saturday afternoons for college and Sunday afternoons for the NFL. While baseball teams offered at least forty or fifty televised games and the Cubs, Mets, and Yankees were on almost every day, the groundbreaking ABC *Monday Night Football* was still three years away and the sport's only cable networks were fifteen or more years in the future. With few exceptions, ABC limited its college games to Saturday afternoons, insisting that broadcasting a prime-time game on Saturday nights could almost never beat out the ratings garnered by *The Lawrence Welk Show* and *The Hollywood Palace*. NBC even went so far as to stop the telecast of a crucial Raiders–Jets contest in favor of a *Heidi* television movie. Even the Superbowl was kept safely on daytime television for fear that it could never match the drawing power of *The Ed Sullivan Show* or *Bonanza*.

While a football fan of 2017—who might be used to five nights a week of prime-time NFL or NCAA games, Saturday and Sunday triple-headers, or even 9:30 a.m. games attended by over 80,000 crazed fans in London's Wembley Stadium—would probably enter a form of addiction withdrawal if reduced to only a Saturday and Sunday afternoon ration of pigskin fever, football was still an integral part of both campus and urban life.

In fall of 1967, college football fans were still arguing over whether Notre Dame coach Ara Parseghian was canny or cowardly the previous November when he ordered the Fighting Irish team to take a knee to preserve a 10–10 tie in what was essentially the championship game of the 1966 season. In what *Sports Illustrated* sarcastically described as "an Upside Down" game, Parseghian and Spartan coach Duffy Daugherty glared at one another as they executed low-risk plays that guaranteed a co-championship of 9–0–1 records. NFL owners and fans, in the meantime, smugly reminded their collegiate counterparts that their version of the game had playoff games that went into sudden-death overtime.

As the new season approached, the Fighting Irish and Spartans bookended the preseason top ten picks as Notre Dame was picked for number one and Michigan State for number ten. As one preseason magazine noted, "Ara Parseghian's carefully assembled record-wrecking grid machine appears to continue leading the national parade as the returning starters and the usual crop of school stars moving up from the freshman team give Notre Dame championship credentials." In a sport that still only offered three seasons of varsity competition, freshman games were followed closely by fans and sports analysts alike, and both the Irish and the Spartans had enjoyed spectacular freshman football seasons in 1966.

As both coaches eyed the hugely publicized game on October 28 at South Bend, events to the south made Daugherty wonder whether he had made a huge mistake in accommodating an old friend in scheduling that friend's team as his season opener. Daugherty's colleague, Bill Yeoman, coached a University of Houston squad, the Cougars, that had not been able to find a league that would accept them for membership, and teams such as Idaho, Tulsa, and Memphis State were not likely to emerge as traditional rivals. Yeoman did happen to have a player named Warren McVea, who was the first African American player on the team, and if Daugherty had bothered to send a scout to any of the Cougars 1966 games (he did not), he would not have so easily looked ahead in the schedule. The Spartans had not yet opened their own season on September 16 when McVea and the Cougars routed a very good Florida State team 33–13. When Houston traveled to East Lansing the next Saturday, 75,833 fans watched in horror as Cougars quarterback Dick Woodall handed off to McVea, passed to McVea, and silenced the crowd as co-national champion Michigan State was sent reeling to a 37–7 defeat, ending virtually any chance for a repeat of 1966 glory.

Michigan State's devastating loss and the refusal of the Notre Dame administration to allow the Fighting Irish to play in a postseason bowl game soon created a seismic shift among sports writers and television network officials as to which emerging teams and players might now gain the national spotlight. As the college football season drove toward a climax, the two vastly different communities of West Lafayette, Indiana, and Los Angeles, California, became the epicenters of the college game that autumn.

At Purdue University in Indiana, football coach Jack Mollenkopf had assembled a Boilermakers squad that some sportswriters felt might unseat league rival Michigan State and perhaps even contest Notre Dame for the powerhouse of the Midwest. Purdue was coming off a very good 8–2 season and had relied on talented quarterback Bob Griese, an All-American who would segue effortlessly into even greater fame in the NFL of the 1970s.

But Griese was gone by 1967 and the offense centered around one of the three players expected to be the finalists for the Heisman Trophy. Leroy Keyes never seemed to get near the bench as offensive and defensive units switched. He led the 1966 team in interceptions, including a 95-yard return against Notre Dame, but also averaged nearly nine yards a carry-on offense. He also completed every pass he tried in relief of Griese. Plus, he sometimes kicked off.

Now Keyes simply had gotten even better. He scored eighteen touchdowns in his first eight games, and in the crucial game against Notre Dame he knocked down an almost sure Irish touchdown pass, then returned to offense to catch six passes in a 28–21 Boilermaker victory.

If Leroy Keyes ruled West Lafayette, Indiana, two players had to share the honors in the Los Angeles area. During much of the 1960s, Trojan fans, who watched with envy every winter as the Bruins established themselves as the greatest powerhouse in college basketball, could at least console themselves that USC football was a superior brand to their crosstown hoops rival. However, Bruins football seemed to be attached to the major spell that surrounded John Wooden as the boys of autumn had their own Lew Alcindor equivalent in quarterback Gary Beban. The All-American candidate and emerging Heisman Trophy finalist had guided the Bruins to a 9–1 record the previous season, and now the Rose Bowl looked promising as Beban's pass-run option plays kept moving the squad closer to the effective championship game against USC on November 18.

Yet in the end, Trojan coach John McKay met UCLA coach Tommy Prothro's challenge with a Heisman Trophy candidate of his own. Orenthal James Simpson had stunned the modest fan base at City College of San Francisco with his 9.5-second speed and his ability to keep defenders away from him. After scoring fifty-four touchdowns for the Bay Area college in just two years, he enrolled at USC and dominated an offense that was laughingly called "OJ to the right, OJ to the left." By late in the season he was rushing thirty times a game for over five yards per carry. Against Notre Dame, he tore open the Fighting Irish defense with thirty-eight carries for 150 yards and a 24–7 thrashing of the expected national champion.

On November 18, 91,000 fans sat in the autumn sunshine while two of the three leading Heisman Trophy contenders squared off for the championship of Los Angeles. Gary Beban admitted that "OJ is going to hurt you sooner or later," but the Bruin quarterback kept the Bruins in the game as he passed for 301 yards and three touchdowns to put UCLA ahead 20–14 late in the game. Then Trojan quarterback Toby Page called a "23 blast" play that let loose Simpson's innate speed and power, and the Trojan score showed the 21–20 final flashing on the scoreboard as the November afternoon waned.

A week later, minus most of the sunshine and warmth of Los Angeles, Leroy Keyes and the Boilermakers traveled the short distance to Bloomington to take on an Indiana University team that they had mauled 51–6 the previous year. Although many Hoosier fans probably expected the basketball court to be the site of most possible revenge for the gridiron disaster, a hugely underdog Indiana football team had already provided some surprises that year, and they pulled off their final surprise on this November afternoon by sending Keyes and company home with a loss. This in turn provided the Bloomington fans with a trip to the Rose Bowl as the new Big Ten champion, a team that had won precisely one game the year before. Of the three primary Heisman Trophy finalists, Leroy Keyes suffered the worst November. His team missed a seemingly sure Rose Bowl invitation and he missed the Heisman. His two California counterparts provided a textbook example of mixed blessings. Gary Beban lost to the Trojans and was forced to watch the Rose Bowl either from the stands or on his living room television. However, he could console himself while watching the game by tapping his new Heisman Trophy, a very acceptable consolation. OJ Simpson played a major role in beating the surprise Indiana team and one year later would have his own Heisman Trophy on his way to a solid football career and a very checkered post-football life.

College football as a sport enjoyed an exciting, star-laden, unpredictable season that boasted everything except a national championship game. The NFL, thanks to the merger, now had a surfeit of championship games

with two still vital league title contests leading to the second edition of a
Super Bowl that many fans hoped would be just a bit more super than the
initial version. The Green Bay Packers were poised to take on all comers,
and the league had changed a bit for the occasion. The major geographical change for 1967 had been the addition of a new franchise in New
Orleans, the first league member that had been an actual major city in the
Southern Confederacy of 1861. This expansion had prompted the NFL
half of the merged leagues to create a new subset below the conference
level, with the introduction of the Central, Coastal, Century, and Capital
divisions, which in turn would create another contest on the road to the
Super Bowl, a Western and Eastern Conference championship game that
would be played on the two days prior to Christmas.

The key question in professional football as the 1967 season began was
centered around the possibility that any NFL team could derail the Green
Bay Packers during the regular season and whether the AFL champion
could make a better showing in the Super Bowl than the Chiefs had in
the inaugural game. National magazines vied with one another to provide
some inside scoop on the vaunted Packers, and *Look* scored a publicity
coup when Vince Lombardi agreed to write an extensive article titled
"Secrets of Winning Football." The martinet/coach of the Packers admitted that "I am highly emotional but I am also highly disciplined, and I
do things by the book. My team is highly emotional, but it is controlled
emotion, released for a purpose. The Packers show that discipline and
will gamble only when they must." Lombardi admitted that many of his
players considered him a madman, and even team leader Bart Starr would
sometimes be criticized in public "not because he needs it, but to impress
someone else who can't take public criticism." This icon of the coaching
profession summarized his success: "The recipe for victory calls for a violent temper, heaps of confidence and a dash of psychology, all simmered
in months of scientific preparation." Defensive tackle Hank Jordan had a
more pithy description of his coach's abilities as he quipped, "I'll say one
thing for Coach, he treats us all the same—like dogs."

While Lombardi was the face of a community-owned Packers team that
ultimately reported to much of the adult population of Green Bay, the

emerging media focus on the AFL side of the league was on the flamboyant and colorful team owner of the Oakland Raiders, Al Davis. Davis had assumed control of the Raiders in 1963 when the team was demoralized by nineteen losses in twenty games, but in four years he had turned the club into a crew of swashbuckling pirates, many of whom had been discarded by other more disciplined teams.

Ben Davidson became one of the poster boys of this ragamuffin crew and had a reputation as possibly the dirtiest player in professional football. Although a quiet father of three little girls off the field, the hulking giant with the impressive mustache sacked sixty-seven players in fourteen games, often (legally) grabbing an offensive lineman with one hand and belting him across the helmet with the other, with a resulting ear-shattering crash and one more stunned member of the quarterback's protective cordon. Fred Arbanas, a star tight end on the Kansas City Chiefs, told a reporter that Davidson "will slam you once or twice on every play and then, he'll hit you late; it doesn't matter to him." Jets offensive lineman Winston Hill said, "He's the number one cheap shot artist of the league. It's all after the whistle with him." While Raiders head coach John Rauch remained rather quiet on Davidson's adventures, owner Al Davis lauded his actions as a key to the personality of one of the most colorful teams in football.

As the NFL season moved toward its climax, the Packers and the Raiders edged ahead of the pack in both wins and publicity. By the time the playoffs had arrived, the semifinalists included the Raiders, the Houston Oilers, the Packers, and their 1966 playoff nemesis, the Dallas Cowboys. The Raiders had raced through their AFL schedule with a sterling 13–1 record, the only blemish being a three-point loss to the rising New York Jets led by the increasingly dangerous passer Joe Namath. Their unlikely opponent on a relatively balmy New Year's Eve in the Bay Area was one of the 1966 season's most woeful teams, the 3–11 Houston Oilers. The Oilers had tied for worst in the AFL with the still new Miami Dolphins and were expected to compete with that team for futility in 1967, especially since they had lost to the Dolphins twice in 1966. Somehow coach Wally Lemm jury-rigged a team centered around unheralded players and castoffs from other squads into the most unheralded surprise of the 1967

season. However, Lemm's magic ended that afternoon as the Raiders rid-
dled the Oilers defense for a 40–7 rout. Daryle Lamonica had led the AFL
in scoring during the regular season with 468 points after coming to the
team in a brilliant Davis-engineered trade, after riding the Bills' bench
for four years. Now he proved his ultimate worth, along with fellow newcomer Hewitt Dixon, who had been a tight end at Denver but switched
to fullback with the Raiders, and halfback Pete Banaszak. The trio helped
rip the Oilers' defensive line to shreds.

On that same New Year's Eve, almost 2,000 miles to the east, the
Packers and the Cowboys took the field in what would be forevermore
be known as the "Frozen Tundra" of Lambeau Field. Vince Lombardi's
famous leadership had been just a bit less than stellar during the regular
season as the Packers reached the championship game with a good but
not great 9–4–1 record. As Packer fans sat in the arctic chill, a Cowboys
team used to warm Texas autumns lined up on a field where the actual
temperature was thirteen degrees below zero with twenty-mile-per-hour
wind gusts sending windchill temperatures down to almost fifty below
zero. Unlike the AFL championship game, the Packers' early 14–0 lead
was cut to 14–10 at halftime as Bart Starr and Don Meredith settled into a
frozen barrage of passing plays, which put the Cowboys ahead 17–14 with
only minutes remaining. Starr launched a final drive from his own 32-yard
line that ended in the shadow of the Dallas goalpost. On two successive
plays, running back Donnie Anderson's momentum resembled an automobile stuck on the ice as his traction failed just short of the end zone.
As the clock wound down to thirteen seconds, Starr called the final play
with steam puffing out of his mouth, and two mammoth lines collided in
an apparent stalemate. At the last possible second, Starr abandoned any
notion of entrusting the ball to another player and, conveyed by a crunch-
ing block by guard Jerry Kramer, dove head first into the frozen turf that
passed as the end zone to give the Packers their third straight NFL championship game and a ticket to the warmer confines of the Orange Bowl
for Super Bowl II.

While the two professional football championship games were the last
major sporting events of calendar year 1967, the season nudged forward

into early 1968. The day after the Oakland Raiders punched their ticket for Super Bowl II in their AFL championship game, a young man who grew up just across the bridge from the Oakland Raiders led his Southern California team to the biggest prize in their sports world, a victory in the Rose Bowl. OJ Simpson had fully emerged from the aimless street corner existence of the slums of San Francisco to lead the Trojans to a 14–3 victory over an Indiana squad that had been a solid pick for the Big Ten cellar but had emerged as the surprise of the college football season.

Yet Simpson's victory would be bittersweet as archrival UCLA player Gary Beban walked away with the ultimate reward in college football. Beban's Bruins would not spend New Year's Day in the sunbaked Rose Bowl, but the quarterback one magazine called "the master of cool football" would postpone Simpson's Heisman Trophy for a year.

Yet a new year was dawning. By the end of 1968, Orenthal James Simpson would be awarded his own Heisman Trophy as he set out from college to his own life of fire and ice.

Epilogue
January 1968

New Year's Day 1968 was a Monday, and most Americans had a three-day weekend. However, within days of the turn of the calendar, even minor changes emerged that hinted that the upcoming year would not simply be a rerun of the previous twelve months. The NBC network, for example, canceled the formerly popular *The Man from U.N.C.L.E.* and replaced it with a cryptically named comedy called *Laugh-In*. At first glance, the show seemed a return to the days of vaudeville, as it starred stand-up comics Dan Rowan and Dick Martin, who sprinkled rapid-fire one-liners throughout the program. Yet the show very much belonged to the late 1960s, as much of the program featured a string of short skits performed by both cast regulars and guest stars. Biting satire of current society and politics frequently put the writers at odds with network executives, who were horrified at the reaction of program sponsors.

At about the same time that *Laugh-In* debuted on NBC, rival ABC launched a new spy show that put the Cold War in a very different perspective. *It Takes a Thief* featured long-time film star Robert Wagner, who made the jump to television playing Alexander Mundy, a convicted jewel thief who is offered a conditional release if he will steal important objects (often microfilms) for the government. Mundy made James Bond look like a team player as he used his missions to attempt to steal some booty for his own bank account, often with the help of a string of either beautiful female SIA agents or equally comely enemy agents, all of whom seemed to adopt the same cavalier attitude for their nation as Mundy did for his employers/jailers.

While *Laugh-In* and *It Takes a Thief* poked fun at the government, the nation's political leaders in January were facing a tightly contested election against the backdrop of growing economic uncertainty, a rise in distrust of leaders, and a war that refused to go away. At the beginning of January, Lyndon Johnson was still clearly the leader of the Democratic Party and could still assume that he would be his party's choice as presidential candidate in November, but there was no certainty about his chances of reelection. For example, *Newsweek* magazine proclaimed that "the Democratics are in the worst trouble since the 1920s when the party split on the League of Nations, Ku Klux Klan, Prohibition, and Al Smith. Yet it is still probable that Lyndon Johnson will be renominated and not inconceivable he will not be reelected." An increasing number of political analysts believed that the modern incarnation of the party, which had largely been formed by Franklin Roosevelt and refined by John Kennedy, was saddled with growing vote losses over Vietnam. Many believed that voters might flock toward other options, from a new Democratic candidate to a victory for the Republicans.

By early 1968, Lyndon Johnson seemed to be in a personal state of transition as the folksy, loud, bragging, bigger-than-life "Daddy" morphed into a more austere, cautious leader who offered fewer massive spending programs while hinting at new strategies to end the Vietnam War. Yet as the president hunkered down, the pool of potential contenders for the Democratic nomination threatened to expand. Senator Eugene McCarthy entered 1968 just over a month after his official challenge to Johnson for the presidential nomination and six weeks from the crucial first-in-the-nation New Hampshire primary election. The ascetic, poetry-writing, hockey-playing Minnesotan began attracting major interest on many college campuses, and his advisors and handlers started forming "clean for Gene" volunteers who, short of beards and hippie clothing, would go door-to-door in the frigid New England winter to inaugurate a guerrilla action against the incumbent president. A *U.S. News and World Report* article predicted that if Johnson ran for reelection, the Democrats would win only twelve states and 110 electoral votes, and the president actually asked staff members to draft a contingency withdrawal speech. Johnson's close ally, Texas governor John Connally, suggested that the president should use his annual State of the Union speech to announce his intentions. A temporary uplift in his approval ratings, largely centered around administration hints that the Vietnam War might soon be ending, provided a temporary reprieve in these actions.

During much of January, the elephant in the room in the upcoming Democratic primaries was Robert Kennedy. Senator Kennedy seemed to be everyone to everybody in the party as the media initiated a barrage of inside articles with titles such as "Bobby To Be or Not To Be" and "Bobby: Will He Run?" Political analysts openly wondered whether the brother of the martyred president "can face four years of exile in the Senate or attempt the bold gamble of openly challenging the sitting president." Some commentators felt that "if he gets in the race, it will be one of the boldest gambles in the history of politics, as he risks alienating the president, splitting the party and possibly ensuring the election of someone like Richard Nixon."

Besides their similarity as photogenic Irish Catholic Democrats with a sense of romanticism softening their hard-core political combativeness, the two contenders for Johnson's seat in the White House caught the imagination of many young people, who were now seriously questioning the wisdom of their elders. While Paul Newman, Art Garfunkel, Lesley Gore, and other pop entertainers began debating the merits of the two contenders for leadership of the Democratic Party, a *Harvard Daily Crimson* poll revealed that of 529 senior students surveyed, 94 percent disapproved of Johnson's policies in Vietnam while 22 percent of the males said they would leave the country or go to jail if they were ordered to Southeast Asia as conscripted servicemen. On the other hand, Colonel Robert Poell, commander of Harvard's ROTC program, noted that 57 percent of the seniors chose not to respond at all, which lessened the impact of the survey.

The state of the popular music world reflected the mixed attitudes of young people toward the reality of late 1960s life. The top-selling single in early 1968 was a lampoon of romantic relationships titled "Judy in Disguise (With Glasses)," a one-hit wonder by John Fred and his Playboy Band that parodied both trippy current songs and traditional romantic ballads by recounting the ambivalence of a young rake who is trying to determine whether the glasses worn by his new love interest is a turn-on or a turn-off. The Beatles were just as evasive in their hugely successful "Hello Goodbye," in which the Fab Four were equally perplexed by the value of their current relationship in the song. The Monkees, who had dominated almost every teen magazine cover for the entire year of 1967, had scored another number one hit, "Daydream Believer," during Christmas week, a song that would remain in the top ten for much of January. Their fantastic run was about to end, however, and they were passed on the way down by the fast-rising teen singer Linda Ronstadt, fronting a rock/country band, the Stone Poneys, who were climbing rapidly up the charts with "Different Drum."

To some extent the Monkees' position as one of the top male groups would be taken by a new group that appeared on stage and on television shows in either Confederate or Union Civil War uniforms. The Union Gap was fronted by Gary Puckett, who provided a powerful voice for unrequited love in the newly released "Woman, Woman," soon to be followed by "Young Girl" and "Lady Willpower." Puckett clearly demonstrated his lead singer status by appearing in either a gray or blue officer's uniform while his band rated only enlisted uniforms.

The growing subgenre of soul music in early 1968 was still led by the incomparable Aretha Franklin, with her "Chain of Fools" reaching number one in January. She received some competition from a new interracial group from England, the Foundations, with "Baby Now That I've Found You," and a new dance-oriented song that reflected how the Bugaloo was pushing the Jerk to the rear with Fantastic Johnny C's "Boogaloo Down Broadway."

As rock music trended toward more controversial themes in a 1968 that produced anthems about placing all adults in concentration camps

("Shape of Things to Come" by Max Frost—the theme from the film *Wild in the Streets*), cannibalism ("Timothy" by the Buoys), and blatant drug use ("Time Has Come Today" by the Chambers Brothers), football fans wondered if the upstart AFL would be able to offer a real challenge to the powerful Green Bay Packers in Super Bowl II.

AFL fans could take comfort in the fact that the Packers had slipped to a good but not sensational 9–4–1 record, while the Raiders seemed to have more swagger and confidence than the Kansas City Chiefs had in Super Bowl I. Yet rumors began to circulate that Vince Lombardi might retire as Packers coach and that the team would be presented with a huge emotional boost in attempting to win his final football game.

The game in Miami presented the same warm day as its predecessor in Los Angeles, and unfortunately for AFL fans, the contest seemed only slightly more exciting than that of the previous year. The Packers drove into Raider territory on their first possession, but the Raiders did gain a temporary moral victory by holding Green Bay to a Don Chandler field goal. A few minutes later, Bart Starr righted the offensive ship when he faked a handoff in the backfield and threw to receiver Boyd Dowler, who scampered down the field as the Raiders defenders fell for the ruse. Raider quarterback Daryle Lamonica came right back with his own drive, one that ended in a touchdown by receiver Bill Miller and brought the score to 13–7.

A second Don Chandler field goal after a stalled Packers drive produced a manageable 16–7 lead for the Packers at halftime. Al Davis focused on the fact that a nine-point lead was not an impossible barrier if the Raiders improved in the second half. On the other side of the field, Vince Lombardi agreed with his counterpart and warned his team of unbelievable embarrassment if they managed to lose this game.

The Packers emerged from the dressing room with renewed fury. A 35-yard pass to Max McGee set up a two-yard score by Donnie Anderson that pushed the lead up to 16 points, soon increased to 26–7 after still another Chandler field goal. As the game seemed to be slipping out of the Raiders' hands, Packers defensive back Herb Adderly intercepted a Lamonica pass and scampered sixty yards to light up the scoreboard with a now insurmountable 33–7 lead. The Raiders gained a minor consolation prize by scoring a late, meaningless touchdown, but Vince Lombardi ended his fantastic run as coach of the Packers with wins in the first two Super Bowls.

Supposedly knowledgeable commentators mused that the ultimate game in professional football was, for the foreseeable future, doomed to be the "Super Bore" or the "Super Joke," as the NFL was asserted to have far more talent that the old AFL, still less than a decade old. However, as commentators chortled about the "endless" superiority of the older league, a brash young man from Beaver Falls, Pennsylvania, who had starred with the Alabama Crimson Tide and spurned smaller NFL offers for a then-sensational $400,000 to play for the New York Jets, was apparently determined to make those analysts eat their words at his first opportunity. Twelve months later, as Johnny Unitas led his 13–1 NFL champion Baltimore Colts into that same Miami Orange Bowl, "Broadway Joe" Namath shocked more than a few fans when he led his buccaneering Jets past the hugely favored Colts, 16–7. That was followed a year and a half later when he led the Jets onto the field for the opening game of *Monday Night Football*.

While American sports fans debated the relative strengths of the NFL and AFL after Super Bowl II, 6,000 American marines were enduring a siege in the village of Khe Sanh, just below the Vietnamese Demilitarized Zone. As an eventual Communist siege force of nearly 40,000 men pounded the base, Lyndon Johnson spent long hours every day peering over a 1/50,000 scale model of the base in the White House Situation Room.

While a large number of American commentators saw the siege as a parallel to the Communist assault on the French garrison at Dien Bien Phu that ousted that nation from Indochina thirteen years earlier, senior American military commanders insisted that, unlike the French, the marines continued to hold the vital high ground and had total command of the air.

What neither American group fully realized was that the siege of Khe Sanh was simply a ploy by Communist General Vo Nguyen Giap to distract the Americans while a massive 84,000-man assault force launched a surprise offensive at the onset of the Vietnamese New Year. Giap's plan was to jettison guerrilla warfare for a bold strike at virtually every city in South Vietnam. He and Ho Chi Minh fully expected the attack would unleash a massive popular uprising in the South that would, in turn, leave the Americans with virtually no allies and a choice between withdrawal or annihilation.

While most Americans would spend a good part of February 1968 viewing the bloody attempt to recapture the imperial capital of Hue from the Communist forces that had seized the city, the other memorable element of the Tet Offensive would actually occur on the final day of January.

Ironically, while the United States fielded an army of over a half-million men in Vietnam by January, there was optimism that the capital city of Saigon could be effectively protected by South Vietnamese forces, with the defense of the American embassy entrusted to a handful of marines. Luckily for the Americans, General Giap only sporadically understood the psychological importance of the center of the American presence in Vietnam, and left the details of the assault to underlings who eventually cobbled together a "T 700" special unit formed around a sparse contingent of eighteen men and one woman.

Just after midnight, as the calendar turned to the last day of January, this tiny force donned red armbands and yellow scarves to "militarize" their casual slacks and sports shirts, climbed into a stolen taxicab and Peugeot truck, and converged on the only months-old embassy garrisoned by a small force of marines who were mostly housed five blocks away. The "Battle of the Embassy" erupted as the assault force blew a hole in the outer wall of the embassy grounds and killed the only two American military police on duty. As the contingent of marines and a few armed civilians on the embassy staff blasted away from the upper floors, a call to Captain Robert O'Brien, billeted with his men a half mile away, brought a relief force cascading through the streets to save their colleagues and friends. In a scene worthy of *Mission Impossible*, one of the embassy chauffeurs turned out to be a Viet Cong agent who helped direct the assault while staff members fumbled through drawers for pistols they had stashed for just such an emergency.

As marine vehicles poured through the embassy gates, the Viet Cong assault force was nearly annihilated, suffering sixteen dead and three wounded at a cost of two American deaths and five injured. Yet as General William Westmoreland arrived in time to step over enemy bodies and congratulate the defenders, newsmen and cameramen began sending home reports and images of a battle-scarred embassy that now looked a bit like the Alamo.

Most of the battle of the Tet Offensive would be fought in February, and by the end of the offensive a Viet Cong casualty total that may have reached 45,000 personnel effectively turned the war into a conflict between American and North Vietnamese regulars. However, the events of that last day of January, when the Communists broke into the seemingly impregnable American embassy and later temporarily captured Saigon's main radio station, shocked more than a few Americans who thought that the United States was close to winning the unpopular conflict.

The first day of the Tet Offensive, January 31, 1968, most likely ended the long 1967, which could be said to have begun on the morning after the 1966 elections. During this fifteen-month period, the odds of Lyndon Johnson being reelected as president of the United States dropped enormously, the map of the Middle East underwent permanent change with the Six-Day War, and international violence seemed endemic. Yet in that same year, at the modest home of a New Jersey college president, the last vestiges of the Cuban Missile Crisis largely ended as President Johnson and Premier Kosygin ate a hearty lunch, congratulated each other on their young grandchildren, and resolved to pull their nations away from the brink of nuclear holocaust. The Boston Red Sox proved that miracles in sports do happen even without fans of losing teams having to sell their souls to the devil to gain a pennant. American television viewers could finally watch all of their favorite programs in living color, as monochrome telecasting retreated to the realm of old films on midnight movies. Jim Morrison shocked and angered Ed Sullivan and possibly much of the adult viewing audience when he sang the uncut version of "Light My Fire" on Sullivan's show, but adults could still safely watch Lawrence Welk and *The Hollywood Palace* and know that no such crass lyrics were likely.

I am finishing this book literally on the eve of one of the most contentious presidential elections in American history. In about five hours, a tiny hamlet in New England will cast the first votes. Much of the excitement of history revolves around the realization that the people of historical narratives had relatively little knowledge of what would happen the next year, let alone the next half century. A time traveler from the year this book depicts might be astonished, confused, or depressed by what has occurred over the past five decades, but I would like to hope that he or she could understand and appreciate that much of what we are as a society really does connect to that now half-century-ago year of fire and ice.

Victor Brooks
Norristown, PA
November 7, 2016

A Note on Sources

M uch like my previous book on America at war and at home in 1944, I envisioned this project as one that would entail extensive research time utilizing the sources that people in 1967 consulted in their attempts to understand a nation and a world engaged in massive upheaval, from college campuses to the jungles of South Vietnam. Therefore, a significant portion of my research activities was spent in the periodicals section of several local (Philadelphia area) university libraries and archives, visits to local used magazine and book stores, and utilization of eBay's treasure trove of period journals, magazines, and artifacts.

In order to get a true feel for living at different ages, genders, and lifestyles in 1967, I held subject searches to a minimum, in favor of reading entire issues of magazines and newspapers, from letters to the editor to advertisements to a huge variety of feature articles. This mix of magazines and journals represents a cross section of what a very print-oriented American public consulted in 1967. *Time, Newsweek, U.S. News and World Report, Life, Look, Fortune, Ebony, Sports Illustrated, Family Circle, Good Housekeeping, Ladies Home Journal, Saturday Evening Post, Sport,* and *TV Guide* were all periodicals with significant reading audiences at a time when there was a limited number of television stations and, of course, no personal computers.

The single most high-profile national event in 1967 was the American engagement in the Vietnam War, and I have attempted to use the widest possible spectrum of books in our nation's most controversial conflict. Two of the most useful works on America's command operations and strategies are Samuel Zaffiri's *Westmoreland: A Biography* (1994), which details the American commander's tightrope walks between an American president who could not avoid micromanaging and a South Vietnamese government embroiled in political feuds in the middle of a battle for national survival. Zaffiri's book also provides an excellent account of Westmoreland's often ill-advised focus on enemy body counts in large-scale operations while largely undervaluing the security of Vietnamese civilians. A valuable first-person account is Phillip B. Davidson's *Vietnam at War* (1990), in which the author, Westmoreland's chief intelligence officer, chronicles the conflict from the emergence of the Viet Minh in 1946 to the fall of Saigon in 1975, with extensive materials on 1967 and the run-up to the Tet Offensive. One of the emerging leaders in the study of the Vietnam War from both a social and military perspective is Andrew Wiest, who coauthored *America and the Vietnam War: Re-examining the Culture and History of a Generation* with Mary Kathryn Barbier and Glenn Robins, which reconsiders the social and cultural aspects of the conflict. Weist was also the sole author of *The Boys of '67: Charlie Company's War in Vietnam,* which focuses on a single army infantry company engaged in combat in 1967.

Marilyn Young emerged as a premier scholar of the Vietnam conflict with her critique of both French and American involvement in Southeast Asia in the *The Vietnam Wars: 1945–1990* (1991), while Douglas Niles focuses on the generally excellent ability of American forces to defeat the enemy in stand-up battles in *A Noble Cause: American Battlefield Victories in Vietnam* (2014). An excellent modern analysis of the true impact of the Tet Offensive is James Robbins's *This Time We Win: Revisiting the Tet Offensive* (2013).

The other major conflict in 1967, the Six-Day War between Israel and a coalition of Arab states, featured both Israeli and generally sympathetic American authors chronicling the actual war. A number of authors also investigated the Israeli attack on the USS *Liberty*, which inflicted a death toll that almost rivaled the fatalities in Vietnam that same week. The political and military run-up to the war is well chronicled by Israeli Foreign Minister Abba Eban's *An Autobiography* (1977). Michael Oren's *Six Days of War: June 1967 and the Making of the Modern Middle East* (2002) and Tom Segev's *1967: Israel, The War, and the Year that Transformed the Middle East* (2005) provide excellent chronicles of the surprising outcome of the conflict. On the other hand, James Ennes's *Assault on the Liberty* (1974) and A. Jay Cristol's *The Liberty Incident: The 1967 Israeli Attach on the U.S. Navy Spy Ship* (2002) chronicle the hugely mixed feelings for an American government that had to deal with a tragedy initiated by an close ally.

The Republican gains in the 1966 congressional elections and the looming presidential election of 1968 received enormous attention in periodicals during 1967 and in books thereafter. Princeton University historian Eric Goldman was granted an extended leave to become a special advisor to President Johnson ten days after the assassination of John F. Kennedy and finished his account of his relationship with the president only months after the 1968 election in *The Tragedy of Lyndon Johnson* (1969). Almost three decades later, UCLA presidential historian Irving Bernstein chronicled the Johnson presidency in *Guns or Butter: The Presidency of Lyndon Johnson* (1996). And Boston University history professor, Robert Dallek, produced his second volume on Johnson in *Flawed Giant: Lyndon Johnson and His Times, 1961–1973* (1998).

The rise of Richard Nixon as the leading contender for the Republican presidential nomination is chronicled in Jules Witcover's *The Resurrection of Richard Nixon* (1970), Rick Perlstein's *Nixonland: The Rise of a President and the Fracturing of America* (2008), and Nixon staffer Patrick Buchanan's *The Greatest Comeback: How Richard Nixon Rose from Defeat to Create the New Majority* (2014).

The Summer of Love encouraged journalists to start emphasizing the growing generation gap in American society and the role of young people in highlighting their differences with adult society. Todd Gitlin provides a guide into the rise of radical politics in the era in *The Sixties: Years of Hope, Days of Rage* (1987), while Steve Gillon approaches the period from a broader demographical and political base in *Boomer Nation: The Largest and Richest Generation Ever, and How It Changed America* (2004).

The year 1967 was one of the more iconic periods in twentieth-century sports, and many athletes from that era wrote accounts of their triumphs or defeats. An excellent example of this is Rico Petrocelli's account of the 1967 Red Sox team in *Tales From The Impossible Dream Red Sox* (2007). The twentieth anniversary of the first Super Bowl provided the impetus for sports writer Richard Brenner to write *The Complete Super Bowl Story* (1987), which provides extra emphasis on Super Bowl I. Much of my research on the year in sports began with the basketball, hockey, baseball, and football preview magazines, the most authoritative of which were produced by sports publishers Street and Smith. The most comprehensive guides were published by *The Sporting News*, including *The Official Baseball Guide for 1968* and *The Official National Basketball Association Guide for 1968*, which included almost every conceivable statistic for those two sports. In turn, *The Sporting News Dope Book* for *1967* supplemented the more conventional premier magazines with diagrams of each Major League Baseball stadium, lists of each team's still relatively limited television schedules, and insights on the backgrounds of the thirty major league team managers.

A major research tool in the discussion of a popular music scene still oriented to singles in 1967 is Record Research Incorporated's massive publication, *Billboard Hot 100 Charts: The Sixties*. This publication, edited and compiled by Joel Whitburn, provides *Billboard* magazine's "top 100" for all fifty-two weeks of 1967 and gives documentary proof on just how eclectic popular music was in that year of fire and ice. The searing music and lyrics of "Light My Fire" by the Doors, "Incense and Peppermints" by Strawberry Alarm Clock, and "White Rabbit" by the Jefferson Airplane were countered by the retro sound of the New Vaudeville Band's "Peek-A-Boo," Harpers Bizarre's "59th Street Bridge Song (Feelin' Groovy)," and Nancy Sinatra's wistful "Sugar Town." Widely divergent essays on the state of popular music in 1967 not only appeared in nearly every national magazine but also in music-oriented publications ranging from the relatively slick format of *Goldmine* to the newly emerging *Crawdaddy* magazine.

In many respects, these varied sources provide their own version of fire and ice, as they range from general support of mainstream American society to intense critiques of almost every aspect of American life. They befit a time in which the nation was looking both forward and backward, alternately thrilled with the relative affluence of the status quo and yet eager to experiment with anything new or novel, from lifestyles to mass entertainment in a continuum that stretched boundaries of accepted behavior and expression far beyond most years in the past.

Index

spy genre, TV and movies, 7–13
St. John's Redmen. *See* St. John's
University
St. John's University, 42
St. Louis, 70, 118–119, 165
St. Louis Blues, 49
St. Louis Browns, 111
St. Louis Cardinals, ix, xxi, 112, 114–116
St. Louis Hawks, 46
Stanky, Eddie, 116–117
Stanley Cup, 47–49
Stanley Cup Finals, 48–49
Stanwyck, Barbara, 7
Star Trek, ix, 13–16
Starr, Bart, 36–39, 170, 172
Starr, Ringo, 68, 71
State University of New York (SUNY),
58, 141
Steed, John (*The Avengers*), 11, 16
Sterling, Robert, 14, 97–106
Stevens, Inger, 127
Stevens, Samantha, xiii
Stevens, Samantha (*Bewitched*), 5
Stone, Sly, 72
Stop Me If You've Heard This One, 2
STP Users Do Not Take Thorazine,
Seconal, or Other Downers for Bad
Trips, 148
Straits of Tiran, 97–98
Stram, Hank, 36
Stroll, the, 66
Students for a Democratic Society, 143,
162
Suez Canal, 98, 103
"Sugar Town," 76–77
Sullivan, Ed, 4, 74
Summer of Love, ix, 71–73, 79, 142–148
"Summer Wine," 77
"Sunday Will Never Be the Same," 81
Super Bowl, xxii, 33–39, 166, 170,
172–173
Super Bowl I, 37–39
Super Bowl II, 170, 172–173
The Supremes, 80

Supremes, 141
"Susan," 83
Susann, Jacqueline, 136
"Sweet Soul Music," 83
Switzerland, 78
Syracuse Nationals. *See* Philadelphia 76ers
Syracuse University, 62
Syria, 101

T
A Tale of Two Cities, 131–132
"Talk to the Animals," 135
Tamba, Tetsuro, 122
Tan Son Nhut, 19, 26–27
Tanaka, "Tiger," 122
Task Force Detroit, 150
Tate, Sharon, 128–129, 136
Taylor, Elizabeth, 134
Taylor, Otis, 36
Technicolor, 121, 125
Teen, ix, 69
Teen Age, ix, 66
Teen Life, 69
Teen Screen, ix, 69
Teen Set, 70
teen surveys, 146
teenagers, in 1960's, xiii–xiv
"Tell It Like It Is," 83
Temple Owls. *See* Temple University
Temple University, 42
The Temptations, 80
Tet Offensive, ix, xv, xvi, 23–24, 85–96,
156–157
Tet offensive, 80
Texas, 172
Texas Western College, 40–41, 44
Texas Western Miners, 149
Texas Western University, 149
Thala, 20
Thanh, Gen. Nguyen Chi, 29, 89,
155–156
Thanh Dien, 26
"Thank the Lord for the Night Time," 77
"Theme From *A Summer Place*," 66

The Who, 75
Who's Afraid of Virginia Woolf? 131, 134
Widmark, Richard, 113, 125
The Wild Wild West, 6
Wild Wild West, xxi, 10
Will (*Lost In Space*), 15–16
Williams, Andy, 66
Williams, Billy, 115
Williams, Dick, 112–113, 116
Williams, Guy, 15–16
Williams, Ted, 112–113
Williamson, Bruce, 134
Williamson, Fred "The Hammer,"
    38–39
Willkie, Wendell, 53
Wills, Maury, 113–114
Willy (*Mission Impossible*), 12
Wilson, Carl, 75
Wilson, Harold, 98–99
Wilson, Scott, 129
"Windy," 82
Winters, Victoria (*Dark Shadows*), 16,
    142
Winwood, Steve, 83
Wonder, Stevie, 83
Woo, Robert, Jr., 139–140
Woo, Sally, 139–140
Wood, Willie, 38
Woodall, Dick, 167
Wooden, John, 39–40, 42–44, 168
Woodstock, 74–75, 80
World Series, 3, 111, 113, 115, 118–
    120
World War I, 24
World War II, xvi, 22, 29, 90, 100,
    122–124, 132–133
"Worried About Today's Young People,"
    141
Wray, Fay, 126
Wrigley Field, 115

X
X, Malcolm, 40

Y
The Yardbirds, 136
Yastrzemski, Carl, 116–120
Yates, Rowdy, 126
"The Yellow Rose of Texas," xv
"Yellow Submarine," 70
Yeoman, Bill, 167
"Yesterday Once More," vii, viii
York, Dick, 5
York, Michael, 134
Yorkin, Bud, 126–128
"You Better Run," 81
"You Got to Me," 77
"You Got What It Takes," 80
"(You Make Me Feel Like) A Natural
    Woman," 80
"You Must Have Been a Beautiful
    Baby," 80
You Only Live Twice (film), 8, 107
You Only Live Twice (film), 122–125
"You Only Live Twice" (song), 77, 122
Young, Cy, 113
Young Americans For Freedom, 162
The Young Rascals, 81
Young Republicans, 143
"You're My Everything," 80
youth movement and war protests,
    142–152
"Youth Quake," 144–152

Z
Zeffirelli, Franco, 134
Zeus, 44
Zimbalist Jr., Efrem, 129
Zombies, xxi
Zorro, 15